*In This Very Life*

# In This Very Life
## The Liberation Teachings of the Buddha

Sayadaw U Pandita

*Translated by* Venerable U Aggacitta
*Edited by* Kate Wheeler

WISDOM PUBLICATIONS · Boston

First published in 1992
2nd Edition 1993

WISDOM PUBLICATIONS
361 Newbury Street, Boston, MA 02115

*Library of Congress Cataloging-in-Publication Data*
Pandita Bivamsa, Ū, 1921-
    In this very life  :   the liberation teachings of the Buddha  /
Sayadaw U. Pandita ;  translated by Venerable U. Aggacitta ;  edited
by Kate Wheeler. — Rev.  ed.
        p.      cm.
    Translation of lectures given in Burmese.
    Includes bibliographical references and index.
    ISBN 0-86171-094-0  :  $19.00
    1. Religious life — Buddhism.   2. Spiritual life — Buddhism.
I. Wheeler, Kate, 1955-      .   II. Title.
BQ5395.P355   1993                                             92-42813
294.3'44 — dc20                                                       CIP


ISBN 0 86171 094 0


Set in Palatino 10½ on 12½ by Wisdom Publications, and
printed and bound by Eurasia Press of Singapore.

# Contents

# Foreword

When Sayadaw U Pandita first came to teach in the United States in 1984, we knew him only by reputation as the successor to Mahāsi Sayadaw of Burma. But in ways that we could not have imagined at the time, his teaching and presence helped to open many new doors of understanding. As a meditation master, he has guided us through the subtleties of practice; as a scholar, he has brought new meaning and life to the timeless words of the Buddha; and as a great spiritual friend, he has inspired us to seek the highest freedom.

Just as the Buddha came from the warrior class of ancient India, so too, is Sayadaw U Pandita a spiritual warrior of our time. His emphasis on heroic effort is joined with a joyous confidence that liberation is possible in this very life. Sayadaw has helped us recognize our own inner capacity to overcome the limitations of the conditioned mind.

This book is a collection of talks from the first three month retreat that Sayadaw taught at the Insight Meditation Society. He describes in detail both the practical journey of awakening and a profound theoretical model of understanding. These discourses reward a thoughtful reading, allowing the familiar aspects of the teachings to mature in our minds, and challenging us with new perspectives on some old and cherished viewpoints.

This book is a treasure house of applied *Dhamma*. May it help to awaken wisdom and compassion in us all.

JOSEPH GOLDSTEIN
*Barre, Massachusetts*

# Acknowledgments

This book came into being through the help of many people.

We want to thank all those who arranged for and supported Sayadaw U Pandita's course at the Insight Meditation Society, Barre, Massachusetts in 1984. Venerable U Aggacitta expertly and lucidly translated Sayadaw U Pandita's discourses. Ron Browning asked that the tapes be transcribed. Evelyn Sweeney patiently transcribed them. U Mya Thaung went over every word of the manuscript, and Eric Kolvig edited one draft of it. We are grateful to Bruce Mitteldorf for his generous contribution toward the printing of this book.

Kate Wheeler steadfastly and very skillfully devoted months to editing the talks – none of this would have been possible without her.

SHARON SALZBERG
*Insight Meditation Society*
*Barre, Massachusetts*

# To the Reader

It is my humble and sincere wish to help you discover for yourself the state of inner peace through the essays in this book, based on the Dhamma, or way of truth, taught by the Buddha and also following the tradition of the late Venerable Mahāsi Sayadaw of Rangoon, Burma. I am trying my best, as far as my wisdom can take me, to provide this service to you.

The publication of these essays helps fulfil five beneficial purposes. First, it may give you access to new aspects of the Dhamma which you might not have heard before. Second, if you have already heard about these subjects, you may be able to consolidate your knowledge of the Dhamma. Third, if you have doubts, these essays may help you to clear them. Fourth, if you have certain pet views and preconceptions which are incorrect, you may be relieved of them by proper and respectful attention to the Dhamma of the Buddha.

The last and perhaps the most fulfilling aspect is that you may be able to tally your own experiences with what is written in this book. If your practice is deep, it can be a joyous and rapturous occasion when you realize that your experiences conform to the theory.

If you do not practice meditation, perhaps these essays can inspire you to begin. Then wisdom, the most potent medicine, can bring you relief from the sufferings of your mind.

I offer you my personal best wishes and encouragement. May you reach liberation, the highest goal.

SAYADAW U PANDITA

# Technical Note

The Pāli terms in this text are meant to introduce a precision of meaning that is not possible in English. It is hoped that readers will pause and reflect in a way they might not, had the terms simply been translated.

Pāli is used this way in Burma and in most of the communities in countries where Vipassanā meditation is practiced. As Pāli words are incorporated into living languages, they inevitably lose endings or suffer other minor changes. The Pāli in this text will differ slightly from academic usage. This reflects the use in Sayadaw U Pandita's native Burma, and more importantly, the refined application of these terms specifically to meditation practice and understanding. For ease of readability, we have used English forms for pluralization or adjectival case.

The first use of a term in the text is italicized and subsequent uses are generally unemphasized. Definitions will be found in the Glossary, pages 280-292.

# 1  Basic Morality and Meditation Instructions

We do not practice meditation to gain admiration from anyone. Rather, we practice to contribute to peace in the world. We try to follow the teachings of the Buddha, and take the instructions of trustworthy teachers, in hopes that we too can reach the Buddha's state of purity. Having realized this purity within ourselves, we can inspire others and share this Dhamma, this truth.

The Buddha's teachings can be summed up in three parts: *sīla*, morality; *samādhi*, concentration; and *paññā*, intuitive wisdom.

Sīla is spoken of first because it is the foundation for the other two. Its importance cannot be overstressed. Without sīla, no further practices can be undertaken. For laypeople the basic level of sīla consists of five precepts or training rules: refraining from taking life, refraining from taking what is not given, refraining from sexual misconduct, refraining from lying, and refraining from taking intoxicating substances. These observances foster a basic purity that makes it easy to progress along the path of practice.

## A BASIC SENSE OF HUMANITY

Sīla is not a set of commandments handed down by the Buddha, and it need not be confined to Buddhist teachings. It actually derives from a basic sense of humanity. For example, suppose we have a spurt of anger and want to harm another being. If we put ourselves in that other being's shoes, and honestly contemplate the action we have been planning, we will quickly answer, "No, I wouldn't want that done to me. That would be cruel and unjust." If we feel this way about some action that we plan, we can be quite sure that the action is unwholesome.

In this way, morality can be looked upon as a manifestation of our sense of oneness with other beings. We know what it feels like to be harmed, and out of loving care and consideration we undertake to avoid harming others. We should remain committed to truthful speech and avoid words that abuse, deceive or slander. As we practice refraining from angry actions and angry speech, then this gross and unwholesome mental state may gradually cease to arise, or at least it will become weaker and less frequent.

Of course, anger is not the only reason we harm other beings. Greed might make us try to grab something in an illegal or unethical way. Or our sexual desire can attach itself to another person's partner. Here again, if we consider how much we could hurt someone, we will try hard to refrain from succumbing to lustful desire.

Even in small amounts, intoxicating substances can make us less sensitive, more easily swayed by gross motivations of anger and greed. Some people defend the use of drugs or alcohol, saying that these substances are not so bad. On the contrary, they are very dangerous; they can lead even a good-hearted person into forgetfulness. Like accomplices to a crime, intoxicants open the door to a host of problems, from just talking nonsense, to inexplicable bursts of rage, to negligence that could be fatal to oneself or others. Indeed, any intoxicated person is unpredictable. Abstaining from intoxicants is therefore a way of protecting all the other precepts.

For those whose devotion makes them wish to undertake a further discipline, there are also sets of eight and ten precepts for laypeople, ten precepts for nuns, and the Vinaya or 227 rules for monks. There is more information about these forms of sīla in the Glossary.

### Refinements During a Retreat

During a meditation retreat it becomes useful to change some of our conduct in ways that support the intensification of meditation practice. In a retreat, silence becomes the appropriate form of right speech, and celibacy that of sexual conduct. One eats lightly to prevent drowsiness and to weaken sensual appetite. The Buddha recommended fasting from noon until the following morning; or, if this is difficult, one could eat only a little in the afternoon. During the time one thus gains to practice, one may well discover that the taste of the Dhamma excels all worldly tastes!

Cleanliness is another support for developing insight and wisdom. You should bathe, keep nails and hair trimmed, and take care to regulate the bowels. This is known as internal cleanliness. Externally, your clothing and bedroom should be tidy and neat. Such observance is said to bring clarity and lightness of mind. Obviously, you do not make cleanliness an obsession. In the context of a retreat, adornments, cosmetics, fragrances, and time-consuming practices to beautify and perfect the body are not appropriate.

In fact, in this world there is no greater adornment than purity of conduct, no greater refuge, and no other basis for the flowering of insight and wisdom. Sīla brings a beauty that is not plastered onto the outside, but instead comes from the heart and is reflected in the entire person. Suitable for everyone, regardless of age, station or circumstance, truly it is the adornment for all seasons. So please be sure to keep your virtue fresh and alive.

Even if we refine our speech and actions to a large extent, however, sīla is not sufficient in itself to tame the mind. A method is needed to bring us to spiritual maturity, to help us realize the real nature of life and to bring the mind to a higher level of understanding. That method is meditation.

MEDITATION INSTRUCTIONS

The Buddha suggested that either a forest place under a tree or any other very quiet place is best for meditation. He said the meditator should sit quietly and peacefully with legs crossed. If sitting with crossed legs proves to be too difficult, other sitting postures may be used. For those with back trouble a chair is quite acceptable. It is true that to achieve peace of mind, we must make sure our body is at peace. So it is important to choose a position that will be comfortable for a long period of time.

Sit with your back erect, at a right angle to the ground, but not too stiff. The reason for sitting straight is not difficult to see. An arched or crooked back will soon bring pain. Furthermore, the physical effort to remain upright without additional support energizes the meditation practice.

Close your eyes. Now place your attention at the belly, at the abdomen. Breathe normally, not forcing your breathing, neither slowing it down nor hastening it, just a natural breath. You will become aware of certain sensations as you breathe in and the abdomen rises, as you breathe out and the abdomen falls. Now sharpen your aim and make sure that the mind is attentive to the entirety of each process. Be aware from the very beginning of all sensations involved in the rising. Maintain a steady attention through the middle and the end of the rising. Then be aware of the sensations of the falling movement of the abdomen from the beginning, through the middle, and to the very end of the falling.

Although we describe the rising and falling as having a beginning, a middle, and an end, this is only in order to show that your awareness should be continuous and thorough. We do not intend you to break these processes into three segments. You should try to be aware of each of these movements from beginning to end as one complete process, as a whole. Do not peer at the sensations with an overfocused mind, specifically looking to discover how the abdominal movement begins or ends.

In this meditation it is very important to have both effort and precise aim, so that the mind meets the sensation directly and powerfully. One helpful aid to precision and accuracy is to make a soft mental note of the object of awareness, naming the sensation by saying the word gently and silently in the mind, like "rising, rising...falling, falling."

*Returning from Wandering*

There will be moments when the mind wanders off. You will start to think of something. At this time, watch the mind! Be aware that you are thinking. To clarify this to yourself, note the thought silently with the verbal label "thinking, thinking," and come back to the rising and falling.

The same practice should be used for objects of awareness that arise at any of what are called the six sense doors: eye, ear, nose, tongue, body, and mind. Despite making an effort to do so, no one can remain perfectly focused on the rising and falling of the abdomen forever. Other objects inevitably arise and become predominant. Thus, the sphere of meditation encompasses all of our experiences: sights, sounds, smells, tastes, sensations in the body, and mental objects such as visions in the imagination or emotions. When any of these objects arise you should focus direct awareness on them, and use a gentle verbal label "spoken" in the mind.

During a sitting meditation, if another object impinges strongly on the awareness so as to draw it away from the rising and falling of the abdomen, this object must be clearly noted. For example, if a loud sound arises during your meditation, consciously direct your attention toward that sound as soon as it arises. Be aware of the sound as a direct experience, and also identify it succinctly with the soft, internal verbal label "hearing, hearing." When the sound fades and is no longer predominant, come back to the rising and falling. This is the basic principle to follow in sitting meditation.

In making the verbal label, there is no need for complex language. One simple word is best. For the eye, ear, and tongue doors we simply say, "Seeing, seeing... Hearing, hearing... Tasting, tasting." For sensations in the body we may choose a slightly more descriptive term like warmth, pressure, hardness, or motion. Mental objects appear to present a bewildering diversity, but actually they fall into just a few clear categories such as thinking, imagining, remembering, planning, and visualizing. But remember that in using the labeling technique, your goal is not to gain verbal skills. Labeling technique helps us to perceive clearly the actual qualities of our experience, without getting immersed in the content. It develops mental power and focus. In meditation we seek a deep, clear, precise awareness of the mind and body. This direct awareness shows us the truth about our lives, the actual nature of mental and physical processes.

Meditation need not come to an end after an hour of sitting. It can be carried out continuously through the day. When you get up from sitting, you must note carefully – beginning with the intention to open the eyes. "Intending, intending... Opening, opening." Experience the mental event of intending, and feel the sensations of opening the eyes. Continue to note carefully and precisely, with full observing power, through the whole transition of postures until the moment you have stood up, and when you begin to walk. Throughout the day you should also be aware of, and mentally note, all other activities, such as stretching, bending your arm, taking a spoon, putting on clothes, brushing your teeth, closing the door, opening the door, closing your eyelids, eating, and so forth. All of these activities should be noted with careful awareness and a soft mental label.

Apart from the hours of sound sleep, you should try to maintain continuous mindfulness throughout your waking hours. Actually this is not a heavy task; it is just sitting and walking and simply observing whatever occurs.

WALKING MEDITATION

During a retreat it is usual to alternate periods of sitting meditation with periods of formal walking meditation of about the same duration, one after another throughout the day. One hour is a standard period, but forty-five minutes can also be used. For formal walking, retreatants choose a lane of about twenty steps in length and walk slowly back and forth along it.

In daily life, walking meditation can also be very helpful. A short period – say ten minutes – of formal walking meditation before sitting serves to focus the mind. Beyond this advantage, the awareness developed in walking meditation is useful to all of us as we move our bodies from place to place in the course of a normal day.

Walking meditation develops balance and accuracy of awareness as well as durability of concentration. One can observe very profound aspects of the Dhamma while walking, and even get enlightened! In fact, a yogi who does not do walking meditation before sitting is like a car with a rundown battery. He or she will have a difficult time starting the engine of mindfulness when sitting.

Walking meditation consists of paying attention to the walking process. If you are moving fairly rapidly, make a mental note of the movement of the legs, "Left, right, left, right" and use your awareness to follow the actual sensations throughout the leg area. If you are moving more slowly, note the lifting, moving and placing of each foot. In each case you must try to keep your mind on just the sensations of walking. Notice what processes occur when you stop at the end of the lane, when you stand still, when you turn and begin walking again. Do not watch your feet unless this becomes necessary due to some obstacle on the ground; it is unhelpful to hold the image of a foot in your mind while you are trying to be aware of sensations. You want to focus on the sensations themselves, and these are not visual. For many people it is a fascinating discovery when they are able to have a pure, bare perception of physical objects such as lightness, tingling, cold, and warmth.

Usually we divide walking into three distinct movements: lifting, moving and placing the foot. To support a precise awareness, we separate the movements clearly, making a soft mental label at the beginning of each movement, and making sure that our awareness follows it clearly and powerfully until it ends. One minor but important point is to begin noting the placing movement at the instant that the foot begins to move downward.

*A New World in Sensations*

Let us consider lifting. We know its conventional name, but in meditation it is important to penetrate behind that conventional concept and to understand the true nature of the whole process of lifting, beginning with the intention to lift and continuing through the actual process, which involves many sensations.

Our effort to be aware of lifting the foot must neither overshoot the sensation nor weakly fall short of this target. Precise and accurate mental aim helps balance our effort. When our effort is balanced and our aim is precise, mindfulness will firmly establish itself on the object of awareness. It is only in the presence of these three factors – effort, accuracy and mindfulness – that concentration develops. Concentration, of course, is collectedness of mind, one-pointedness. Its characteristic is to keep consciousness from becoming diffuse or dispersed.

As we get closer and closer to this lifting process, we will see that it is like a line of ants crawling across the road. From afar the line may appear to be static, but from closer up it begins to shimmer and vibrate. And from even closer the line breaks up into individual ants, and we see that our notion of a line was just an illusion. We now accurately perceive the line of ants as one ant after another ant, after another ant. Exactly like this, when we look accurately at the lifting process from beginning to end, the mental factor or quality of consciousness called "insight" comes nearer to the object of observation. The nearer insight comes, the clearer the true nature of the lifting process can be seen. It is an amazing fact about the human mind that when insight arises and deepens through *vipassanā*, or insight, meditation practice, particular aspects of the truth about existence tend to be revealed in a definite order. This order is known as the progress of insight.

The first insight which meditators commonly experience is to begin to comprehend – not intellectually or by reasoning, but quite intuitively – that the lifting process is composed of distinct mental and material phenomena occurring together, as a pair. The physical sensations, which are material, are linked with, but different from, the awareness, which is mental. We begin to see a whole succession of mental events and physical sensations, and to appreciate the conditionality that relates mind and matter. We see with the greatest freshness and immediacy that mind causes matter – as when our intention to lift the foot initiates the physical sensations of movement, and we see that matter causes mind – as when a physical sensation of strong heat generates a wish to move our walking meditation into a shady spot. The insight into cause and effect can take a great variety of forms; but when it arises, our life seems far more simple to us than ever before. Our life is no more than a chain of mental and physical causes and effects. This is the second insight in the classical progress of insight.

As we develop concentration we see even more deeply that these phenomena of the lifting process are impermanent, impersonal, appearing and disappearing one by one at fantastic speed. This is the next level of insight, the next aspect of existence that concentrated awareness becomes capable of seeing directly. There is no one behind what is happening; the phenomena arise and pass away as an empty process, according to the law of cause and effect. This illusion of movement and solidity is like a movie. To ordinary perception it seems full of characters and objects, all the semblances of a world. But if we slow the movie down we will see that it is actually composed of separate, static frames of film.

*Discovering the Path by Walking*

When one is very mindful during a single lifting process – that is to say, when the mind is with the movement, penetrating with mindfulness into the true nature of what is happening – at that moment, the path to liberation taught by the Buddha opens up. The Buddha's Noble Eightfold Path, often known as the Middle Way or Middle Path, consists of the eight factors of right view or understanding, right thought or aim, right speech, right action, right livelihood, right effort, right mindfulness and right concentration. During any moment of strong mindfulness, five of the eight path factors come alive in consciousness. There is right effort; there is mindfulness; there is one-pointedness or concentration; there is right aim; and as we begin to have insight into the true nature of the phenomena, right view also arises. And during a moment when these five factors of the Eightfold Path are present, consciousness is completely free from any sort of defilement.

As we make use of that purified consciousness to penetrate into the true nature of what is happening, we become free of the delusion or illusion of self; we see only bare phenomena coming and going. When insight gives us intuitive comprehension of the mechanism of cause and effect, how mind and matter are related to one another, we free ourselves of misconceptions about the nature of phenomena. Seeing that each object lasts only for a moment, we free ourselves of the illusion of permanence, the illusion of continuity. As we understand impermanence and its underlying unsatisfactoriness, we are freed from the illusion that our mind and body are not suffering.

This direct seeing of impersonality brings freedom from pride and conceit, as well as freedom from the wrong view that we have an abiding self. When we carefully observe the lifting process, we see mind and body as unsatisfactory and so are freed from craving. These three states of mind – conceit, wrong view and craving – are called "the perpetuating *dhammas*." They help to perpetuate existence in *saṃsāra*, the cycle of craving and suffering which is caused by ignorance of ultimate truth. Careful attention in walking meditation shatters the perpetuating dhammas, bringing us closer to freedom.

You can see that noting the lifting of one's foot has incredible possibilities! These are no less present in moving the foot forward and in placing it on the ground. Naturally, the depth and detail of awareness described in these walking instructions should also be applied to noting the abdominal movement in sitting, and all other physical movements.

*Five Benefits of Walking Meditation*

The Buddha described five additional, specific benefits of walking meditation. The first is that one who does walking meditation will have the stamina to go on long journeys. This was important in the Buddha's time, when *bhikkhus* and *bhikkhunīs*, monks and nuns, had no form of transportation other than their feet and legs. You who are meditating today can consider yourselves to be bhikkhus, and can think of this benefit simply as physical strengthening.

The second benefit is that walking meditation brings stamina for the practice of meditation itself. During walking meditation a double effort is needed. In addition to the ordinary, mechanical effort needed to lift the foot, there is also the mental effort to be aware of the movement – and this is the factor of right effort from the Noble Eightfold Path. If this double effort continues through the movements of lifting, pushing and placing, it strengthens the capacity for that strong, consistent mental effort all yogis know is crucial to vipassanā practice.

Thirdly, according to the Buddha, a balance between sitting and walking contributes to good health, which in turn speeds progress in practice. Obviously it is difficult to meditate when we are sick. Too much sitting can cause many physical ailments. But the shift of posture and the movements of walking revive the muscles and stimulate circulation, helping prevent illness.

The fourth benefit is that walking meditation assists digestion. Improper digestion produces a lot of discomfort and is thus a hindrance to practice. Walking keeps the bowels clear, minimizing sloth and torpor. After a meal, and before sitting, one should do a good walking meditation to forestall drowsiness. Walking as soon as one gets up in the morning is also a good way to establish mindfulness and to avoid a nodding head in the first sitting of the day.

Last, but not least, of the benefits of walking is that it builds durable concentration. As the mind works to focus on each section of the movement during a walking session, concentration becomes continuous. Every step builds the foundation for the sitting that follows, helping the mind

stay with the object from moment to moment – eventually
to reveal the true nature of reality at the deepest level. This
is why I use the simile of a car battery. If a car is never
driven, its battery runs down. A yogi who never does
walking meditation will have a difficult time getting anywhere when he or she sits down on the cushion. But
one who is diligent in walking will automatically carry
strong mindfulness and firm concentration into sitting
meditation.

I hope that all of you will be successful in completely
carrying out this practice. May you be pure in your precepts, cultivating them in speech and action, thus creating
the conditions for developing samādhi and wisdom.

May you follow these meditation instructions carefully,
noting each moment's experience with deep, accurate and
precise mindfulness, so that you will penetrate into the true
nature of reality. May you see how mind and matter
constitute all experiences, how these two are interrelated
by cause and effect, how all experiences are characterized
by impermanence, unsatisfactoriness and absence of self so
that you may eventually realize *nibbāna* – the unconditioned
state that uproots mental defilements – here and now.

THE INTERVIEW

Vipassanā meditation is like planting a garden. We have
the seed of clear and complete vision, which is the mindfulness with which we observe phenomena. In order to
cultivate this seed, nurture the plant, and reap its fruit of
transcendent wisdom, there are five procedures we must
follow. These are called the Five Protections, or the Five
*Anuggahitas*.

*The Five Protections*

As gardeners do, we must build a fence around our little
plot to protect against large animals, deer and rabbits, who
might devour our tender plant as soon as it tries to sprout.
This first protection is *sīlā-nuggahita*, morality's protection against gross and wild behavior which agitates the

mind and prevents concentration and wisdom from ever appearing.

Second, we must water the seed. This means listening to discourses on the Dhamma and reading texts, then carefully applying the understanding we have gained. Just as overwatering will rot a seed, our goal here is only clarification. It is definitely not to bewilder ourselves, getting lost in a maze of concepts. This second protection is called *sutā-nuggahita.*

The third protection is the one I will dwell on here. It is *sākacchā-nuggahita*, discussion with a teacher, and it is likened to the many processes involved in cultivating a plant. Plants need different things at different times. Soil may need to be loosened around the roots, but not too much, or the roots will lose their grip in the soil. Leaves must be trimmed, again with care. Overshadowing plants must be cut down. In just this way, when we discuss our practice with a teacher, the teacher will give different instructions depending on what is needed to keep us on the right path.

The fourth protection is *samathā-nuggahita*, the protection of concentration, which keeps off the caterpillars and weeds of unwholesome states of mind. As we practice we make a strong effort to be aware of whatever is actually arising at the six sense doors – eye, ear, nose, tongue, body and mind – in the present moment. When the mind is sharply focused and energetic in this way, greed, hatred and delusion have no opportunity to creep in. Thus, concentration can be compared to weeding the area around the plant, or to applying a very wholesome and natural type of pesticide.

If these first four protections are present, insights have the opportunity to blossom. However, yogis tend to become attached to early insights and unusual experiences related to strong concentration. Unfortunately, this will hinder their practice from ripening into the deeper levels of vipassanā. Here, the fifth protection, *vipassanā-nuggahita*, comes into play. This is meditation which continues forcefully at a high level, not stopping to dawdle in the enjoyment of peace of mind nor other pleasures of concentration. Craving for these pleasures is called *nikanti tanhā*. It is subtle, like cobwebs, aphids, mildew, tiny spiders – sticky little things that can eventually choke off a plant's growth.

Even if a yogi gets caught in such booby traps, however, a good teacher can find out about this in the interview and nudge him or her back onto the straight path. This is why discussing one's experiences with a teacher is such an important protection for meditation practice.

## The Interview Process

During an intensive vipassanā retreat, personal interviews are held as often as possible, ideally every day. Interviews are formally structured. After the yogi presents his or her experiences as described below, the teacher may ask questions relating to particular details before giving a pithy comment or instruction.

The interview process is quite simple. You should be able to communicate the essence of your practice in about ten minutes. Consider that you are reporting on your research into yourself, which is what vipassanā actually is. Try to adhere to the standards used in the scientific world: brevity, accuracy and precision.

First, report how many hours of sitting you did and how many of walking in the most recent twenty-four-hour period. If you are quite truthful and honest about this, it will show the sincerity of your practice. Next, describe your sitting practice. It is not necessary to describe each sitting in detail. If sittings are similar, you may combine their traits together in a general report. Try using details from the clearest sitting or sittings. Begin your description with the primary object of meditation, the rise and fall of the abdomen. After this you may add other objects that arose at any of the six sense doors.

After describing the sitting, go into your walking practice. Here you must only describe experiences directly connected with your walking movements – do not include a range of objects as you might in reporting a sitting. If you use the three-part method of lifting, moving and placing in your walking meditation, try to include each segment and the experiences you had with it.

*What Occurred, How You Noted It, What Happened to It*

For all of these objects, indeed with any object of meditation, please report your experience in three phases. One, you identify what occurred. Two, you report how you noted it. And three, you describe what you saw, or felt, or understood; that is, what happened when you noted it.

Let us take as an example the primary object, the rising and falling movement of the abdomen. The first thing to do is to identify the occurrence of the rising process.

"Rising occurred."

The second phase is to note it, give it a silent verbal label.

"I noted it as 'rising'."

The third phase is to describe what happened to the rising.

"As I noted 'rising,' this is what I experienced, the different sensations I felt. This was the behavior of the sensations at that time."

Then you continue the interview by using the same three-phase description for the falling process and the other objects that arise during sitting. You mention the object's occurrence, describe how you noted it, and relate your subsequent experiences until the object disappears or your attention moves elsewhere.

Perhaps an analogy will serve to clarify. Imagine that I am sitting in front of you, and suddenly I raise my hand into the air and open it so that you can see that I am holding an apple. You direct your attention toward this apple; you recognize it and (because this is an analogy) you say the word "apple" to yourself. Now you go on to discern that the apple is red, round and shiny. At last I slowly close my hand so that the apple disappears.

How would you report your experience of the apple, if the apple were your primary object of meditation? You would say, "The apple appeared. I noted it as 'apple' and

I noticed that it was red, round and shiny. Then the apple slowly disappeared."

Thus, you would have reported in a precise way on the three phases of your involvement with the apple. First, there was the moment when the apple appeared and you became able to perceive it. Second, you directed your attention to the apple and recognized what it was; since you were "practicing meditation" with the apple, you made the particular effort to label it verbally in your mind. Third, you continued attending to the apple and discerned its qualities, as well as the manner of its passing out of your awareness. This three-step process is the same one you must follow in actual vipassanā meditation, except, of course, that you observe and report on your experiences of the rising and falling of your abdomen. One warning: your duty to observe the fictitious apple does not extend to imagining the apple's juiciness or visualizing yourself eating it! Similarly, in a meditation interview, you must restrict your descriptions to what you have experienced directly, rather than what you may imagine, visualize and opine about the object.

As you can see, this style of reporting is a guide for how awareness should be functioning in actual vipassanā meditation. For this reason, meditation interviews are helpful for an additional reason beyond the chance to receive a teacher's guidance. Yogis often find that being required to produce a report of this kind has a galvanizing effect on their meditation practice, for it asks them to focus on their experiences as clearly as they possibly can.

### Awareness, Accuracy, Perseverance

It is not enough to look at the object indifferently, haphazardly, or in an unmindful, automatic way. This is not a practice where you mindlessly recite some mental formula. You must look at the object with full commitment, with all of your heart. Directing your whole attention toward the object, as accurately as possible, you keep your attention there so that you can penetrate into the object's true nature.

Despite our best efforts, the mind may not always be so well-behaved as to remain with our abdomen. It wanders off. At this point a new object, the wandering mind, has arisen. How do we handle this? We become aware of the wandering. This is the first phase. Now the second phase: we label it as "wandering, wandering." How soon after its arising were we aware of the wandering? One second, two minutes, half an hour? And what happens after we label it? Does the wandering mind disappear instantly? Does the mind just keep on wandering? Or do the thoughts reduce in intensity and eventually disappear? Does a new object arise before we have seen the disappearance of the old one? If you cannot note the wandering mind at all, you should tell the teacher about this, too.

If the wandering mind disappears, you come back to the rising and falling. You should make a point to describe whether you are able to come back to it. In your reports it is good, also, to say how long the mind usually remained with the rising and falling movements before a new object arose.

Pains and aches, unpleasant sensations, are sure to arise after some time of sitting. Say an itch suddenly appears – a new object. You label it as "itching." Does the itch get worse or remain the same? Does it change or disappear? Do new objects arise, such as a wish to scratch? All this should be described as precisely as possible. It is the same with visions and sights, sounds and tastes, heat and cold, tightness, vibrations, tinglings, the unending procession of objects of consciousness. No matter what the object, you only have to apply the same three-step principle to it.

All of this process is done as a silent investigation, coming very close to our experience – not asking ourselves a lot of questions and getting lost in thought. What is important to the teacher is whether you could be aware of whatever object has arisen, whether you had the accuracy of mind to be mindful of it, and the perseverance to observe it fully. Be honest with your teacher. If you are unable to find the object, or note it, or experience anything at all after making a mental label, it may not always mean that you are practicing poorly! A clear and precise report enables the teacher to assess your practice; then point out mistakes or make corrections to put you back on the right path.

May you benefit from these interview instructions. May a teacher someday help you help yourself.

# 2  Cutting Through to Ultimate Reality by Sharpening the Controlling Faculties

❦ Vipassanā meditation can be seen as a process of developing certain positive mental factors until they are powerful enough to dominate the state of the mind quite continuously. These factors are called "the controlling faculties", and they are five in number: faith, effort or energy, mindfulness, concentration, and wisdom. Especially in an intensive retreat setting, proper practice develops strong and durable faith, powerful effort, deep concentration, penetrative mindfulness, and the unfolding of more and more profound insight or wisdom. This final product, intuitive wisdom or paññā, is the force in the mind which cuts through into the deepest truth about reality, and thus liberates us from ignorance and its results: suffering, delusion, and all the forms of unhappiness.

For this development to occur, however, the appropriate causes must be present. Nine causes lead to the growth of the controlling faculties; they are listed here, and will be discussed in more detail below. The first cause is attention directed toward the impermanence of all objects of consciousness. The second is an attitude of care and respect in meditation practice. The third is maintaining an unbroken continuity of awareness. The fourth cause is an environment that supports meditation. The fifth is remembering circumstances or behavior that have been helpful in one's past meditation practice so that one can maintain or recreate those conditions, especially when difficulties may arise. The sixth is cultivating the qualities of mind which lead toward enlightenment. The seventh is willingness to work intensely in meditation practice. The eighth is patience and perseverance in the face of pain or other obstacles. The ninth and last cause for the development of the controlling faculties is a determination to continue practicing until one reaches the goal of liberation.

A yogi can travel far in this practice if he or she fulfills even just the first three causes for the controlling faculties to arise. That is, the yogi's mental state will come to be characterized by faith, energy, mindfulness, concentration and wisdom if she or he is aware of the passing away of mental and physical phenomena meticulously, respectfully, and with persistent continuity. Under these conditions, the inner hindrances to meditation will soon be removed. The controlling faculties will calm the mind and clear it of disturbances. If you are such a yogi, you will experience a tranquility you may never have felt before. You may be filled with awe. "Fantastic, it's really true! All those teachers talk about peace and calm and now I'm really experiencing it!" Thus faith, the first of the controlling faculties, will have arisen out of your practice.

This particular kind of faith is called "preliminary veri- fied faith." Your own experience leads you to feel that the further promises of the Dhamma may actually be true.

With faith comes a natural inspiration, an upsurge of energy. When energy is present, effort follows. You will say to yourself, "This is just the beginning. If I work a little harder, I'll have experiences even better than this." A renewed effort guides the mind to hit its target of obser- vation in each moment. Thus mindfulness consolidates and deepens.

Mindfulness has the uncanny ability to bring about concentration, one-pointedness of mind. When mindfulness penetrates into the object of observation moment by mo- ment, the mind gains the capacity to remain stable and undistracted, content within the object. In this natural fash- ion, concentration becomes well-established and strong. In general, the stronger one's mindfulness, the stronger one's concentration will be.

With faith, effort, mindfulness and concentration, four of the five controlling faculties have been assembled. Wisdom, the fifth, needs no special introduction. If the first four factors are present, wisdom or insight unfolds of itself. One begins to see very clearly, intuitively, how mind and matter are separate entities, and begins also to understand in a very special way how mind and matter are connected by cause and effect. Upon each insight, one's verified faith deepens.

A yogi who has seen objects arising and passing away from moment to moment feels very fulfilled. "It's fabulous. Just moment after moment of these phenomena with no self behind them. No one at home." This discovery brings a sense of great relief and ease of mind. Subsequent insights into impermanence, suffering and absence of self have a particularly strong capacity to stimulate faith. They fill us with powerful conviction that the Dhamma as it has been told to us is authentic.

Vipassanā practice can be compared to sharpening a knife against a whetstone. One must hold the blade at just the right angle, not too high or too low, and apply just the right amount of pressure. Moving the knife blade consistently against the stone, one works continuously and until the first edge has been developed. Then one flips the knife over to sharpen the other edge, applying the same pressure at the same angle. This image is given in the Buddhist scriptures. Precision of angle is like meticulousness in practice, and pressure and movement are like continuity of mindfulness. If meticulousness and continuity are really present in your practice, rest assured that in a short time your mind will be sharp enough to cut through to the truth about existence.

## ONE: ATTENTION TO IMPERMANENCE

The first cause for development of the controlling faculties is to notice that everything which arises will also dissolve and pass away. During meditation one observes mind and matter at all the six sense doors. One should approach this process of observation with the intention to notice that everything which appears will, in turn, dissolve. As you are no doubt aware, this idea can only be confirmed by actual observation.

This attitude is a very important preparation for practice. A preliminary acceptance that things are impermanent and transitory prevents the reactions that might occur when you discover these facts – sometimes painfully – through your own experience. Without this acceptance, moreover, a student might spend considerable time with the contrary assumption, that the objects of this world might be permanent, an assumption that can block the development of insight. In the beginning you can take impermanence on faith. As practice deepens, this faith will be verified by personal experience.

### Two: CARE AND RESPECT

The second basis for strengthening the controlling faculties is an attitude of great care in pursuing the meditation practice. It is essential to treat the practice with the utmost reverence and meticulousness. To develop this attitude it may be helpful to reflect on the benefits you are likely to enjoy through practice. Properly practiced, mindfulness of body, feelings, mind and mind objects leads to the purification of the mind, the overcoming of sorrow and lamentation, the complete destruction of physical pain and mental distress, and the attainment of nibbāna. The Buddha called it *satipaṭṭhāna* meditation, meaning meditation on the four foundations of mindfulness. Truly it is priceless!

Remembering this, you may be inspired to be very careful and attentive toward the objects of awareness that arise at the six sense doors. On a meditation retreat, you should also try to slow down your movements as much as possible, appreciating the fact that your mindfulness is at an infant stage. Slowing down gives mindfulness the chance to keep pace with the movements of the body, noting each one in detail.

The scriptures illustrate this quality of care and meticulousness with the image of a person crossing a river on a very narrow footbridge. There is no railing, and swift water runs below. Obviously, this person cannot skip and run across the bridge. He or she must go step by step, with care.

A meditator can also be compared to a person carrying a bowl brimful of oil. You can imagine the degree of care that is required not to spill it. This same degree of mindfulness should be present in your practice.

This second example was given by the Buddha himself. It seems there was a group of monks residing in a forest, ostensibly practicing meditation. They were sloppy, though. At the end of a sitting, they would leap up suddenly and unmindfully. Walking from place to place, they were careless; they looked at the birds in the trees and the clouds in the sky, not restraining their minds at all. Naturally they made no progress in practice.

When the Buddha came to know of this, his investigation showed that the fault lay in the monks' lack of respect and reverence for the Dhamma, for the teaching, and for meditation. The Buddha then approached the monks and spoke to them about the image of carrying a bowl of oil. Inspired by his *sutta*, or discourse, the monks resolved thereafter to be meticulous and careful in all that they did. As a result they were enlightened in a short time.

You can verify this result in your own experience on a retreat. Slowing down, moving with great care, you will be able to apply a quality of reverence in noting your experience. The slower you move, the faster you will progress in your meditation.

Of course, in this world one must adapt to the prevailing circumstances. Some situations require speed. If you cruise the highway at a snail's pace, you might end up dead or in jail. At a hospital, in contrast, patients must be treated with great gentleness and allowed to move slowly. If doctors and nurses hurry them along so that the hospital's work can be finished more efficiently, the patients will suffer and perhaps end up on a mortuary slab.

Yogis must comprehend their situation, wherever they are, and adapt to it. On retreat, or in any other situation, it is good to be considerate and to move at a normal speed if others are waiting behind you. However, you must also understand that one's primary goal is to develop mindfulness, and so when you are alone it is appropriate to revert to creeping about. You can eat slowly, you can wash your face, brush your teeth and bathe with great mindfulness – as long as no one is waiting in line for the shower or tub.

## THREE: UNBROKEN CONTINUITY

Persevering continuity of mindfulness is the third essential factor in developing the controlling faculties. One should try to be with the moment as much as possible, moment after moment, without any breaks in between. In this way mindfulness can be established, and its momentum can increase. Defending our mindfulness prevents the *kilesas*, the harmful and painful qualities of greed, hatred and delusion, from infiltrating and carrying us off into oblivion. It is a fact of life that the kilesas cannot arise in the presence of strong mindfulness. When the mind is free of kilesas, it becomes unburdened, light and happy.

Do whatever is necessary to maintain continuity. Do one action at a time. When you change postures, break down the movement into single units and note each unit with the utmost care. When you arise from sitting, note the intention to open the eyelids, and then the sensations that occur when the lids begin to move. Note lifting the hand from the knee, shifting the leg, and so on. Throughout the day, be fully aware of even the tiniest actions – not just sitting, standing, walking and lying, but also closing your eyes, turning your head, turning doorknobs and so forth.

Apart from the hours of sleeping, yogis on retreat should be continuously mindful. Continuity should be so strong, in fact, that there is no time at all for reflection, no hesitation, no thinking, no reasoning, no comparing of one's experiences with the things one has read about meditation – just time enough to apply this bare awareness.

The scriptures compare practicing the Dhamma to start-ing a fire. In the days before the invention of matches or magnifying glasses, fire had to be started by the primitive means of friction. People used an instrument like a bow, held horizontally. In its looped string they entwined a vertical stick whose point was inserted into a slight depres-sion in a board, which was in turn filled with shavings or leaves. As people moved the bow back and forth, the stick's point twirled, eventually igniting the leaves or shavings. Another method was simply to roll that same stick between the palms of the hands. In either case, people rubbed and rubbed until sufficient friction accumulated to ignite the shavings. Imagine what would happen if they rubbed for ten seconds and then rested for five seconds to think about it. Do you think a fire would start? In just this way, a continuous effort is necessary to start the fire of wisdom.

Have you ever studied the behavior of a chameleon? The scriptures use this lizard to illustrate discontinuous practice. Chameleons approach their goals in an interesting way. Catching sight of a delicious fly or a potential mate, a chameleon rushes suddenly forward, but does not arrive all at once. It scurries a short distance, then stops and gazes at the sky, tilting its head this way and that. Then it rushes ahead a bit more and stops again to gaze. It never reaches its destination in the first rush.

People who practice in fits and starts, being mindful for a stretch and then stopping to daydream, are chameleon yogis. Chameleons manage to survive despite their lack of continuity, but a yogi's practice may not. Some yogis feel called to reflect and think each time they have a new experience, wondering which stage of insight they have reached. Others do not need novelty, they think and worry about familiar things.

"I feel tired today. Maybe I didn't sleep enough. Maybe I ate too much. A little nap might be just the ticket. My foot hurts. I wonder if a blister is developing. That would affect my whole meditation! Maybe I should just open my eyes and check." Such are the hesitations of chameleon yogis.

FOUR: SUPPORTIVE CONDITIONS

The fourth cause for developing the controlling faculties is to make sure that suitable conditions are met for insights to unfold. Proper, suitable and appropriate activities can bring about insight knowledge. Seven types of suitability should be met in order to create an environment that is supportive of meditation practice.

The first suitability is that of place. A meditative environment should be well-furnished, well-supported, a place where it is possible to gain insight.

Second is what is known as suitability of resort. This refers to the ancient practice of daily alms rounds. A monk's place of meditation should be far enough from a village to avoid distraction, but near enough so that he can depend on the villagers for daily alms food. For lay yogis, food must be easily and consistently available, yet perhaps not distractingly so. Under this heading, one should avoid places which ruin one's concentration. This means busy, active places where the mind is likely to be distracted from its meditation object. In short, a certain amount of quiet is important, but one must not go so far from the noises of civilization that one cannot obtain what one needs to survive.

The third suitability is that of speech. During a retreat, suitable speech is of a very limited kind and quantity. The commentaries define it as listening to Dhamma talks. We can add participating in Dhamma discussions with the teacher – that is, interviews. It is essential at times to engage in discussions of the practice, especially when one is confused or unsure about how to proceed.

But remember that anything in excess is harmful. I once taught in a place where there was a potted plant which my attendant was overzealous in watering. All its leaves fell off. A similar thing could happen to your samādhi if you get involved in too many Dhamma discussions. And one should carefully evaluate even the discourses of one's teacher. The general rule is to exercise discretion as to whether what one is hearing will develop the concentration that has already arisen, or cause to arise concentration that has not yet arisen. If the answer is negative, one should avoid the situation, perhaps even choosing not to attend the teacher's discourses or not requesting extra interviews.

Yogis on intensive retreat should of course avoid any kind of conversation as much as possible, especially chatting about worldly affairs. Even serious discussion of the Dhamma is not always appropriate during intensive practice. One should avoid debating points of dogma with fellow yogis on retreat. Thoroughly unsuitable during retreats are conversations about food, place, business, the economy, politics and so forth; these are called "animal speech."

The purpose of having this kind of prohibition is to prevent distractions from arising in the yogi's mind. Lord Buddha, out of deep compassion for meditating yogis, said, "For an ardent meditator, speech should not be indulged. If indeed speech is resorted to frequently, it will cause much distraction."

Of course it may become really necessary to talk during a retreat. If so, you should be careful not to exceed what is absolutely necessary to communicate. You should also be mindful of the process of speaking. First there will be a desire to speak. Thoughts will arise in the mind as to what to say and how to say it. You should note and carefully label all such thoughts, the mental preparation for speaking; and then the actual act of speaking itself, the physical movements involved. The movements of your lips and face, and any accompanying gestures, should be made the objects of mindfulness.

Some years ago in Burma there was a high-ranking government official who had just retired. He was a very ardent Buddhist. He had read a lot of Buddhist scriptures and literature in the fine translations available in Burmese and had also spent some time meditating. His practice was not strong, but he had a lot of general knowledge and he wanted to teach, so he became a teacher.

One day he came to the center in Rangoon to meditate. When I give instructions to yogis, usually I explain the practice and then compare my instructions to the scriptural texts, trying to reconcile any apparent differences. This gentleman immediately began to ask me, "From where did this quotation come and what is its reference?" I advised him politely to forget about this concern and to continue his meditation, but he could not. For three days in a row, he did the same thing at each interview.

Finally I asked him, "Why are you here? Did you come here to be my student, or to try to teach me?" It seemed to me he had only come to show off his general knowledge, not because he wished to meditate.

The man said airily, "Oh, I'm the student and you're the teacher."

I said, "I've been trying to let you know this in a subtle way for three days, but I must now be more direct with you. You are like the minister whose job it was to marry off brides and bridegrooms. On the day it was his turn to get married, instead of standing where the bridegroom should stand, he went up to the altar and conducted the ceremony. The congregation was very surprised." Well, the gentleman got the point; he admitted his error and thereafter became an obedient student.

Yogis who truly want to understand the Dhamma will not seek to imitate this gentleman. In fact, it is said in the texts that no matter how learned or experienced one may be, during a period of meditation one should behave like a person who is incapable of doing things out of his or her own initiative, but is also very meek and obedient. In this regard, I'd like to share with you an attitude I developed in my youth. When I am not skilled, competent or experienced in a particular field, I do not intrude in a situation. Even if I am skilled, competent and experienced in a field, I do not intrude unless someone asks for my advice.

The fourth suitability is that of person, which chiefly relates to the meditation teacher. If the instruction given by one's teacher helps one to progress, developing concentration that has already arisen, or bringing about concentration that has not yet arisen, then one can say that this teacher is suitable.

Two more aspects of suitability of person have to do with the community that supports one's practice, and one's own relationship with the community of other people. In an intensive retreat, yogis require a great deal of support. In order to develop their mindfulness and concentration, they abandon worldly activities. Thus, they need friends who can perform certain tasks that would be distracting for a yogi in intensive practice, such as shopping for and preparing food, repairing the shelter, and so on. For those engaged in group practice, it is important to consider one's own effect on the community. Delicate consideration for other yogis is quite helpful. Abrupt or noisy movements can be very disruptive to others. Bearing this in mind, one can become a suitable person with respect to other yogis.

The fifth area of suitability, of food, means that the diet one finds personally appropriate is also supportive to progress in meditation. However, one must bear in mind that it is not always possible to fill one's every preference. Group retreats can be quite large, and meals are cooked for everyone at once. At such times, it is best to adopt an attitude of accepting whatever is served. If one's meditation is disturbed by feelings of lack or distaste, it is all right to try to rectify this if convenient.

### The Story of Mātikamātā

Once sixty monks were meditating in the forest. They had a laywoman supporter named Mātikamātā, who was very devout. She tried to figure out what they might like, and every day she cooked enough food for all of them. One day Mātikamātā approached the monks and asked whether a lay person could meditate as they did. "Of course," she was told, and they gave her instructions. Happily she went back and began to practice. She kept up her meditation even while she was cooking for the monks and carrying out her household chores. Eventually she reached the third stage of enlightenment, *anāgāmī* or nonreturner; and because of the great merit she had accumulated in the past, she also had psychic powers such as the deva eye and deva ear – i.e. the abilities to see and hear distant things – and the ability to read people's minds.

Filled with joy and gratitude, Mātikamātā said to herself, "The Dhamma I've realized is very special. I'm such a busy person, though, looking after my household chores as well as feeding the monks every day, I'm sure those monks have progressed much further than I." With her psychic powers she investigated the meditation progress of the sixty monks, and saw to her shock that none of them had had even the vaguest ghost of a vipassanā insight.

"What's wrong here?" Mātikamātā wondered. Psychically, she looked into the monks' situation to determine where the unsuitability lay. It was not in the place they were meditating. It was not because they weren't getting along – but it was that they were not getting the right food! Some of the monks liked sour tastes, others preferred the salty. Some liked hot peppers and others liked cakes, and still others preferred vegetables. Out of great gratitude for the meditation instructions she had received from them, which had led her to profound enlightenment, Mātikamātā began to cater to each monk's preference. As a result, all of the monks soon became *arahants*, fully enlightened ones.

This woman's rapid and deep attainments, as well as her intelligence and dedication, provide a good model for people like parents and other caretakers, who serve the needs of others, but who do not need to relinquish aspirations for deep insights.

While on this subject, I would like to talk about vegetarianism. Some hold the view that it is moral to eat only vegetables. In Theravāda Buddhism there is no notion that this practice leads to an exceptional perception of the truth.

The Buddha did not totally prohibit the eating of meat. He only lay down certain conditions for it. For example, an animal must not be killed expressly for one's personal consumption. The monk Devadatta asked him to lay down a rule expressly forbidding the eating of meat, but the Buddha, after thorough consideration, refused to do so.

In those days as now, the majority of people ate a mixture of animal and vegetable food. Only Brahmins, or the upper caste, were vegetarian. When monks went begging for their livelihood, they had to take whatever was offered by donors of any caste. To distinguish between vegetarian and carnivorous donors would have affected the spirit of this activity. Furthermore, both Brahmins and members of other castes were able to join the order of monks and nuns. The Buddha took this fact into consideration as well, with all of its implications.

Thus, one needn't restrict oneself to vegetarianism to practice the Dhamma. Of course, it is healthy to eat a balanced vegetarian diet, and if your motivation for not eating meat is compassion, this impulse is certainly wholesome. If, on the other hand, your metabolism is adjusted to eating meat, or if for some other reason of health it is necessary for you to eat meat, this should not be considered sinful or in any way detrimental to the practice. A law that cannot be obeyed by the majority is ineffective.

The sixth type of suitability is that of weather. Human beings have a fantastic ability to adapt to weather. No matter how hot or cold it may be, we devise methods of making ourselves comfortable. When these methods are limited or unavailable, one's practice can be disrupted. At such times it may be better to practice in a temperate climate, if possible.

The seventh and last kind of suitability is that of posture. Posture here refers to the traditional four postures: sitting, standing, walking and lying down. Sitting is best for *samatha* or tranquillity meditation. In the tradition of Mahāsī Sayadaw, vipassanā practice is based on sitting and walking. For any type of meditation, once momentum builds, posture does not really matter; any of the four is suitable.

Beginning yogis should avoid the lying and the standing postures. The standing posture can bring about pain in a short while: tightness and pressure in the legs, which can disrupt the practice. The lying posture is problematic because it brings on drowsiness. In it there is not much effort being made to maintain the posture, and there is too much comfort.

Investigate your own situation to find out whether the seven types of suitability are present. If they are not, perhaps you should take steps to ensure they are fulfilled, so that your practice can develop. If this is done with the aim of making progress in your practice, it will not be self-centered.

## FIVE: REAPPLYING HELPFUL CONDITIONS FROM THE PAST

The fifth way of sharpening the controlling faculties is to bring about the completion of meditative insight using what is called "the sign of samādhi." This refers to circumstances in which good practice has occurred before: good mindfulness and concentration. As we all know, practice is an up and down affair. At times we are high up in the clouds of samādhiland; at other times, we're really depressed, assaulted by kilesas, not mindful of anything. Using the sign of samādhi means that when you are up in those clouds, when mindfulness is strong, you should try to notice what circumstances led to this good practice. How are you working with the mind? What are the specific circumstances in which this good practice is occurring? The next time you get into a difficult situation, you may be able to remember the causes of good mindfulness and establish them again.

## SIX: CULTIVATING THE FACTORS THAT LEAD TO ENLIGHTENMENT

The sixth way of sharpening the controlling faculties is cultivating the factors of enlightenment: mindfulness, investigation, energy, rapture or joy, tranquility, concentration, and equanimity. These qualities of mind, or mental factors, are actually the causes which bring about enlightenment. When they are present and alive in one's mind, the moment of enlightenment is being encouraged, and may be said to be drawing nearer. Furthermore, the seven factors of enlightenment belong to what is known as "noble path and fruition consciousness." In Buddhism, we speak of "consciousnesses" when we mean specific, momentary types of consciousness – particular mental events, with recognizable characteristics. Path and fruition consciousness are the linked mental events that constitute an enlightenment experience. They are what is occurring when the mind shifts its attention from the conditioned realm to nibbāna, or unconditioned reality. The result of such a shift is that certain defilements are uprooted, so that the mind is never the same afterwards.

While working to create the conditions for path and fruition consciousness, a yogi who understands the factors of enlightenment can use them to balance her or his meditation practice. The enlightenment factors of *effort, joy,* and *investigation* uplift the mind when it becomes depressed, while the factors of *tranquility, concentration,* and *equanimity* calm the mind when it becomes hyperactive.

Many times a yogi may feel depressed and discouraged, having no mindfulness, thinking that his or her practice is going terribly badly. Mindfulness may not be able to pick up objects as it has in the past. At such a time it is essential for a yogi to pull out of this state, brighten the mind. He or she should go in search of encouragement and inspiration. One way to do this is by listening to a good Dhamma talk. A talk can bring about the enlightenment factor of joy or rapture; or it can inspire greater effort, or it can deepen the enlightenment factor of investigation by providing knowledge about practice. These three factors of enlightenment – rapture, effort and investigation – are most helpful in facing depression and discouragement.

Once an inspiring talk has brought up rapture, energy or investigation, you should use this opportunity to try to focus the mind very clearly on objects of observation, so that the objects appear very clearly to the mind's eye.

At other times, yogis may have an unusual experience, or for some other reason may find themselves flooded with exhilaration, rapture and joy. The mind becomes active and overenthusiastic. On a retreat you can spot such yogis beaming, walking around as if they were six feet above the ground. Due to excess energy, the mind slips; it refuses to concentrate on what is happening in the present moment.

If attention touches the target object at all, it immediately goes off on a tangent.

If you find yourself excessively exhilarated, you should restore your equilibrium by developing the three enlightenment factors of tranquility, concentration and equanimity. A good way to start is by realizing that your energy is indeed excessive; and then reflecting, "There's no point in hurrying. The Dhamma will unfold by itself. I should just sit back coolly and watch with gentle awareness." This stimulates the factor of tranquility. Then, once the energy is cooled, one can begin to apply concentration. The practical method of doing this is to narrow down the meditation. Instead of noting many objects, cut down to concentrate more fully on a few. The mind will soon renew its normal, slower pace. Lastly, one can adopt a stance of equanimity, cajoling and soothing the mind with reflections like, "A yogi has no preferences. There's no point in hurrying. The only thing that matters is for me to watch whatever is happening, good or bad."

If you can keep your mind in balance, soothing excitement and lightening up depression, you can be sure that wisdom will shortly unfold on its own.

Actually, the person best qualified to rectify imbalances in practice is a competent meditation teacher. If he or she keeps steady track of students through interviews, a teacher can recognize and remedy the many kinds of excesses that yogis are susceptible to.

I would like to remind all yogis never to feel discouraged when they think something is wrong with their meditation. Yogis are like babies or young children. As you know, babies go through various stages of development. When babies are in a transition from one stage of development to another, they tend to go through a lot of psychological and physical upheaval. They seem to get irritated very easily and are difficult to care for. They cry and wail at odd times. An inexperienced mother may worry about her baby during periods like this. But truly, if infants don't go through this suffering they will never mature and grow up. Babies' distress is often a sign of developmental progress. So if you feel your practice is falling apart, do not worry. You may be just like that little child who is in a transition between stages of growth.

## SEVEN: COURAGEOUS EFFORT

The seventh way of developing the controlling faculties is to practice with courageous effort, so much so that you are willing to sacrifice your body and life in order to continue the practice uninterrupted. This means giving rather less consideration toward the body than we tend to be accustomed to give to it. Rather than spending time beautifying ourselves or catering to our wishes for greater comfort, we devote as much energy as possible to going forward in meditation.

Although it may feel very youthful right now, our body becomes completely useless when we die. What use can one make of a corpse? The body is like a very fragile container which can be used as long as it is intact, but the moment it drops on the floor, it is of no further help to us.

While we are alive and in reasonably good health, we have the good fortune to be able to practice. Let us try to extract the precious essence from our bodies before it is too late, before our bodies become useless corpses! Of course, it is not our aim to hasten this event. We should also try to be sensible, and to maintain this body's health, if only for our practice to continue.

You might ask what essence one can extract from the body. A scientific study was once made to determine the market value of the substances composing the human body: iron, calcium and so on. I believe it came to less than one American dollar, and the cost of extracting all those components was many times greater than this total value. Without such a process of extraction, a corpse is valueless, beyond providing compost for the soil. If a dead person's organs can be used for transplants into living bodies, this is good; but in this case, progress toward becoming an entirely lifeless and valueless corpse has only been delayed.

The body can be looked at as a rubbish dump, disgusting and full of impurities. Uncreative people have no use for things they might find in such a dump, but an innovative person understands the value of recycling. He or she may take a dirty, smelly thing off the rubbish heap and clean it and be able to use it again. There are many stories of people who have made millions from the recycling business.

From this rubbish heap we call our body, we can nonetheless extract gold through the practice of the Dhamma. One form of gold is sīla, purity of conduct, the ability to tame and civilize one's actions. After further extraction, the body yields up the controlling faculties of faith, mindfulness, effort, concentration and wisdom. These are priceless jewels which can be extracted from the body through meditation. When the controlling faculties are well-developed, the mind resists domination by greed, hatred and delusion. A person whose mind is free of these painful, oppressive qualities experiences an exquisite happiness and peace that cannot be bought with money. His or her presence becomes calm and sweet, so that others feel uplifted. This inner freedom is independent of all circumstances and conditions, and it is only available as a result of ardent meditation practice.

Anyone can understand that painful mental states do not vanish just because we wish them to do so. Who has not wrestled with a desire they knew would hurt someone if they indulged it? Is there anyone who has never been in an irritable, grumpy mood and wished they were feeling happy and contented instead? Has anyone failed to experience the pain of being confused? It is possible to uproot the tendencies which create pain and dissatisfaction in our lives, but for most of us it is not easy. Spiritual work is as demanding as it is rewarding. Yet we should not be discouraged. The goal and result of vipassanā meditation is to be free from all kinds, all shades and all levels of mental and physical suffering. If you desire this kind of freedom, you should rejoice that you have an opportunity to strive to achieve it.

The best time to strive is right now. If you are young, you should appreciate your good situation, for young people have the most energy to carry out the meditation practice. If you are older you may have less physical energy, but perhaps you have seen enough of life to have gained wise consideration, such as a personal understanding of life's fleetingness and unpredictability.

## "Urgency Seized Me"

During the Buddha's time there was a young bhikkhu, or monk, who had come from a wealthy family. Young and robust, he'd had the chance to enjoy a wide variety of sense pleasures before his ordination. He was wealthy, he had many friends and relatives, and his wealth made available to him the full panoply of indulgences. Yet he renounced all this to seek liberation.

One day when the king of that country was riding through the forest, he came across this monk. The king said, "Venerable sir, you are young and robust; you are in the prime of youth. You come from a wealthy family and have lots of opportunities to enjoy yourself. Why did you leave your home and family to wear robes and live in solitude? Don't you feel lonely? Aren't you bored?"

The monk answered, "O great king, when I was listening to the Buddha's discourse that leads to arousing spiritual urgency, a great sense of urgency seized me. I want to extract the optimum utility from this body of mine in time before I die. That is why I gave up the worldly life and took these robes."

If you still are not convinced of the need to practice with great urgency, without attachment to body or life, the Buddha's words may also be helpful for you.

One should reflect, he said, on the fact that the whole world of beings is made up of nothing but mind and matter which have arisen but do not stay. Mind and matter do not remain still for one single moment; they are in constant flux. Once we find ourselves in this body and mind, there is nothing we can do to prevent growth from taking place. When we are young we like to grow, but when we are old we are stuck in an irreversible process of decline.

We like to be healthy, but our wishes can never be guaranteed. We are plagued by sickness and illness, by pain and discomfort, throughout our existence. Immortal life is beyond our reach. All of us will die. Death is contrary to what we would wish for ourselves, yet we cannot prevent it. The only question is whether death will come sooner or later.

Not a single person on earth can guarantee our wishes regarding growth, health or immortality. People refuse to accept these facts. The old try to look young. Scientists develop all manner of cures and contraptions to delay the process of human decay. They even try to revive the dead! When we are sick we take medicines to feel better. But even if we get well, we will get sick again. Nature cannot be deceived. We cannot escape old age and death.

This is the main weakness of beings: beings are devoid of security. There is no safe refuge from old age, disease and death. Look at other beings, look at animals, and most of all, look at yourself.

If you have practiced deeply, these facts will come as no surprise to you. If you can see with intuitive insight how mental and physical phenomena arise endlessly from moment to moment, you know there is no refuge anywhere that you can run to. There is no security. Yet, if your insight has not reached this point, perhaps reflecting on the precariousness of life will cause some urgency to arise in you, and give you a strong impulse to practice. Vipassanā meditation can lead to a place beyond all these fearsome things.

Beings have another great weakness: lack of possessions. This may sound strange. We are born. We begin procuring knowledge right away. We obtain credentials. Most of us get a job, and buy many items with the resulting wages. We call these our possessions, and on a relative level, that is what they are – no doubt about it. If possessions really belonged to us, though, we would never be separated from them. Would they break, or get lost, or stolen the way they do if we owned them in some ultimate sense? When human beings die there is nothing we can take with us. Everything gained, amassed, stored up and hoarded is left behind. Therefore it is said that all beings are possessionless.

All of our property must be left behind at the moment of death. Property is of three types, the first of which is immovable property: buildings, land, estates, and so forth. Conventionally these belong to you, but you must leave them behind when you die. The second type of property is moveable property: chairs, toothbrushes and clothing – all the things you carry along as you travel about during your existence on this planet. Then there is knowledge: arts and sciences, the skills you use to sustain your life and that of others. As long as we have a body in good working order, this property of knowledge is essential. However, there is no insurance against losing that either. You may forget what you know, or you may be prevented from practicing your specialty by a government decree or some other unfortunate event. If you are a surgeon you could badly break your arm, or you could meet with some other kind of attack on your well-being which leaves you too neurotic to continue your livelihood.

None of these kinds of possessions can bring any security during existence on earth, let alone during the afterlife. If one can understand that we possess nothing, and that life is extremely transitory, then we will feel much more peaceful when the inevitable comes to pass.

### Our Only True Possession

However, there are certain things that follow human beings through the doors of death. This is *kamma* (Sanskrit: *karma*), the results of our actions. Our good and bad kammas follow us wherever we are; we cannot get away from them even if we want to.

Believing that kamma is your only true possession brings a strong wish to practice the Dhamma with ardor and thoroughness. You will understand that wholesome and beneficial deeds are an investment in your own future happiness, and harmful deeds will rebound upon you. Thus, you will do many things based on noble considerations of benevolence, generosity, and kindness. You will try to make donations to hospitals, to people suffering from calamity. You will support members of your family, the aged, the handicapped and underprivileged, your friends, and others who need help. You will want to create a better society by maintaining purity of conduct, taming your speech and actions. You will bring about a peaceful environment as you strive to meditate and tame the obsessive kilesas that arise in the heart. You will go through the stages of insight and eventually realize the ultimate goal. All of these meritorious deeds of *dāna*, of giving; of *sīla*, morality; and of *bhāvanā*, mental development or meditation – they will follow you after death, just as your shadow follows you wherever you go. Do not cease to cultivate the wholesome!

All of us are slaves of craving. It is ignoble, but it is true. Desire is insatiable. As soon as we get something, we find it is not as satisfying as we thought it would be, and we try something else. It is the nature of life, like trying to scoop up water in a butterfly net. Beings cannot become contented by following the dictates of desire, chasing after objects. Desire can never satisfy desire. If we understand this truth correctly, we will not seek satisfaction in this self-defeating way. This is why the Buddha said that contentment is the greatest wealth.

There is a story of a man who worked as a basket weaver. He was a simple man who enjoyed weaving his baskets. He whistled and sang and passed the day happily as he worked. At night he retired to his little hut and slept well. One day a wealthy man passed by and saw this poor wretched basket weaver. He was filled with compassion and gave him a thousand dollars. "Take this," he said, "and go enjoy yourself."

The basket weaver took the money with much appreciation. He had never seen a thousand dollars in his life. He took it back to his ramshackle hut and was wondering where he could keep it. But his hut was not very secure.

He could not sleep all night because he was worrying about robbers, or even rats nibbling at his cash.

The next day he took his thousand dollars to work, but he did not sing or whistle because he was worrying so much about his money again. Once more, that night he did not sleep, and in the morning he returned the thousand dollars to the wealthy man, saying, "Give me back my happiness."

You may think that Buddhism discourages you from seeking knowledge or credentials, or from working hard to earn money so you can support yourself and family and friends and contribute to worthy causes and institutions. No. By all means, make use of your life and your intelligence, and obtain all these things legally and honestly. The point is to be contented with what you have. Do not become a slave of craving: that is the message. Reflect on the weaknesses of beings so that you can get the most from your body and life before you are too sick and old to practice and can only depart from this useless corpse.

### EIGHT: PATIENCE AND PERSEVERANCE

If you practice with heroic effort, entertaining no considerate attachment to body or life, you can develop the liberating energy which will carry you through the higher stages of practice. Such a courageous attitude contains within itself not only the seventh, but also the eighth means of developing the controlling faculties. This eighth quality is patience and perseverance in dealing with pain, especially painful sensations in the body.

All yogis are familiar with the unpleasant sensations that can come up during the course of a single sitting, the suffering of the mind in reaction to these sensations, and on top of that, the mind's resistance to being controlled as it must be in the practice.

An hour's sitting requires a lot of work. First, you try to keep your mind on the primary object as much as possible. This restraint and control can be very threatening to the mind, accustomed as it is to running wild. The process of maintaining attention becomes a strain. This strain of the mind, resisting control, is one form of suffering.

When the mind fills with resistance, often the body reacts also. Tension arises. In a short time you are besieged by painful sensations. What with the initial resistance and this pain on top of it, you've got quite a task on your hands. Your mind is constricted, your body is tight, you lose the patience to look directly at the physical pain. Now your mind goes completely bonkers. It may fill with aversion and rage. Your suffering is now threefold: the mind's initial resistance; the actual physical pain; and the mental suffering that results from physical suffering.

This would be a good time to apply the eighth cause for strengthening the controlling faculties, patience and perseverance, and try to look at the pain directly. If you are not prepared to confront pain in a patient way, you only leave open the door to the kilesas, like greed and anger. "Oh, I hate this pain. If only I could get back the wonderful comfort I had five minutes ago." In the presence of anger and greed, and in the absence of patience, the mind becomes confused and deluded as well. No object is clear, and you are unable to see the true nature of pain.

At such a time you will believe that pain is a thorn, a hindrance in your practice. You may decide to shift position in order to "concentrate better." If such movement becomes a habit, you will lose the chance to deepen your meditation practice. Calmness and tranquility of mind have their foundation in stillness of body.

Constant movement is actually a good way to conceal the true nature of pain. Pain may be right under your nose, the most predominant element of your experience, but you move your body so as not to look at it. You lose a wonderful opportunity to understand what pain really is.

In fact we have been living with pain ever since we were born on this planet. It has been close to us all our lives. Why do we run from it? If pain arises, look on it as a precious opportunity really to understand something familiar in a new and deeper way.

At times when you are not meditating, you can exercise patience toward painful sensations, especially if you are concentrating on something you are interested in. Say you are a person who really loves the game of chess. You sit in your chair and look very intently at the chessboard, where your opponent has just made a fantastic move, putting you in check. You may have been sitting on that chair for two hours, yet you will not feel your cramped position as you try to work out the strategy to escape from your predicament. Your mind is totally lost in thought. If you do feel the pain, you may very well ignore it until you have achieved your goal.

It is even more important to exercise patience in the practice of meditation, which develops a much higher level of wisdom than does chess, and which gets us out of a more fundamental kind of predicament.

*Strategies for Dealing with Pain*

- The degree of penetration into the true nature of phenomena depends very much on the level of concentration we can develop. The more one-pointed the mind, the more deeply it can penetrate and understand reality. This is particularly true when one is being aware of painful sensations. If concentration is weak, we will not really feel the discomfort which is always present in our bodies. When concentration begins to deepen, even the slightest discomfort becomes so very clear that it appears to be magnified and exaggerated. Most human beings are myopic in this sense. Without the eyeglasses of concentration, the world appears hazy, blurry and indistinct. But when we put them on, all is bright and clear. It is not the objects that have changed; it is the acuity of our sight.

When you look with the naked eye at a drop of water, you do not see much. If you put a sample under the microscope, however, you begin to see many things happening there. Many things are dancing and moving, fascinating to watch. If in meditation you are able to put on your glasses of concentration, you will be surprised at the variety of changes taking place in what would appear to be a stagnant and uninteresting spot of pain. The deeper the concentration, the deeper your understanding of pain. You will be more and more enthralled the more clearly you can see that these painful sensations are in a constant state of flux, from one sensation to another, changing, diminishing, growing stronger, fluctuating and dancing. Concentration and mindfulness will deepen and sharpen. At times when the show becomes utterly fascinating, there is a sudden and unexpected end to it, as though the curtain is dropped and the pain just disappears miraculously.

One who is unable to arouse enough courage or energy to look at pain will never understand the potential that lies in it. We have to develop courage of mind, heroic effort, to look at pain. Let's learn not to run from pain, but rather to go right in.

When pain arises, the first strategy is to send your attention straight toward it, right to the center of it. You try to penetrate its core. Seeing pain as pain, note it persistently, trying to get under its surface so that you do not react.

Perhaps you try very hard, but you still become fatigued. Pain can exhaust the mind. If you cannot maintain a reasonable level of energy, mindfulness and concentration, it is time to gracefully withdraw. The second strategy for dealing with pain is to play with it. You go into it and then you relax a bit. You keep your attention on the pain, but you loosen the intensity of mindfulness and concentration. This gives your mind a rest. Then you go in again as closely as you can; and if you are not successful you retreat again. You go in and out, back and forth, two or three times.

If the pain is still strong and you find your mind becoming tight and constricted despite these tactics, it is time for a graceful surrender. This does not mean shifting your physical position just yet. It means shifting the position of your mindfulness. Completely ignore the pain and put your mind on the rising and falling or whatever primary object you are using. Try to concentrate so strongly on this that the pain is blocked out of your awareness.

*Healing Body and Mind*

We must try to overcome any timidity of mind. Only if you have the strength of mind of a hero will you be able to overcome pain by understanding it for what it really is. In meditation many kinds of unbearable physical sensations can arise. Nearly all yogis see clearly the discomfort that has always existed in their bodies, but magnified by concentration. During intensive practice pain also frequently resurfaces from old wounds, childhood mishaps, or chronic illnesses of the past. A current or recent illness can suddenly get worse. If these last two happen to you, you can say that Lady Luck is on your side. You have the chance to overcome an illness or chronic pain through your own heroic effort, without taking a drop of medicine. Many yogis have totally overcome and transcended their health problems through meditation practice alone.

About fifteen years ago there was a man who'd been suffering from gastric troubles for many years. When he went to his checkup, the doctor said he had a tumor and needed surgery. The man was afraid that the operation would be unsuccessful and he might die.

So he decided to play it safe in case he did die. "I had better go meditate," he said to himself. He came to practice under my guidance. Soon he began to feel a lot of pain. At first it was not bad, but as he made progress in practice and reached the level of insight connected with pain, he had a severe, unbearable, torturous attack. He told me about it and I said, "Of course you are free to go home to see your doctor. However, why don't you stay a few more days?"

He thought about it and decided there still was no guarantee he would survive the operation. So he decided to stay and meditate. He took a teaspoon of medicine every two hours. At times the pain got the better of him; at times he overcame the pain. It was a long battle, with losses on both sides. But this man had enormous courage.

During one sitting the pain was so excruciating that his whole body shook and his clothes were soaked in sweat. The tumor in his stomach was getting harder and harder, more and more constricted. Suddenly his idea of his stomach disappeared as he was looking at it. Now there was just his consciousness and a painful object. It was very painful but it was very interesting. He kept on watching and there was just the noting mind and the pain, which got more and more excruciating.

Then there was a big explosion like a bomb. The yogi said he could even hear a loud sound. After that it was all over. He got up from his sitting drenched in sweat. He touched his belly, but in the place where his tumor once protruded, there was nothing. He was completely cured. Moreover, he had completed his meditation practice, having had an insight into nibbāna.

Soon afterwards this man left the center and I asked him to let me know what the doctor said about the gastric problem. The doctor was shocked to see that the tumor was gone. The man could forget the strict diet he had followed for twenty years, and to this day he is alive and in good health. Even the doctor became a vipassanā yogi!

I have come across innumerable people who have recovered from chronic headaches, heart trouble, tuberculosis, even cancer and severe injuries sustained at an early age. Some of them had been declared incurable by doctors. All of these people had to go through tremendous pain. But they exercised enormous perseverance and courageous effort, and they healed themselves. More important, many also came to understand far more deeply the truth about reality by observing pain with tenacious courage and then breaking through to insight.

You should not be discouraged by painful sensations. Rather, have faith and patience. Persevere until you understand your own true nature.

NINE: UNWAVERING COMMITMENT

The ninth and last factor leading to the development of the controlling faculties is the quality of mind that keeps you walking straight to the end of the path without becoming sidetracked, without giving up your task.

What is your objective in practicing meditation? Why do you undergo the threefold training of sīla, samādhi and paññā? It is important to appreciate the goal of meditation practice. It is even more important to be honest with yourself, so that you can know the extent of your commitment to that goal.

## Good Deeds and Our Highest Potential

Let us reflect on sīla. Having this amazing opportunity to be born on this planet as human beings, understanding that our wondrous existence in this world comes about as a result of good deeds, we should endeavor to live up to the highest potential of humanity. The positive connotations of the word "humanity" are great loving-kindness and compassion. Would it not be proper for every human being on this planet to aspire to perfect these qualities? If one is able to cultivate a mind filled with compassion and loving-kindness, it is easy to live in a harmonious and wholesome way. Morality is based on consideration for the feelings of all beings, others as well as oneself. One behaves in a moral way not only to be harmless toward others, but also to prevent one's own future sorrow. We all should avoid actions that will lead to unfavorable consequences, and walk the path of wholesome actions, which can free us forever from states of misery.

Kamma is our only true property. It will be very helpful if you can take this view as a basic foundation for your behavior, for your practice, for your life as a whole. Whether good or bad, kamma follows us everywhere, in this life and the next. If we perform skillful, harmonious actions, we will be held in high esteem in this very life. Wise persons will praise us and hold us in affection, and we will also be able to look forward to good circumstances in our future lives, until we attain final nibbāna.

Committing bad or unskillful actions brings about dishonor and notoriety even in this life. Wise people will blame us and look down upon us. Nor in the future will we be able to escape the consequences of our deeds.

In its powerful potential to bring good and bad results, kamma can be compared to food. Some foods are suitable and healthy, while others are poisonous to the body. If we understand which foods are nutritious, eating them at the proper time and in proper amounts, we can enjoy a long and healthy life. If, on the other hand, we are tempted by foods which are unhealthy and poisonous, we must suffer the consequences. We may fall sick and suffer a great deal. We may even die.

## Beautiful Acts

Practicing dāna or generosity can lessen the greed that arises in the heart. The five basic sīla precepts help control the emotions and very gross defilements of greed and hatred. Observing the precepts, the mind is controlled to the extent that it does not manifest through the body and perhaps not even through speech.

If you can be perfect in precepts, you may appear to be a very holy person, but inside you may still be tortured by eruptions of impatience, hatred, covetousness and scheming. Therefore, the next step is bhāvanā, which means in Pāli "the cultivation of exceptionally wholesome mental states." The first part of bhāvanā is to prevent unwholesome states from arising. The second part is the development of wisdom in the absence of these states.

### Blissful Concentration and its Flaws

*Samatha bhāvanā,* or concentration meditation, has the power to make the mind calm and tranquil and to pull it far away from the kilesas. It suppresses the kilesas, making it impossible for them to attack. Samatha bhāvanā is not unique to Buddhism. It can be found in many other religious systems, particularly in Hindu practices. It is a commendable undertaking in which the practitioner achieves purity of mind during the time he or she is absorbed in the object of meditation. Profound bliss, happiness and tranquility are achieved. At times even psychic powers can be cultivated through these states. However, success in samatha bhāvanā does not at all mean that one gains an insight into the true nature of reality in terms of mind and matter. The kilesas have been suppressed but not uprooted; the mind has not yet penetrated the true nature of reality. Thus, practitioners are not freed from the net of samsāra, and may even fall into states of misery in the future. One can attain a great deal through concentration and yet still be a loser.

After the Buddha's supreme enlightenment, he spent forty-nine days in Bodh Gaya enjoying the bliss of his liberation. Then he started to think about how he could communicate this profound and subtle truth to other beings. He looked around and saw that most of the world was covered by a thick layer of dust, of kilesas. People were wallowing in deepest darkness. The immensity of his task dawned on him.

Then it occurred to him that there were two-people who would be quite receptive to his teaching, whose minds were quite pure and clear of the kilesas. In fact, they were two of his former teachers, the hermits Ālāra the Kalāma and Udaka the Rāmaputta. Each of them had a large number of followers due to their attainments in concentration. The Buddha had mastered each of their teachings in turn, but had realized that he was seeking something beyond what they taught.

Yet both of these hermits' minds were very pure. Ālāra the Kalāma had mastered the seventh level of concentration, and Udaka the Rāmaputta the eighth, or highest, level of absorption. The kilesas were kept far from them, even during the times when they were not actually practicing their absorptions. The Buddha felt certain they would become completely enlightened if only he would speak a few significant words of Dhamma to them.

Even as the Buddha considered in this way, an invisible *deva*, a being from a celestial realm, announced to him that both of the hermits had died. Ālāra the Kalāma had passed away seven days before, and Udaka the Rāmaputta only the previous night. Both had been reborn in the formless world of the brahmas, where mind exists but matter does not. Therefore the hermits no longer had ears for hearing nor eyes for seeing. It was impossible for them to see the

Buddha or to listen to the Dhamma; and, since meeting with a teacher and listening to the Dhamma are the only two ways to discover the right way of practice, the two hermits had missed their chance to become fully enlightened.

The Buddha was moved. "They have suffered a great loss," he said.

• *Liberating Intuition*

What exactly is missing from concentration meditation? It simply cannot bring the understanding of truth. For this we need vipassanā meditation. Only intuitive insight into the true nature of mind and matter can free one from the concept of ego, of a person, of self or "I." Without this insight, which comes about through the process of bare awareness, one cannot be free from these concepts.

• Only an intuitive understanding of the mechanism of cause and effect – that is, seeing the link of recurrence of mind and matter – can free one from the delusion that things happen without a cause. Only by seeing the rapid arising and disappearance of phenomena can one be released from the delusion that things are permanent, solid and continuous. Only by experiencing suffering in the same intuitive way can one deeply learn that samsāric existence is not worth clinging to. Only the knowledge that mind and matter just flow by according to their own natural laws with no one, and nothing, behind them, can impress upon one's mind that there is no *atta*, or self essence.

Unless you go through the various levels of insight and eventually realize nibbāna, you will not understand true happiness. With nibbāna as the ultimate goal of your practice, you should try to maintain a high level of energy, not stopping or surrendering, never retreating until you reach your final destination.

First you will make the effort needed to establish your meditation practice. You focus your mind on the primary object of meditation, and you return to this object again and again. You set up a routine of sitting and walking practice. This is called "Launching Energy;" it puts you on the path and gets you moving forward.

Even if obstacles arise, you will stick with your practice, overcoming all obstacles with perseverance. If you are bored and lethargic, you summon up ardent energy. If you feel pain, you overcome the timid mind that prefers to withdraw and is unwilling to face what is happening. This is called "Liberating Energy," the energy necessary to liberate you from indolence. You will not retreat. You know you will just keep walking until you reach your goal.

After that, when you have overcome the intermediate difficulties and perhaps have found yourself in a smooth and subtle space, you will not become complacent. You will go into the next gear, putting in the effort to lift your mind higher and higher. This is an effort which neither decreases nor stagnates, but is in constant progress. This is called "Progressive Effort," and it leads to the goal you desire.

Therefore, the ninth factor conducive to sharpening the controlling faculties actually means applying successive levels of energy so that you neither stop nor hesitate, surrender nor retreat, until you reach your final goal and destination.

As you go along in this way, making use of all of the nine qualities of mind described above, the five controlling faculties of faith, energy, mindfulness, concentration and wisdom will sharpen and deepen. Eventually they will take over your mind and lead you on to freedom.

I hope you can examine your own practice. If you see that it is lacking in some element, make use of the above information to your own benefit.

Please walk straight on until you reach your desired goal.

# 3  *The Ten Armies of Māra*

Meditation can be seen as a war between wholesome and unwholesome mental states. On the unwholesome side are the forces of the kilesas, also known as "The Ten Armies of Māra." In Pāli, Māra means killer. He is the personification of the force that kills virtue and also kills existence. His armies are poised to attack all yogis; they even tried to overcome the Buddha on the night of his enlightenment.

Here are the lines the Buddha addressed to Māra, as recorded in the *Sutta Nipāta:*

> Sensual pleasures are your first army,
> Discontent your second is called.
> Your third is hunger and thirst,
> The fourth is called craving.
> Sloth and torpor are your fifth,
> The sixth is called fear,
> Your seventh is doubt,
> Conceit and ingratitude are your eighth,
> Gain, renown, honor and whatever fame
>    is falsely received (are the ninth),
> And whoever both extols himself and
>    disparages others (has fallen victim
>    to the tenth).
> That is your army, Namuci [Māra],
>    the striking force of darkness.
> One who is not a hero cannot conquer it,
>    but having conquered it, one obtains
>    happiness.

To overcome the forces of darkness in our own minds, we have the wholesome power of *satipaṭṭhāna vipassanā* meditation, which gives us the sword of mindfulness, as well as strategies for attack and defense.

In the Buddha's case, we know who won the victory. Now, which side will win over you?

### FIRST ARMY: SENSE PLEASURE

Sense pleasure is the First Army of Māra. Due to previous good actions in sensual or material realms, we find ourselves reborn in this world. Here, as in other sensual spheres, beings are faced with a wide assortment of appealing sense objects. Sweet sounds, rich smells, beautiful ideas, and other delightful objects touch all our six sense doors. As a natural result of encountering these objects, desire arises. Pleasant objects and desire are the two bases of sense pleasure.

Our attachments to family, property, business and friends also constitute the First Army. Normally for a sentient being, this army is very difficult to overcome. Some humans fight it by becoming monks and nuns, leaving behind their families and all that they cling to. Yogis on retreat leave behind their family and occupation temporarily, in order to combat the force of attachment which ties us to the six kinds of sense objects.

Anytime you practice meditation, especially in a retreat, you leave behind a large number of pleasant things. Even with this narrowing in range, though, you still find that some parts of your environment are more desirable than others. At this time it is useful to recognize that you are dealing with Māra, the enemy of your freedom.

### SECOND ARMY: DISSATISFACTION

The Second Army of Māra is dissatisfaction with the holy life, with the meditation practice in particular. On a retreat, you may find yourself dissatisfied and bored: with the hardness or the height of your cushion, with the food you are given, with any of the elements of your life during the time of practice. Some issue crops up and, as a result, you cannot quite immerse yourself in the delight of meditation. You may begin to feel that this is actually the fault of the practice.

To combat this discontent, you must become an *abhirati*, a person who is delighted in and devoted to the Dhamma. Having found and implemented the correct method of practice, you begin to overcome the hindrances. Rapture, joy and comfort will arise naturally from your concentrated mind. At this time you realize that the delight of the Dhamma is far superior to sense pleasures. This is the attitude of an abhirati. However, if you are not thorough and careful in your practice, you will not find this subtle and wonderful taste of the Dhamma, and any difficulty in your practice will cause aversion to arise in you. Then Māra will be victorious.

The overcoming of difficulty in vipassanā practice is, again, like warfare. The yogi will use an offensive, defensive or a guerrilla style of combat depending on his or her abilities. If he or she is a strong fighter, the yogi will advance. If weak, he or she may withdraw temporarily, but not in a helter-skelter fashion, reeling and running in disorder. Rather, the withdrawal will be strategic, planned and executed with the aim of gathering strength to win the battle at last.

Sometimes discontent with the environmental or other supports of meditation practice is not entirely Māra's fault – not entirely due to the wanderings of a greedy mind. Nonetheless, pervasive discontent may interfere with meditative progress. To allow for meditation, certain necessities of life must be available. Yogis must have proper shelter and meals, as well as sundry other help. With these requirements met they can proceed wholeheartedly to practice meditation. The need for a suitable environment is the fourth of nine causes for development of the controlling faculties, and was discussed at length in the preceding chapter. If you find a deficiency in your environment that you are certain is hindering your meditation, it is all right to take reasonable steps to correct it. Of course, you should be honest with yourself and others; make sure that you are not merely succumbing to Māra's Second Army.

### THIRD ARMY: HUNGER AND THIRST

Is food the problem? Perhaps a yogi has to overcome desire and dissatisfaction, only to be attacked again by Māra's Third Army, hunger and thirst. In the days of old and even now, Buddhist monks and nuns have depended for their food on the generosity of lay people. The normal practice for a monk is to go for an alms round every day in the community or village that supports him. Sometimes a monk may live in a secluded area and take all his support from a small group of families. One day his needs will be well taken care of, another day not. The same goes for lay yogis. At a retreat, the food is not quite like home. You do not get the sweet things you are fond of; or the sour, salty and rich foods you are accustomed to. Agitated by missing such tastes, you cannot concentrate and thus are unable to see the Dhamma.

In the world also, one can spend a lot of money in a restaurant and then not like the dish. Rarely, in fact, do human beings get everything precisely as they like. They may hunger and thirst not only for food, but also for clothing, entertainment, and activities either reassuringly familiar, or exotically exciting. This notion of hunger and thirst relates to the entire range of needs and requirements.

If you are easily contented, adopting an attitude of being grateful for whatever you receive, Māra's Third Army will not bother you very much. One cannot always do everything one wishes to do, but it is possible to try to remain within what is beneficial and appropriate. If you concentrate your energy on furthering your meditation practice, you will be able to taste the real taste of the Dhamma, which is incomparably satisfying. At such a time, the Third Army of Māra will seem an army of toy soldiers to you.

Otherwise it is hard to adjust to hunger and thirst. They are uncomfortable feelings which no one really welcomes.

When they strike, if there is no mindfulness, the mind inevitably begins to scheme. You come up with fantastic justifications for getting what you want – for the sake of your practice! Your mental health! To aid your digestion! Then you begin moving around to get the things you desire. Your body gets involved in satisfying your craving.

FOURTH ARMY: CRAVING

Craving is the Fourth Army of Māra. At times a monk's bowl may not be quite full at the end of his normal alms round, or some of the things most suitable for his diet have not yet appeared in it. Instead of going home to the monastery, he may decide to continue his alms round. Here is a new route, as yet untried – on it he might get the tidbit he desires. New routes like this can grow quite long.

Whether one is a monk or not, one might be familiar with this pattern. First comes craving, then planning, then moving about to materialize these schemes. This whole process can be very exhausting to mind and body.

FIFTH ARMY: SLOTH AND TORPOR

Thus, the Fifth Army of Māra marches in. It is none other than sloth and torpor, drowsiness. The difficulties caused by sloth and torpor are worth dwelling on, for they are surprisingly great. Torpor is the usual translation of the Pāli word *thīna*, which actually means a weak mind, a shrunken and withered, viscous and slimy mind, unable to grasp the meditation object firmly.

As thīna makes the mind weak, it automatically brings on weakness of body. The sluggish mind cannot keep your sitting posture erect and firm. Walking meditation becomes a real drag, so to speak. The presence of thīna means that *ātāpa*, the fiery aspect of energy, is absent. The mind becomes stiff and hard; it loses its active sharpness.

Even if a yogi has good energy to begin with, sloth can envelop him or her so that an additional burst of energy will be required to burn it away. All the positive forces of mind are at least partially blocked. The wholesome factors of energy and mindfulness, aim and contact, are enveloped in the shroud of weakness; their functions are retarded. This situation as a whole is spoken of as *thīna middha,* thīna being the mental factor of torpor, and *middha* referring to the condition of the consciousness as a whole when the factor of torpor is present.

In one's practical experience, it is not worthwhile to try to distinguish between the two components of thina and middha. The general state of mind is familiar enough. Like imprisonment in a tiny cell, sloth is a restricted state in which no wholesome factor is free to carry on its proper activity. This obstruction of wholesome factors is why sloth and torpor together are called a hindrance. Eventually Māra's Fifth Army can bring one's practice to a complete standstill. A twitching sensation comes to the eyelids, the head suddenly nods forward... How can we overcome this noxious state? Once when the Venerable Mahā Moggallāna, one of the Buddha's two chief disciples, was meditating in the forest, thina middha arose. His mind shrank and withered, as unworkable as a piece of butter that hardens in the cold. At this point the Lord Buddha looked into the Venerable Mahā Moggallāna's mind. Seeing his plight, he approached and said, "My son Mahā Moggallāna, are you drowsy, are you sleepy, are you nodding?"

The elder replied, "Yes, Lord, I am nodding." He was frank and candid in his reply. The Buddha said, "Listen, my son, I will now teach you eight techniques of overcoming sloth and torpor."

● *Eight Ways to Stay Awake*

The first is to change one's attitude. When torpor attacks, one may be tempted to surrender to thoughts like, "I'm so sleepy. It's not doing me any good just to sit here in a daze. Maybe I'll lie down for a minute and gather my energy." As long as you entertain such thoughts, the mental state of sloth and torpor will be encouraged to remain.

If, on the other hand, one states decisively, "I'll sit through this sloth and torpor, and if it recurs I still won't give in to it," this is what the Buddha meant by changing one's attitude. Such determination sets the stage for overcoming the Fifth Army of Māra.

Another occasion to change one's attitude is when meditation practice becomes quite easy and smooth. There comes a point where you have more or less mastered following the rise and fall of the abdomen, and not much effort is needed to observe it well. It is quite natural to relax, sit back and watch the movement very coolly. Due to this relaxation of effort, sloth and torpor easily creep in. If this happens, you should either try to deepen your mindfulness, looking more carefully into the rise and fall, or else increase the number of objects of meditation.

There is a specific technique for adding more objects. It requires greater effort than simply watching the abdomen, and thus it has a revivifying effect. The mental labels to use are, "rising, falling, sitting, touching." When you note "sitting," you shift your awareness to the sensations of the entire body in the sitting posture. Noting "touching," you focus on the touch sensations at one or more small areas, about the size of a quarter. The buttocks are convenient. During this "touching" note you should always return to the same chosen areas, even if you cannot always find sensations there. The heavier the state of sloth, the more touch points you should include, up to a maximum of six or so. When you have run through the course of touch points, return attention to your abdomen and repeat the series of notes from the beginning. This change of strategy can be quite effective; but it is not infallible.

The second antidote to drowsiness is to reflect on inspiring passages you remember or have learned by heart, trying to fathom their deepest meanings. Perhaps you have lain awake at night pondering the meaning of some event. If so, you understand the function of the Buddha's second antidote to sloth and torpor. In Buddhist psychology, when thinking is analyzed in terms of its components, one component is the mental factor of *vitakka*, or aim. This mental factor has the capacity to open and refresh the mind, and is the specific antidote to sloth and torpor.

The third strategy for dealing with sloth is to recite those same passages aloud. If you are meditating in a group, it goes without saying that you should recite only loud enough for your own benefit.

Resort to more drastic measures if your mind still has not perked up. Pull on your ears; rub your hands, arms, legs and face. This stimulates the circulation and so freshens you up a bit.

If drowsiness persists, get up mindfully and wash your face. You could put in some eye-drops to refresh yourself. If this strategy fails, you are advised to look at a lighted object, such as the moon or an electric bulb; this should lighten up your mind. Clarity of mind is a kind of light. With it, you can make a renewed attempt to look clearly at the rising and falling from beginning to end. If none of these techniques work, then you should try some brisk walking meditation with mindfulness. Finally, a graceful surrender would be to go to bed.

If sloth and torpor are persistent over a long period, constipation could be responsible; if this is the case, consider measures to gently clear the bowels.

SIXTH ARMY: FEAR

The Sixth Army of Māra is fear and cowardliness. It easily attacks yogis who practice in a remote place, especially if the level of ardent effort is low after an attack of sloth and torpor. Courageous effort drives out fear. So does a clear perception of the Dhamma which comes as a result of effort, mindfulness and concentration. The Dhamma is the greatest protection available on earth: faith in, and practice of, the Dhamma are therefore the greatest medicines for fear. Practicing morality ensures that one's future circumstances will be wholesome and pleasant; practicing concentration means that one suffers less from mental distress; and practicing wisdom leads toward nibbāna, where all fear and danger have been surpassed. Practicing the Dhamma, you truly care for yourself, protect yourself, and act as your own best friend.

Ordinary fear is the sinking form of anger. You cannot face the problem, so you show no reaction outwardly and wait for the opportunity to run away. But if you can face your problems directly, with an open and relaxed mind, fear will not arise. On a meditation retreat, yogis who have lost touch with the Dhamma feel fear and lack of confidence in relating to other yogis and their teacher. For example, some yogis are severely attacked by sloth and torpor. Such people have been known to sleep through five hour-long sittings in a row. They may have only a few minutes of clear awareness in an entire day. Such yogis tend to feel inferior, shy and embarrassed, especially if they begin to compare their own practice to that of other yogis who seem to be in deep samādhi all the time. At times in Burma, torpid yogis slip away for a couple of days and miss their interviews. A few slip all the way home! They are like schoolchildren who have not done their homework. If such yogis would apply courageous effort, their awareness would become hot like the sun, burning off the clouds of sleepiness. Then they could face their teachers boldly, ready to report what they have seen for themselves in the light created by Dhamma practice.

No matter what problem you may encounter in your meditation practice, try to have the courage and honesty to report it to your teacher. Sometimes yogis may feel that their practice is falling apart, when actually it is going fine. A teacher who is trustworthy and well-qualified can help you to overcome such insecurities, and you can continue on the path of Dhamma with energy, faith and confidence.

SEVENTH ARMY: DOUBT

Sloth and torpor is only one reason why yogis may begin to doubt their own capacities. Doubt is the Seventh Army of Māra, dreadful and fearsome. When a yogi begins to slip in his or her practice, he or she will probably begin to lose self-confidence. Pondering the situation does not usually lead to improvement. Instead, doubt arises and slowly spreads: first as self-doubt, then as doubt of the method of practice. It may even extend to becoming doubt of the teacher. Is the teacher competent to understand this situation? Perhaps this yogi is a special case and needs a special new set of instructions. The experiences narrated by fellow yogis must be imaginary. Every conceivable aspect of practice becomes dubious.

The Pāli word for this Seventh Army is *vicikicchā*, which means more than simple doubt. It is the exhaustion of mind that comes about through conjecture. A yogi attacked by sloth and torpor, for example, will not be able to muster the continuous attention that fosters intuitive vipassanā insight. If such a yogi were mindful, he or she might experience mind and matter directly, and see that these two are connected by cause and effect. If no actual observation is made, however, the true nature of mind and matter will remain obscure. One simply cannot understand what one hasn't yet seen. Now this unmindful yogi begins to intellectualize and reason: "I wonder what mind and matter are composed of, what their relationship is." Unfortunately, he or she can only interpret experiences based on a very immature depth of knowledge, mixed up with fantasy. This is an explosive mixture. Since the mind is unable to penetrate into the truth, agitation arises, and then perplexity, indecisiveness, which is another aspect of vicikicchā. Excessive reasoning is exhausting.

Immaturity of insight prevents a yogi from reaching a firm and convinced position. Instead, his or her mind is condemned to run about among various options. Remembering all the meditative techniques he or she has heard of, a yogi might try a bit from here and a bit from there. This person falls into a great pot of chop suey, perhaps to drown. Vicikicchā can be a terrible obstacle in practice. The proximate cause of doubting conjecture is lack of proper attention, an improper adjustment of the mind in its search for truth. Proper attention, then, is the most direct cure for doubt. If you look correctly and in the right place, you will see what you are looking for: the true nature of things. Having seen this for yourself, you will have no more doubt about it.

To create the proper conditions for wise attention, it is important to have a teacher who can put you on the path leading to truth and wisdom. The Buddha himself said that one who is intent on finding the truth should seek out a reliable and competent teacher. If you cannot find a good teacher and follow his or her instructions, then you must turn to the plethora of meditation literature available today. Please be cautious, especially if you are an avid reader. If you gain a general knowledge of many techniques and then try to put them all together, you will probably end up disappointed, and even more doubtful than when you started. Some of the techniques may even be good ones, but since you will not have practiced them with proper thoroughness, they will not work and you will feel skeptical of them. Thus you will have robbed yourself of the opportunity to experience the very real benefits of meditation practice. If one cannot practice properly, one cannot gain personal, intuitive, real understanding of the nature of phenomena. Not only will doubt increase, but the mind will become very hard and stiff, attacked by *kodha*, aversion and associated mental states. Frustration and resistance might be among them.

## The Thorny Mind

Kodha makes the mind hard and rigid as a thorn. Under its influence, a yogi is said to be pricked by the mind, like a traveler thrashing through a bramble thicket, suffering at every step. Since kodha is a great impediment in many yogis' meditation practice, I will deal with it in some detail in hopes that readers can learn to overcome it. In general, it results from two kinds of mental states: firstly from doubt, and secondly from what are known as "the mental fetters."

There are five kinds of doubt which lead to the thorny mind. A yogi is pricked by doubt regarding the Buddha, the great master who showed the path to enlightenment. One doubts the Dhamma, the path that leads to liberation; and the sangha, the noble ones who have uprooted some or all of the kilesas. Next come doubts of oneself, of one's own morality and method of practice. Last is doubt of fellow yogis, including one's teacher. When so many doubts are present, the yogi is filled with anger and resistance: his or her mind becomes thorny indeed. He or she will probably feel quite unwilling actually to practice this meditation, seeing it as dubious and unreliable.

All is not lost, however. Wisdom and knowledge are medicine for this state of vicikicchā. One form of knowledge is reasoning. Often persuasive words can coax a doubting yogi from the brambles: a teacher's reasoning, or an inspiring and well-constructed discourse. Returning to the clear path of direct observation, such yogis breathe great sighs of relief and gratitude. Now they have the chance to gain personal insight into the true nature of reality. If they do attain insight, then a higher level of wisdom becomes their medicine for the thorny mind.

Failure to return to the path, however, may allow doubt to reach its incurable stage.

## The Five Mental Fetters

The thorny mind arises not only from doubt, but also from another set of causes known as the five mental fetters. When these mental fetters are present, the mind suffers from hard and prickling states of aversion, frustration and resistance. But these fetters can be overcome. Vipassanā meditation clears them automatically from the mind. If they do manage to intrude upon one's practice, identifying them is the first step toward recovering a broad and flexible mental state.

The first mental fetter is to be chained to the various objects of the senses. Desiring only pleasant objects, one will be dissatisfied with what is really occurring in the present moment. The primary object, the rising and falling of the abdomen, may seem inadequate and uninteresting in comparison with one's fantasies. If this dissatisfaction occurs, one's meditative development will be undermined.

The second fetter is over-attachment to one's own body, sometimes spoken of as excessive self-love. A variation is the projection of attachment and possessiveness onto

The Ten Armies of Mara 75

another person and his or her body. This is the third fetter, and it is such a common situation that I hardly need elaborate.

Excessive self-love can be a significant hindrance in the course of practice. When one sits for extended periods, unpleasant sensations invariably arise, some of them rather intense. You may begin to wonder about your poor legs. Will you ever walk again? You may decide to open your eyes and stretch. At this point, continuity of attention usually breaks apart; momentum is lost. Tender consideration for one's own body can sometimes supplant the courage we need to probe into the actual nature of pain.

Personal appearance is another area where this second fetter can arise. Some human beings depend on stylish clothes and makeup to feel happy. If ever they lose access to these external supports (perhaps on a retreat where makeup and flamboyant fashions are inappropriate distractions), these people feel as if something is missing, and worry can interfere with their progress. The fourth fetter of mind is to be chained to food. Some people like to eat large amounts, others have many whims and preferences. People whose first concern is the satisfaction of their bellies tend to find greater bliss in snoozing than in practicing mindfulness. A few yogis have the opposite problem, worrying constantly about gaining weight. They, too, are chained to what they eat.

The fifth fetter of mind is to practice with the goal of gaining rebirth in a deva world. Besides effectively basing one's practice on craving for sensual pleasures, this is also to set one's sights much too low. For information on the disadvantages of deva life, see the last chapter of this book, "Chariot to Nibbāna."

By diligent practice one overcomes these five fetters. By the same means, one overcomes doubt and the anger that follows it. Relieved from thorny discomfort, the mind becomes crystal clear and bright. This bright mind is happy to make the preliminary effort that sets your feet on the path of practice, the steady effort that moves you along into deeper meditation, and the culminating effort that brings liberation at the higher stages of practice. This three-fold effort – actually directed toward keeping the mind alert and observant – is the best and most natural defense strategy against Māra's Seventh Army of doubt. Only when the mind slips from the object, as it will in times of slackening effort, do the conjectures and equivocations of doubt have a chance to set in.

• *Faith Clarifies the Mind*

The quality of faith, or *saddhā*, also has the power to clarify the mind and clear away clouds of doubt or aversion. Imagine a pail of murky river water, full of sediment. Some chemical substances, such as alum, have the power to make suspended particles settle quickly, leaving clear water behind. Faith works just like this. It settles impurities, and brings a sparkling clarity to the mind.

A yogi ignorant of the virtues of the Triple Gem – the Buddha, Dhamma and Sangha – will doubt its value as well as that of the meditation practice, and will be overcome by the Seventh Army of Māra. Such a yogi's mind is like a bucket of murky river water. But informed of these virtues through reading, discussions and Dhamma talks, a yogi can gradually settle doubts and begin to arouse faith.

With faith comes the desire to meditate, the willingness to exert energy in order to reach the goal. Strong faith is the foundation of sincerity and commitment. Sincerity of practice and commitment to the Dhamma will of course lead to the development of effort, mindfulness and concentration. Then wisdom will unfold in the form of the various stages of vipassanā insight.

When circumstances and conditions are right in meditation, wisdom unfolds quite naturally of itself. Wisdom, or insight, occurs when one sees the specific and common characteristics of mental and physical phenomena. Individual characteristics mean the specific traits of mind and matter as experienced directly within you. These are color, shape, taste, smell, loudness, hardness or softness, temperature, movement, and different states of mind. Common

characteristics are general to all the manifestations of mind and matter. Objects may differ greatly from one another in terms of individual essence or individual characteristics,
• yet all are united by the universal traits of impermanence, suffering and absence of an abiding self or essence.

Both these types of characteristics, specific and common, will be understood clearly and unquestionably through the insight that arises naturally out of bare awareness. One attribute of this wisdom or insight is the quality of brightness. It lightens one's field of awareness. Wisdom is like a floodlight breaking into pitch darkness, revealing what was invisible up to now – the specific and common qualities of all objects and mental states. By wisdom's light, you will see these aspects of any activity you are involved in, be it seeing, smelling, tasting, touching, feeling through the body, or thinking.

• The behavioral aspect of wisdom is nonconfusion. When insight is present, the mind is no longer confused by mistaken concepts about, or delusive perceptions of, mind and matter.

Seeing clearly, bright and unconfused, the mind begins to fill with a new kind of faith, known as verified faith.
• Verified faith is neither blind nor unfounded. It comes directly from personal experience of reality. One might compare it to the faith that raindrops will get us wet. The scriptures formally characterize this kind of faith as a decision based on direct personal experience. Thus, we see a very close association between faith and wisdom.

Verified faith does not arise because you hear statements you find plausible. No comparative study, scholastic research nor abstract reasoning can bring it. Nor is it shoved down your throat by some sayadaw, roshi, rinpoche, or spiritual group. Your own direct, personal, intuitive experience brings about this firm and durable kind of faith.

The most important way to develop and realize verified faith is practice in conformity with instructions from the scriptures. The satipaṭṭhāna method of meditation is sometimes viewed as narrow and oversimplified. It may appear so from the outside, but when wisdom begins to unfold during deep practice, personal experience shatters this myth of narrowness. Vipassanā brings a wisdom that is far from narrow. It is panoramic and expansive.

In the presence of faith one can spontaneously notice that the mind has become crystal clear and is free from disturbances and pollution. At this time, too, the mind fills with peace and clarity. The function of verified faith is to bring together the five controlling faculties discussed in the last chapter – faith, energy, mindfulness, concentration and wisdom – and to clarify them. They become alert and effective, and their active properties will be more efficiently deployed to bring about a calm, powerful, incisive meditative state – one which is bound to be successful in overcoming not only the Seventh, but all the other nine armies of Māra as well.

### Four Powers which Motivate Successful Practice

In practice as much as in worldly endeavors, a vigorous and strong-minded person is quite sure of accomplishing whatever she or he desires. Vigor and strength of mind are only two of the four powers which motivate a successful practice. *Chanda* is willingness, the first power. *Viriya* is energy, or vigor, the second. Strength of mind is third, and wisdom or knowledge is the fourth. If these four factors provide the driving force for practice, one's meditation will unfold whether one has any desire to gain results from it or not. One can even reach nibbāna in this way.

The Buddha gave a rather homely example which illustrates just how the results of meditation are attained. If mother hen lays an egg with a sincere wish for it to hatch, but then runs off and leaves the egg exposed to nature's elements, the egg will soon rot. If, on the other hand, mother hen is conscientious in her duties toward the egg, sitting on it for long periods every day, the warmth of her body will keep the egg from rotting and will also permit the chick within to grow. Sitting on the egg is mother hen's most important duty. She must do this in the proper way, with her wings slightly spread out to protect the nest from rain. She must also take care not to sit heavily and crack her egg. If she sits in proper style and for sufficient time, the egg will naturally receive the warmth it needs to hatch. Inside the shell, an embryo develops beak and claws. Day by day the shell grows thinner. During mother hen's brief excursions from the nest, the chick inside may see a light that slowly brightens. After three weeks or so, a healthy yellow chick pecks its way out of its claustrophobic space. This result happens regardless of whether the hen foresaw the outcome. All she did was sit on the egg with sufficient regularity.

Mother hens are very dedicated and committed to their task. At times they would rather be hungry and thirsty than get up from the egg. If they do have to get up, they go about their errands as efficiently as possible and then return to their sitting practice.

I am not recommending that you skip meals, or stop drinking liquids, or cease going to the bathroom. I would simply like you to be inspired by the hen's patience and persistence. Imagine if she became fickle and restless, sitting for a few minutes and then going out to do something else for a few minutes. Her egg would quickly rot, and the chick would lose its chance for life.

So, too, for the yogi. If during sitting meditation, you are prone to giving in to all those whims to scratch, to shift, to squirm, then the heat of energy will not be continuous enough to keep the mind fresh and free from attacks by the rotting influence of mental obscurations and difficulties such as the five mental fetters mentioned above: sense desire, attachment to our own bodies and to the bodies of others, gluttony, and craving for future sensual pleasures as a result of meditation practice.

A yogi who tries to be mindful in each moment generates a persistent stream of energy, like the persistent heat of mother hen's body. This heat aspect of energy prevents the mind from rotting from its exposure to kilesa attacks, and it also permits insight to grow and mature through its developmental stages.

All five of the mental fetters arise in the absence of attention. If one is not careful when there is contact with a pleasurable sense object, the mind will be filled with craving and clinging – the first mental fetter. With mindfulness, however, sense desire is overcome. Similarly, if one can penetrate the true nature of the body, attachment to it disappears. Our infatuation with the bodies of others diminishes in turn. Thus the second and third mental fetters are broken. Close attention to the whole process of eating cuts through gluttony, the fourth mental fetter. If one carries out this whole practice with the aim of realizing nibbāna, hankering after mundane pleasures one might obtain in the afterlife will also disappear – wishing for rebirth in subtle realms is the fifth fetter of mind. Thus, continuous mindfulness and energy overcome all five fetters. When these fetters are broken, we are no longer bound in a dark, constricted mental state. Our minds are freed to emerge into the light.

With continued effort, mindfulness and concentration, the mind slowly fills with the warmth of the Dhamma which keeps it fresh and scorches the kilesas. The Dhamma's fragrance penetrates throughout, and the shell of ignorance grows thinner and more translucent. Yogis begin to understand mind and matter and the conditionality of all things. Faith based on direct experience arises. They understand directly how mind and matter are interrelated by a process of cause and effect, rather than being moved by the actions and decisions of an independent self. By inference, they realize that this same causal process existed in the past and will continue into the future. As practice deepens, one gains deep confidence, no longer doubting oneself and one's practice, other yogis or teachers. The mind is filled with gratitude for the Buddha, the Dhamma and the sangha.

Then one begins to see the appearing and disappearing of things, and realizes their impermanent nature, their suffering and lack of a permanent self. Upon the occurrence of such insights, ignorance of these aspects disappears.

Like the chick about to hatch, at this point you will see a lot of light coming through the shell. Awareness of objects moves ahead at a faster and faster pace; you will be filled with a sort of energy you have never experienced before, and great faith will arise.

If you continue to incubate your wisdom, you will be led forward to the experience of nibbāna – *magga phala*, path and fruition consciousnesses. You will emerge from the shell of darkness. Just like the chick who, filled with enthusiasm to find itself in the great world, runs about the sunny farmyard with its mother, so too will you be filled with happiness and bliss. Yogis who have experienced nibbāna feel a unique, newfound happiness and bliss. Their faith, energy, mindfulness and concentration become particularly strong.

I hope you will take this analogy of mother hen into deep consideration. Just as she hatches her chicks without hopes or desire, merely carrying out her duties in a conscientious way, so may you well incubate and hatch your practice.

May you not become a rotten egg.

*Captain of My Own Ship*

I have spent a lot of time here on doubt and related problems because I know they are quite serious, and I want to help you avoid them. I know personally how much suffering doubt can cause. When I was twenty-eight or twenty-nine years old I began to meditate under the Venerable Mahāsī Sayadaw, my predecessor and the head of the lineage of Mahāsī Sāsana Yeiktha, the meditation center in Rangoon. After about a week at the meditation center, I began to feel quite critical of my fellow meditators. Some monks who were supposed to be meditating were not perfect in their morality; they did not seem scrupulous or meticulous to me. The lay meditators, too, seemed to communicate and move about in an uncivilized, impolite manner. Doubt began to fill my mind. Even my teacher, one of Mahāsī Sayadaw's assistants, came under the fire of my critical mind. This man never smiled and was sometimes abrupt and harsh. I felt that a meditation teacher should be filled with softness and solicitude.

A competent meditation teacher can make quite an educated guess about a yogi's situation, based on experience with many yogis as well as on scriptural study. The master who was teaching me was no exception. He saw my practice begin to regress. Guessing that a doubt attack was responsible, he gave me a very gentle and skillful scolding. Afterwards I went back to my room and did some soul-searching. I asked myself, "Why did I come here? To criticize others and test the teacher? No."

I realized that I had come to the center to get rid of as many as I could of the kilesas I had accumulated through my journey in samsāra. I hoped to accomplish this goal by practicing the Dhamma of the Buddha in the meditative tradition of the center where I was. This reflection was a great clarification for me.

A simile popped into my mind. It was as if I had been on a sailboat. Out at sea I had been caught in a raging storm. Huge waves rose up and crashed down again on every side. Blown from left to right, up and down, I rocked helplessly in the mighty ocean. Around me other boats were in the same predicament. Instead of managing my own boat, I had been barking orders at the other captains: "Better put up the sails! Hey, you! Better take them down." If I had remained a busybody, I might well have found myself at the bottom of the ocean.

This is what I learned for myself. After that I worked very hard and entertained no more doubts in my mind. I even became a favorite of my teacher. I hope you can benefit from this experience of mine.

EIGHTH ARMY: CONCEIT AND INGRATITUDE

Having overcome doubt, the yogi begins to realize some aspects of the Dhamma. Unfortunately, the Eighth Army of Māra lies in wait, in the form of conceit and ingratitude. Conceit arises when yogis begin to experience joy, rapture, delight, and other interesting things in practice. At this point they may wonder whether their teacher has actually attained this wondrous stage yet, whether other yogis are practicing as hard as they are, and so forth.

Conceit most often happens at the stage of insight when yogis perceive the momentary arising and passing away of phenomena. It is a wonderful experience of being perfectly present, seeing how objects arise and pass away at the very moment when mindfulness alights on them. At this particular stage, a host of defilements can arise. They are specifically known as the *vipassanā kilesas*, defilements of insight. Since these defilements can become a harmful obstacle, it is important for yogis to understand them clearly. The scriptures tell us that *māna* or conceit has the characteristic of bubbly energy, of a great zeal and enthusiasm arising in the mind. One overflows with energy and is filled with self-centered, self-glorifying thoughts like, "I'm so great, no one can compare with me."

A prominent aspect of conceit is stiffness and rigidity. One's mind feels stiff and bloated, like a python that has just swallowed some other creature. This aspect of māna is also reflected as tension in the body and posture. Its victims get big-headed and stiff-necked, and thus may find it difficult to bow respectfully to others.

*Forgetting Others' Help*

Conceit is really a fearsome mental state. It destroys gratitude, making it difficult to acknowledge that one owes any kind of debt to another person. Forgetting the good deeds others have done for us in the past, one belittles them and denigrates their virtues. Not only that, but one also actively conceals the virtues of others so that no one will hold them in esteem. This attitude toward one's benefactors is the second aspect of conceit, rigidity being the first.

All of us have had benefactors in our lives, especially in childhood and younger days. Our parents, for example, gave us love, education and the necessities of life at a time when we were helpless. Our teachers gave us knowledge. Friends helped us when we got into trouble. Remembering our debts to those who have helped us, we feel humble and grateful, and we hope for a chance to help them in turn. It is precisely this gentle state that defeats Māra's Eighth Army.

Yet it is very common to find people who don't recognize the good that has been done for them in the past. Perhaps a lay person finds himself or herself in trouble, and a compassionate friend offers help. Thanks to this help, the person manages to improve his or her circumstances. Later, however, he or she may demonstrate no gratitude at all, may even turn and speak harshly to the erstwhile benefactor. "What have you ever done for me?" Such behavior is far from unknown in this world.

Even a monk may become arrogant, feeling he has reached fame and popularity as a teacher only through his own hard work. He forgets his preceptors and teachers, who may have helped him since his childhood days as a novice. They will have taught him the scriptures, provided him with the requisites of life, instructed him in meditation, given him advice, and admonished him when appropriate, so that he grew up to be a responsible, cultured, civilized young monk.

Come the age of independence, this monk may reveal great talent. He gives good Dhamma talks that are well received by the audience. People respect him, give him many presents and invite him to distant places to teach. Having reached a high station in life, the monk may become rather arrogant. One day, perhaps, his old teacher approaches him and says, "Congratulations! I've been watching you ever since you were a small novice. Having helped you in so many ways, it does my heart good to see you doing so well." The young monk snaps back, "What have you done for me? I worked hard for this."

Problems can occur in the Dhamma family as in any human family. In any family, one should always adopt a positive, loving and compassionate attitude toward resolving difficulties. Imagine how it could be if the members of the world family could get together with love and compassion and consideration for each other when a disagreement arises.

In this world there are ways of solving problems which may not be very fruitful but are unfortunately widespread. Instead of acting directly and from fellowship and love, a family member might start to wash dirty linen in public; might belittle other family members; or criticize their personalities and virtues, either directly or indirectly.

Before hurling insults and accusations at another family member, one should consider one's own state of mind and circumstances. The tendency to lash out, defame and belittle is an aspect of conceit. The scriptures illustrate it with the image of a person enraged, taking up a handful of excrement to fling at his or her opponent. This person befouls himself or herself even before the opponent. So, if there are matters on which we disagree, please let us all try to exercise patience and forgiveness in the spirit of the good-hearted.

Imagine a traveler on a long and arduous journey. In the middle of a long hot day he or she comes across a tree by the side of the road, a leafy tree with deep cool shade. The traveler is delighted, and lies down at the roots of this tree for a nice nap. If the traveler cuts down the tree before he goes on his or her way, this is what the scriptures call ungrateful. Such a person does not understand the benevolence a friend has shown.

We have a responsibility to do more than refrain from chopping down our benefactors. It is true that in this world there are times when we cannot repay what we owe to those who have helped us. We will nonetheless be regarded as a good-hearted person if we can at least remember their acts of benevolence. If we can find a way to repay our debt, we should of course do so. It is quite irrelevant whether our benefactor is more virtuous than we, or is a rascal, or happens to be our equal in virtue. The only requirement for him or her to gain the status of benefactor is to have helped us in the past.

Once upon a time, a man worked very hard to support his mother. As it turned out, she was a promiscuous woman. She tried to hide this from her son, but eventually some gossiping villagers disclosed her activities to him. He answered, "Run along, friends. As long as my mom is happy, whatever she chooses to do is fine. My only duty is to work and support her."

This was a very intelligent young man. He understood the limits of his own responsibility: to repay his debt of gratitude to her who had borne and suckled him. Beyond this, his mother's behavior was her own business.

This man was one of the two types of rare and precious people in the world. The first type of rare and precious person is a benefactor: one who is benevolent and kind, who helps another person for noble reasons. The Buddha was one of these, sparing no effort to help beings liberate themselves from the sufferings of saṃsāra. All of us owe him grateful remembrance, and we might even consider our diligence in practice to be a form of repayment. The second type of rare and precious person is the one who is grateful, who appreciates the good that has been done for him or her, and who tries to repay it when the time is ripe. I hope you will be both types of rare and precious person, and will not succumb to the Eighth Army of Māra.

NINTH ARMY: GAIN, PRAISE, HONOR, UNDESERVED FAME

The Ninth Army of Māra is gain, praise, honor and undeserved fame. When you attain some depth of practice, your manner and behavior will improve. You will become venerable and impressive. You may even start to share the Dhamma with others, or your experience of the Dhamma may manifest outwardly in another way, perhaps in clear expositions of the scriptures. People may feel deep faith in you and may bring you gifts and donations. Word may spread that you are an enlightened person, that you give great Dhamma discourses.

At this point it would be very easy for you to succumb to the Ninth Army of Māra. The honor and respect these people direct toward you could go to your head. You might begin to subtly or overtly try to extract bigger and better donations from your followers. You might decide that you deserve renown because you really are superior to other people. Or, insincere ambition might supplant a genuine wish to help others as your motivation for teaching, for sharing whatever wisdom you have reached in your own practice. Your reflections might run as follows: "Oh, I'm pretty great. I'm popular with many people. I wonder if anyone else is as great as I am. Can I get my devotees to buy me a new car?"

The first battalion of the Ninth Army is material gain: the gifts one receives from devotees and admirers. The reverence of these same people is the second battalion; the third battalion is fame or renown.

In the outer world, Māra's Ninth Army attacks mostly those yogis who've had a good result in meditation. But it is quite unnecessary to have a band of followers. Wishes for gain can attack the most ordinary yogi, in the form of desires for grander accommodations or new outfits to wear while on a retreat. One might feel proud of one's practice and begin wishing to be acknowledged as a great yogi. People whose practice is not very deep are most susceptible to deluding themselves about their own achievements. A yogi who has had an interesting experience or two, but little depth, can become overconfident. He or she may quickly want to step out onto the Dhamma scene and teach other people, thus becoming the object of admiration and praise. Such persons will teach a pseudo-vipassanā that is not in accordance with the texts, nor with deep practical experience. They may actually harm their students.

*Sincerity*

To vanquish this Ninth Army, the motivation behind your effort must be sincere. If you begin practicing only with the hope of getting donations, reverence, or fame, you will never make any progress. Frequent reexamination of motives can be very helpful. If you make genuine, sincere progress and later succumb to greed for gain, you will become intoxicated and negligent. It is said that a person who is intoxicated and negligent will continue a life of peacelessness and be overcome by much suffering. Satisfied with cheap gain, this person forgets the purpose of meditation, performs unskillful actions and fails to cultivate wholesomeness. Her or his practice will regress.

Perhaps, though, we believe there is an end to suffering and that we can attain this end by practicing the Dhamma. This is the sincere motivation that prevents us from falling into greed for worldly gain and fame. Life means coming into being. For humans it means a very painful birth process, with death waiting at the end. In between these two events, we experience falling sick, accidents, the pain of aging. There is also emotional pain, not getting what we desire, depressions and losses, unavoidable associations with persons and objects we dislike. To be freed from all this pain, we sit in meditation, practicing the Dhamma, the path that ends in the supramundane release of nibbāna. Some of us go to retreats, leaving behind worldly activities such as business, education, social obligations and the pursuit of pleasure, because we have faith that suffering can come to an end. Actually, we can legitimately consider as a retreat any place where you strive to extinguish the kilesas. When you go to such a place, even if it is the corner of the living room set aside for meditation, the Pāli word for you is *pabbajita*, meaning "one who has gone forth from the world in order to extinguish the kilesas."

Why would one want to extinguish them? Kilesas, or defilements, have a tremendous power to torture and oppress those who are not free of them. They are likened to a fire which burns and tortures and torments. When kilesas arise in a being, they burn him or her; they bring exhaustion, torment and oppression. There is not a single good thing to be said about the kilesas.

### The Three Types of Kilesas

Kilesas are of three kinds: the defilements of transgression, the defilements of obsession, and the latent or dormant defilements.

Defilements of transgression occur when people cannot keep the basic precepts, and perform actions of killing, stealing, sexual misconduct, lying and intoxication.

The second class of kilesas is a bit more subtle. One may not outwardly commit any immoral action, but one's mind will be obsessed with desires to kill and destroy, hurt and harm other beings physically or otherwise. Obsessive wishes may fill the mind: to steal property, manipulate people, deceive others to obtain some desired object. If you have ever experienced this kind of obsession, you know it is a very painful state. If a person fails to control the obsessive kilesas, he or she is likely to hurt other beings in one way or another.

Dormant or latent kilesas are ordinarily not apparent. They lie hidden, waiting for the right conditions to assault the helpless mind. Dormant kilesas may be likened to a person deeply asleep. As such a person awakes, when his or her mind begins to churn, it is as if the obsessive kilesas have arisen. When the person stands up from bed and becomes involved in the day's activities, this is like moving from the obsessive kilesas to the kilesas of transgression.

These three aspects can also be discovered in a matchstick. Its phosphorus tip is like the dormant kilesas. The flame that results from striking is like the obsessive kilesas. The forest fire that ensues from careless handling of the flame is like the kilesas of transgression.

### ▲ Extinguishing the Kilesas' Fire

If you are sincere in applying sīla, samādhi and paññā, you can overcome, extinguish and give up all three kinds of kilesas. Sīla puts aside the kilesas of transgression; samādhi suppresses the obsessive ones; and wisdom uproots latent or dormant kilesas which are the cause of the other two. As you practice in this way, you can gain new kinds of happiness.

By practicing sīla, the delight of sensual pleasures is replaced by the happiness that comes from sincerity of conduct, morality. Due to the absence of the kilesas of transgression, a moral person lives a relatively pure, clean and blissful life. We practice sīla by keeping the five basic precepts mentioned in the first chapter; and more generally by following the morality group of the Noble Eightfold

Path: Right Action, Right Speech and Right Livelihood, all of which are based on not harming others or oneself.

You may wonder whether true purity of conduct is possible in the world. Of course it is! However, it is much easier to be pure in one's precepts in a retreat, where situations are simplified and temptations are kept to a minimum. This is especially true if one wishes to practice more than the basic five precepts, or if one is a monk or nun and therefore obliged to follow many rules. On retreat one can achieve a very high success rate for any of these difficult endeavors.

Purity of conduct is only a first step. If we want to extinguish more than the coarse kilesas, some internal practice is necessary. The obsessive kilesas are vanquished by the samādhi, or the concentration group of the Noble Eightfold Path: which consists of Right Effort, Right Mindfulness and Right Concentration. A continuous and persistent effort is needed to note and be aware of the objects that arise in each moment, without straying away. This kind of endeavor is difficult to maintain in a worldly context.

With continuous moment-to-moment effort, mindfulness and concentration, the obsessive kilesas can be kept far from the mind. The mind can enter into the object of meditation and stay there, unscattered. The obsessive kilesas have no chance to arise, unless there is a momentary slip in the practice. Freedom from these kilesas brings about a state of mind known as *upasama sukha*, the well-being and bliss of tranquility which results from freedom from the oppressive kilesas. The mind is free from lust, greed, anger, agitation. When one has known this happiness, one sees it as superior to sense pleasure and considers it a worthwhile exchange to have put aside sensual joys to obtain it.

There is a better kind of happiness even than this, so one should not become complacent. Taking a further step, one can practice wisdom. With wisdom, the dormant kilesas can be abandoned momentarily and perhaps also permanently. When mindfulness is well developed along with its associated factors, such as energy and concentration, one begins to understand very intuitively the nature of mind and matter. The wisdom group of the Noble Eightfold Path, Right View and Right Thought, begins to be fulfilled as one naturally moves through the successive stages of insight. At every occurrence of insight, the dormant kilesas are extinguished. Through the gradual progress of insight, one may attain the noble path consciousness in which dormant kilesas are permanently extinguished.

Thus with deep practice the torture of the kilesas will diminish, will perhaps even disappear forever.

In this case, gain and respect and fame will come very naturally to you, but you will not get caught in them. They will seem paltry compared to the noble goal and dedication of your practice. Since you are sincere, you will never stop adding to your foundation of morality. You will make use of gain and fame in a fitting way, and will continue with your practice.

TENTH ARMY: SELF-EXALTATION AND DISPARAGING OTHERS

All of us have some awareness of the fact of suffering. It is present in birth, in life and in death. Painful experiences in life often lead us to want to overcome suffering and live in freedom and peace. Perhaps it is this wish, this faith, or perhaps even a firm conviction of this that led you to read this book.

In the course of our practice, this fundamental aim may be undermined by certain by-products of the practice itself. We have discussed how gain, respect and fame can become obstacles to liberation. So, too, can the closely related problems of self-exaltation and disparaging others, the Tenth Army of Māra. This is a battle faced by meditation masters.

Self-exaltation often attacks after some gain in practice, perhaps a feeling of maturity in our precepts. We might become quite cocky, looking around and saying, "Look at that person. They're not keeping the precepts. They're not as holy as I am, not as pure." If this happens, we have fallen victim to the Tenth Army of Māra. This last army is perhaps the most lethal of all. In the Buddha's time there was even a man, Devadatta, who tried to kill the Buddha under its influence. He had grown proud of his psychic powers, his attainments in concentration and his position as a disciple. Yet when subversive thoughts came, he had no mindfulness, no defense against them.

## The Essence of the Holy Life

It is possible to take delight in our own purity without disparaging others, and without self-aggrandizement. A simile might be useful here. Consider a valuable timber tree whose core is the most precious part. We can compare this tree with the holy life described by the Buddha: sīla, samādhi, paññā.

In cross section the tree trunk is revealed to be made of the precious core, the woody tissue, the inner bark and finally the thin epidermis of outer bark. A tree also has branches and fruits.

The holy life is composed of sīla, samādhi and paññā; it includes the path and fruition attainments or experiences of nibbāna. There are also psychic powers, including, we might say, the psychic power of penetrating into the true nature of reality by vipassanā insight. Then there are the gain, respect, and fame which can come to one through the practice.

One woodcutter may go into the forest seeking the tree's pith for some important purpose. Finding this big, handsome timber tree, he or she cuts off all the branches and takes them home. There the woodcutter finds that the branches and leaves are useless for the intended purpose. This is like a person satisfied with gain and fame.

Another person may strip the thin outer bark from the tree. This is like a yogi who, content with purity of conduct, does not work to develop the mind any further.

A third yogi, perhaps a bit more intelligent, realizes that morality is not the end of the road: there is mental development to be considered. He or she may take up some form of meditation and work very hard. Attaining one-pointedness of mind, this yogi feels great. The mind is still and content, full of bliss and rapture. Such a person may even master the jhānas, or absorption states of deep concentration. Then the thought comes: "Boy am I feeling great, but the person next to me is as restless as ever." This yogi feels he or she has attained the essence of vipassanā and the holy life. But instead she or he has only been attacked by the Tenth Army of Māra. This is like a woodcutter who is content with the inner bark of the tree and has not yet touched the core.

More ambitious, another yogi determines to develop the psychic powers. He or she attains them and is filled with pride. Moreover, it is a lot of fun to play with those new abilities. The thought may come, "Wow, this is far out. It must be the essence of the Dhamma. Not everyone can do it, either. That woman over there can't see what's right under her nose, the devas and hell beings." If this person does not break free from the Tenth Army of Māra, he or she will become intoxicated and negligent in developing wholesome states of mind. His or her life will be accompanied by great suffering.

• Psychic powers are not truly liberating, either. In this present age, many people are inspired by certain individuals who have developed paranormal psychic powers. For some reason even a small display of psychic ability seems to draw a great deal of faith from people. It was the same in the Buddha's time. In fact, there was once a layman who approached the Buddha with the suggestion that the Buddha should campaign for his teaching on a basis of demonstrating psychic power. For this purpose the Buddha should widely deploy all of his disciples who had psychic powers and ask them to demonstrate miracles to the people. "People will be really impressed," the layman said. "You'll get a lot of followers that way."

The Buddha refused. Three times the request was repeated, and three times it was refused. Finally the Buddha said, "Layman, there are three types of psychic powers. One is the power to fly in the air and dive into the earth, and to perform other superhuman feats. The second is the power to read other people's minds. You can tell a person, 'Ah, on such and such a day you were thinking that, and you went out to do this.' People can be very impressed with this. But there is a third psychic power, the power of instruction, whereby one can tell another, 'Ah, you have such-and-such a behavior that is not good. It is unwholesome, unskillful, not conducive to your welfare or that of others. You should abandon that and practice in such a way as to cultivate wholesome actions. Then you should meditate as I will now instruct you.' Now, this power to guide another person on the right path is the most important psychic power.

"O layman, if the first two powers are displayed to persons who have faith in vipassanā, it will not undermine their faith. But there are those who are not by nature faithful, and they would say, 'Well, that's nothing very special. I know of other sects and other religious systems wherein people can also attain such powers, through mantras and other esoteric practices.' People like that will misunderstand my teaching.

"The third type of psychic power is best, that of being able to instruct others, O layman. When one can say, 'This is bad, do not do it. You should cultivate good speech and behavior. This is the way to cleanse your mind of kilesas. This is how to meditate. This is the way to attain the bliss of nibbāna, which liberates you from all suffering,' this, O layman, is the best psychic power."

By all means, go ahead and try to attain psychic powers if this interests you. It is not essential, but it does not contradict vipassanā practice; there's no one to stop you, and the achievement certainly is not anything one can scoff at. Just do not mistake psychic powers for the essence of the teachings. A person who attains psychic powers and then believes he or she has reached the end of the spiritual path is much deluded. Such people seek the pith of the timber tree but are satisfied to reach only the woody outer layer. Bringing it home, they will find it of no use. So, after you attain psychic powers, please go on and develop the various vipassanā insights, successive path and fruition moments, until the realization of arahantship.

When mindfulness and concentration are well-developed, the vipassanā insight that penetrates into the various levels of the true nature of things will arise. This is also a form of psychic knowledge, but it is not yet the end of the path.

You may eventually attain the *sotāpatti* path, the noble consciousness of the stream entrant, which is the first stage of enlightenment. Path consciousness, the first dip into nibbāna, uproots certain kilesas forever. You may continue to practice and also develop the fruition consciousness. When this consciousness arises, the mind dwells in the bliss of nibbāna. It is said that this liberation is unbounded by time. Once you have put forth the effort to attain it, you can return to it at any time.

However, these lower attainments still fall short of the Buddha's purpose, which was to attain full enlightenment, that final liberating consciousness which extinguishes all suffering forever.

After he had finished constructing the simile of the timber tree, the Buddha said, "The benefit of my teaching does not lie simply in gain, respect and fame. The benefit of my teaching does not lie merely in purity of conduct. It does not lie merely in the attainment of the jhānas. It does not lie merely in the attainment of psychic powers. It has as its essence the total liberation from kilesas that is attainable at any time."

I hope you will gather up strength, energy and a great deal of courage to face the Ten Armies of Māra, and to vanquish all of them with merciless compassion, so that you may be able to go through the various vipassanā insights. May you at least attain the noble consciousness of the stream entrant in this very life, and after that, may you be liberated totally and finally from suffering.

# 4 *The Seven Factors of Enlightenment*

## BECOMING A NOBLE ONE

One does not become enlightened by merely gazing into the sky. One does not become enlightened by reading or studying the scriptures, nor by thinking, nor by wishing for the enlightened state to burst into one's mind. There are certain necessary conditions or prerequisites which cause enlightenment to arise. In Pāli these are known as the *bojjhangas,* or factors of enlightenment, and there are seven of them.

The word bojjhanga is made up of *bodhi,* which means enlightenment or an enlightened person, and *anga,* causative factor. Thus a bojjhanga is a causative factor of an enlightened being, or a cause for enlightenment. A second sense of the word bojjhanga is based on alternative meanings of its two Pāli roots. The alternative meaning of bodhi is the knowledge that comprehends or sees the Four Noble Truths: the truth of universal suffering or unsatisfactoriness; the truth that desire is the cause of this suffering and dissatisfaction; the truth that there can be an end to this suffering; and the truth of the path to the end of this suffering, or the Noble Eightfold Path. The second meaning of anga is part or portion. Thus, the second meaning of bojjhanga is the specific part of knowledge that sees the Four Noble Truths.

All vipassanā yogis come to understand the Four Noble Truths to some extent, but true comprehension of them requires a particular, transforming moment of consciousness, known as path consciousness. This is one of the culminating insights of vipassanā practice. It includes the experience of nibbāna. Once a yogi has experienced this, he or she deeply knows the Four Noble Truths, and thus is considered to contain the bojjhangas inside him or herself. Such a person is called noble. Thus, the bojjhangas or enlightenment factors also are parts or qualities of a noble person. Sometimes they are known as the *sambojjhangas*, the prefix *sam-* meaning full, complete, correct, or true. The prefix is an honorific and intensifier, and adds no crucial difference in meaning.

These seven factors of enlightenment, or seven qualities of a noble person, are: mindfulness, investigation, effort, rapture, calm, concentration and equanimity. In Pāli, the list would be *sati, dhamma vicaya, viriya, pīti, passaddhi, samādhi, upekkhā*. These seven can be found in all phases of vipassanā practice. But if we take as a model the progressive stages of insight, we can say that the seven enlightenment factors begin to be very clear at the stage of insight where a yogi begins to see the arising and passing of phenomena.

How can one develop these factors in himself or herself? By means of satipaṭṭhāna meditation. The Buddha said, "Oh bhikkhus, if the four foundations of mindfulness are practiced persistently and repeatedly, the seven types of bojjhangas will be automatically and fully developed."

Practicing the four foundations of mindfulness does not mean studying them, thinking of them, listening to discourses about them, nor discussing them. What we must do is be directly and experientially aware of the four foundations of mindfulness, the four bases on which mindfulness can be established. The *Satipaṭṭhāna Sutta* names them: first, the sensations of the body; second, feeling – the painful, pleasant or neutral quality inherent in each experience; third, the mind and thought; and fourth, all other objects of consciousness – things seen, heard, tasted and so forth. The Buddha said, furthermore, that one should practice this awareness not intermittently, but rather persistently and repeatedly. This is exactly what we try to do in vipassanā meditation. The tradition of vipassanā meditation taught and developed by Mahāsī Sayadaw is oriented toward developing fully the seven factors of enlightenment, and eventually experiencing noble path consciousness, in accordance with the Buddha's instructions.

## MINDFULNESS: THE FIRST ENLIGHTENMENT FACTOR

Sati, mindfulness, is the first factor of enlightenment. "Mindfulness" has come to be the accepted translation of sati into English. However, this word has a kind of passive connotation which can be misleading. "Mindfulness" must be dynamic and confrontative. In retreats, I teach that mindfulness should leap forward onto the object, covering it completely, penetrating into it, not missing any part of it. To convey this active sense, I often prefer to use the words "observing power" to translate sati, rather than "mindfulness." However, for the sake of ease and sim-plicity, I will consistently use the word "mindfulness" in this volume, but I would like my readers to remember the dynamic qualities it should possess.

Mindfulness can be well understood by examining its three aspects of characteristic, function and manifestation. These three aspects are traditional categories used in the *Abhidhamma,* the Buddhist description of consciousness, to describe factors of mind. We will use them here to study each of the enlightenment factors in turn.

### Nonsuperficiality

The *characteristic* of mindfulness is nonsuperficiality. This suggests that mindfulness is penetrative and profound. If we throw a cork into a stream, it simply bobs up and down on the surface, floating downstream with the current. If we throw a stone instead, it will immediately sink to the very bed of the stream. So, too, mindfulness ensures that the mind will sink deeply into the object and not slip superficially past it.

Say you are watching your abdomen as the object of your satipaṭṭhāna practice. You try to be very firm, focusing your attention so that the mind will not slip off, but rather will sink deeply into the processes of rising and falling. As the mind penetrates these processes, you can comprehend the true natures of tension, pressure, movement and so on.

## Keeping the Object in View

The *function* of mindfulness is to keep the object always in view, neither forgetting it nor allowing it to disappear. When mindfulness is present, the occurring object will be noted without forgetfulness.

In order for nonsuperficiality and nondisappearance, the characteristic and function of mindfulness, to appear clearly in our practice, we must try to understand and practice the third aspect of mindfulness. This is the *manifestation* aspect, which develops and brings along the other two. The chief ✳ manifestation of mindfulness is confrontation: it sets the mind directly face to face with the object.

## Face to Face with the Object

It is as if you are walking along a road and you meet a traveler, face to face, coming from the opposite direction. When you are meditating, the mind should meet the object ✳ in just this way. Only through direct confrontation with an object can true mindfulness arise.

They say that the human face is the index of character. If you want to size up a person, you look at his or her face very carefully and then you can make a preliminary judgment. If you do not examine the face carefully and instead become distracted by other parts of his or her body, then your judgment will not be accurate.

In meditation you must apply a similar, if not sharper, degree of care in looking at the object of observation. Only ✗ if you look meticulously at the object can you understand its true nature. When you look at a face for the first time, you get a quick, overall view of it. If you look more carefully, you will pick up details – say, of the eyebrows, eyes and lips. First you must look at the face as a whole, and only later will details become clear.

Similarly, when you are watching the rising and falling of your abdomen, you begin by taking an overall view of these processes. First you bring your mind face to face with the rising and falling. After repeated successes you will find yourself able to look closer. Details will appear to you effortlessly, as if by themselves. You will notice different sensations in the rise and fall, such as tension, pressure, heat, coolness, or movement.

As a yogi repeatedly comes face to face with the object, his or her efforts begin to bear fruit. Mindfulness is activated and becomes firmly established on the object of observation. There are no misses. The objects do not fall away from view. They neither slip away nor disappear, nor are they absent-mindedly forgotten. The kilesas cannot infiltrate this strong barrier of mindfulness. If mindfulness can be maintained for a significant period of time, the yogi can discover a great purity of mind because of the absence of kilesas. Protection from attack by the kilesas is a second aspect of the manifestation of mindfulness. When mindfulness is persistently and repeatedly activated, wisdom arises. There will be insight into the true nature of body and mind. Not only does the yogi realize the true experiential sensations of the rise and fall, but she or he also comprehends the individual characteristics of the various physical and mental phenomena happening inside herself or himself.

*Seeing the Four Noble Truths*

The yogi may see directly that all physical and mental phenomena share the characteristic of suffering. When this happens, we say that the First Noble Truth is seen.

When the First Noble Truth has been seen, the remaining three are also seen. Thus it is said in the texts, and we can observe the same in our own experience. Because there is mindfulness at the moment of occurrence of mental and physical phenomena, no craving arises. With this abandoning of craving, the Second Noble Truth is seen. Craving is the root of suffering, and when craving is absent, suffering, too, disappears. Seeing the Third Noble Truth, the cessation of suffering, is fulfilled when ignorance and the other kilesas fall away and cease. All this occurs on a provisional or moment-to-moment basis when mindfulness and wisdom are present. Seeing the Fourth Noble Truth refers to the development of the Eightfold Path factors. This development occurs simultaneously within each moment of mindfulness. We will discuss the factors of the Eightfold Path in more detail in the next chapter, "Chariot to Nibbāna."

Therefore, on one level, we can say that the Four Noble Truths are seen by the yogi at any time when mindfulness and wisdom are present. This brings us back to the two definitions of bojjhanga given above. Mindfulness is part of the consciousness that contains insight into the true nature of reality; it is a part of enlightenment knowledge. It is present in the mind of one who knows the Four Noble Truths. Thus, it is called a factor of enlightenment, a bojjhanga.

## Mindfulness is the Cause of Mindfulness

The first cause of mindfulness is nothing more than mindfulness itself. Naturally, there is a difference between the weak mindfulness that characterizes one's early meditative efforts and the mindfulness at higher levels of practice, which becomes strong enough to cause enlightenment to occur. In fact, the development of mindfulness is a simple momentum, one moment of mindfulness causing the next.

## Four More Ways to Develop Mindfulness

Commentators identify four additional factors which help develop and strengthen mindfulness until it is worthy of the title bojjhanga.

### 1. Mindfulness and Clear Comprehension

The first is *satisampajañña*, usually translated as "mindfulness and clear comprehension." In this term, sati is the mindfulness activated during formal sitting practice, watching the primary object as well as others. *Sampajañña*, clear comprehension, refers to mindfulness on a broader basis: mindfulness of walking, stretching, bending, turning around, looking to one side, and all the other activities that make up ordinary life.

## 2. Avoiding Unmindful People

Dissociation from persons who are not mindful is the second way of developing mindfulness as an enlightenment factor. If you are doing your best to be mindful, and you run across an unmindful person who corners you into some long-winded argument, you can imagine how quickly your own mindfulness might vanish.

## 3. Choosing Mindful Friends

The third way to cultivate mindfulness is to associate with mindful persons. Such people can serve as strong sources of inspiration. By spending time with them, in an environment where mindfulness is valued, you can grow and deepen your own mindfulness.

## 4. Inclining the Mind Toward Mindfulness

The fourth method is to incline the mind toward activating mindfulness. This means consciously taking mindfulness as a top priority, alerting the mind to return to it in every situation. This approach is very important; it creates a sense of unforgetfulness, of non-absentmindedness. You try as much as possible to refrain from those activities that do not particularly lead to the deepening of mindfulness. Of these there is a wide selection, as you probably know.

As a yogi only one task is required of you, and that is to be aware of whatever is happening in the present moment. In an intensive retreat, this means you set aside social relationships, writing and reading, even reading scriptures. You take special care when eating not to fall into habitual patterns. You always consider whether the times, places, amounts and kinds of food you eat are essential or not. If they are not, you avoid repeating the unnecessary pattern.

### INVESTIGATION: THE SECOND ENLIGHTENMENT FACTOR

We say that the mind is enveloped by darkness, and as soon as insight or wisdom arises, we say that the light has come. This light reveals physical and mental phenomena so that the mind can see them clearly. It is as if you were

in a dark room and were given a flashlight. You can begin
to see what is present in the room. This image illustrates
the second enlightenment factor, called "investigation" in
English and *dhamma vicaya sambojjhanga* in Pāli.

The word "investigation" may need to be elucidated. In
meditation, investigation is not carried out by means of the
thinking process. It is intuitive, a sort of discerning insight
that distinguishes the characteristics of phenomena. *Vicaya*
is the word usually translated as "investigation"; it is also
a synonym for "wisdom" or "insight." Thus in vipassanā
practice there is no such thing as a proper investigation
which uncovers nothing. When vicaya is present, investigation and insight coincide. They are the same thing.

What is it we investigate? What do we see into? We see
into dhamma. This is a word with many meanings that can
be experienced personally. Generally when we say
"dhamma" we mean phenomena, mind and matter. We
also mean the laws that govern the behavior of phenomena.
When "Dhamma" is capitalized, it refers more specifically
to the teaching of the Buddha, who realized the true nature
of "dhamma" and helped others to follow in his path. The
commentaries explain that in the context of investigation,
the word "dhamma" has an additional, specific meaning.
It refers to the individual states or qualities uniquely present in each object, as well as the common traits each object
may share with other objects. Thus, individual and common
traits are what we should be discovering in our practice.

### Knowing the True Nature of Dhammas

The characteristic of investigation is the ability to know,
through discernment by a nonintellectual investigation, the
true nature of dhammas.

### Dispelling Darkness

The function of investigation is to dispel darkness. When
dhamma vicaya is present, it lights up the field of awareness, illuminating the object of observation so that the mind
can see its characteristics and penetrate its true nature. At
a higher level, investigation has the function of totally

removing the envelope of darkness, allowing the mind to penetrate into nibbāna. So you see, investigation is a very important factor in our practice. When it is weak, or absent, there is trouble.

*Dissipating Confusion*

As you walk into a pitch-dark room, you may feel a lot of doubt. "Am I going to trip over something? Bang my shins? Bang into the wall?" Your mind is in confusion because you do not know what things are in the room, or where they are located. Similarly, when dhamma vicaya is absent, the yogi is in a state of chaos and confusion, filled with a thousand and one doubts. "Is there a person, or is there no person? Is there a self, or no self? Am I an individual or not? Is there a soul, or is there no soul? Is there a spirit or not?"

You, too, may have been plagued by doubts like this. Perhaps you doubted the teaching of impermanence, suffering, and absence of self. "Are you sure that everything is impermanent? Maybe some things aren't quite so unsatisfactory as others. Maybe there's a self-essence we haven't found yet." You may feel that nibbāna is a fairy tale invented by your teachers, that it does not really exist.

The manifestation of investigation is the dissipation of confusion. When dhamma vicaya sambojjhanga arises, everything is brightly lit, and the mind sees clearly what is present. Seeing clearly the nature of mental and physical phenomena, you no longer worry about banging into the wall. Impermanence, unsatisfactoriness and absence of self will become quite clear to you. Finally, you may penetrate into the true nature of nibbāna, such that you'll not need to doubt its reality.

*Ultimate Realities*

Investigation shows us the characteristics of *paramattha dhamma*, or ultimate realities, which simply means objects that can be experienced directly without the mediation of concepts. There are three types of ultimate realities: physical phenomena, mental phenomena, and nibbāna.

Physical phenomena are composed of the four great elements, earth, fire, water and air. Each element has separate characteristics which are peculiar to and inherent in it.

When we say "characterized" we could also say "experienced as," for we experience the characteristics of each of these four elements in our own bodies, as sensations.

Earth's specific or individual characteristic is hardness. Water has the characteristic of fluidity and cohesion. Fire's characteristic is temperature, hot and cold. Air, or wind, has characteristics of tightness, tautness, tension or piercing, and an additional dynamic aspect, movement.

Mental phenomena also have specific characteristics. For example, the mind, or consciousness, has the characteristic of knowing an object. The mental factor of *phassa*, or contact, has the characteristic of impingement.

Please bring your attention right now to the rising and falling of your abdomen. As you are mindful of the movement, you may perhaps come to know that it is composed of sensations. Tightness, tautness, pressure, movement – all these are manifestations of the wind element. You may feel heat or cold as well, the element of fire. These sensations are objects of your mind; they are the dhammas which you investigate. If your experience is perceived directly, and you are aware of the sensations in a specific way, then we can say dhamma vicaya is present.

Investigation can also discern other aspects of the Dhamma. As you observe the rising and falling movements, you may spontaneously notice that there are two distinct processes occurring. On the one hand are physical phenomena, the sensations of tension and movement. On the other hand is consciousness, the noting mind which is aware of these objects. This is an insight into the true nature of things. As you continue to meditate, another kind of insight will arise. You will see that all dhammas share characteristics of impermanence, unsatisfactoriness and absence of self. The factor of investigation has led you to see what is universal in nature, in every physical and mental object.

With the maturation of this insight into impermanence, unsatisfactoriness and absence of self, wisdom becomes able to penetrate nibbāna. In this case, the word dhamma takes nibbāna as its referent. Thus, dhamma vicaya can also mean discerning insight into nibbāna.

There is something outstanding about nibbāna in that it has no characteristics in common with phenomena that can be perceived. It has specific characteristics of its own, however: permanence, eternity, nonsuffering, bliss and happiness. Like other objects, it is called *anatta*, nonself, but the nonself nature of nibbāna is different from the nonself of ordinary phenomena in that it does not rest upon suffering and impermanence. It rests instead on bliss and permanence. When the mind penetrates nibbāna, this distinction becomes evident through dhamma vicaya, the investigative discerning insight into the dhamma, which has led us to this place and now allows us to see it clearly.

### Spontaneous Insight is the Cause of Investigation

We might be interested in knowing how we can get this factor of investigation to arise. According to the Buddha, there is only one cause of it: there must be a spontaneous insight, a direct perception. To realize such an insight, you must activate mindfulness. You must be aware in a penetrative manner of whatever arises. Then the mind can gain insight into the true nature of phenomena. This accomplishment requires wise attention, appropriate attention. You direct the mind toward the object, mindfully. Then you will have that first insight or direct perception. The factor of investigation arises, and because of it, further insights will follow naturally in order, as a child progresses from kindergarten through high school and college and finally graduates.

### Seven More Ways to Develop Investigation

The commentaries speak of seven additional ways to support the arising of investigation as a factor of enlightenment.

## 1. Asking Questions

The first is to ask questions about the Dhamma and the practice. This means finding a person who is knowledgeable about the Dhamma and speaking with him or her. There is no doubt that Westerners can quite easily fulfil this first requirement. They are adept at asking complicated questions. This capacity is good; it will lead to the development of wisdom.

## 2. Cleanliness

The second support is cleanliness of what are called the internal and external bases. These are nothing more than the body and the environment. Keeping the internal base, or body, clean means bathing regularly, keeping hair and nails well groomed, and making sure the bowels are free of constipation. Keeping the external base clean means wearing clean and neat clothes and sweeping, dusting and tidying your living quarters. This helps the mind become bright and clear. When the eyes fall upon dirt and untidiness, mental confusion tends to arise. But if an environment is clean, the mind becomes bright and clear. This mental state is ideally conducive to the development of wisdom.

## 3. A Balanced Mind

The third support for the arising of investigation is balancing the controlling faculties of faith, wisdom, mindfulness, energy and concentration. We treated them at length in an earlier chapter. Four of these five faculties are paired: wisdom and faith, effort and concentration. The practice depends in fundamental ways upon the equilibrium of these pairs.

If faith is stronger than wisdom, one is apt to become gullible or to be carried away by excessive devotional thoughts, a hindrance to practice. Yet, on the other hand, if knowledge or intelligence is in excess, a cunning and manipulative mind results. One can deceive oneself in many ways, even about the truth.

The balance between effort and concentration works like this: if one is overenthusiastic and works too hard, the mind becomes agitated and cannot focus properly on the object of observation. Slipping off, it wanders about, causing much frustration. Too much concentration, however, can lead to laziness and drowsiness. When the mind is still and it seems easy to remain focused on the object, one might begin to relax and settle back. Soon one dozes off.

This balancing of faculties is an aspect of meditation that teachers must understand quite thoroughly in order to guide their students. The most basic way of maintaining balance, and of reestablishing it when it is lost, is to strengthen the remaining controlling faculty, mindfulness.

### 4-5. Avoiding Fools, Making Friends with the Wise

The fourth and fifth supports for investigation are to avoid foolish, unwise persons and to associate with wise ones. What is a wise person? One person may be learned in the scriptures. Another may be able to think things through with great clarity. If you associate with these people, your theoretical learning will surely increase and you will cultivate a philosophical attitude. This activity is not at all bad. Another sort of wise person, however, can give you knowledge and wisdom beyond what is found in books. The scriptures tell us that the minimum prerequisite defining such a person is that he or she must have practiced meditation and reached the stage of insight into the arising and passing away of all phenomena. If one has not reached this stage, it goes without saying that one should never try to teach meditation, since associating with one's students will not foster the arising of dhamma vicaya in them.

### 6. Reflection on Profound Truth

The sixth support for investigation is reflection on profound Dhamma. This instruction to think about something might seem contradictory. Basically it means reflecting on the nature of physical and mental phenomena from the vipassanā point of view: as aggregates, elements and faculties, all of them impersonal.

### 7. Total Commitment

The last important support for the arising of investigation is total commitment to cultivating this factor of enlightenment. One should always have the inclination toward investigation, toward direct intuitive insight. Remember that it is not necessary to rationalize or intellectualize your experiences. Just practice meditation, so that you can gain a firsthand experience of your own mind and body.

## COURAGEOUS EFFORT: THIRD FACTOR OF ENLIGHTENMENT

The third enlightenment factor, effort or *viriya*, is the energy expended to direct the mind persistently, continuously, toward the object of observation. In Pāli, viriya is defined as *vīrānaṁ bhāvo*, which means "the state of heroic ones." This gives us an idea of the flavor, the quality, of effort in our practice. It should be courageous effort.

People who are hardworking and industrious have the capacity to be heroic in whatever they do. It is effort itself, in fact, that gives them a heroic quality. A person endowed with courageous effort will be bold in going forward, unafraid of the difficulties he or she may encounter in executing a chosen task. Commentators say that the characteristic of effort is an enduring patience in the face of suffering or difficulty. Effort is the ability to see to the end no matter what, even if one has to grit one's teeth.

Yogis need patience and acceptance from the very beginning of practice. If you come to a retreat, you leave behind the pleasant habits and hobbies of ordinary life. You sleep little, on makeshift mattresses in tiny cells. Then you get up and spend the day trying to sit immobile and cross-legged, hour upon hour. On top of the sheer austerity of practice, you must be patient with your mind's dissatisfaction, its longing for the good things of home.

Anytime you actually get down to the work of meditation, moreover, you are likely to experience bodily resistance and some level of pain. Say you are trying to sit still for an hour with your legs crossed. Just fifteen minutes into the sitting, a nasty mosquito comes and bites you. You itch. On top of that, your neck is a bit stiff and there's a creeping numbness in your foot. You may start to feel irritated. You are used to a luxurious life. Your body is so pampered and spoonfed that you usually shift its position whenever it feels the slightest discomfort. Now, alas, your body must suffer. And because it is suffering, you suffer as well.

Unpleasant sensations have the uncanny ability to exhaust and wither the mind. The temptation to give up can be very great. Your mind may fill with rationalizations: "I'll just move my foot a tiny inch; it'll improve my concentration." It may be only a matter of time before you give in.

## Patient Endurance

You need courageous effort, with its characteristic of forbearance in the face of difficulty. If you raise your energy level, the mind gains strength to bear with pain in a patient and courageous way. Effort has the power to freshen the mind and keep it robust, even in difficult circumstances. To increase your energy level, you can encourage yourself, or perhaps seek out the inspiration of a spiritual friend or guide. Fed with a bit more energy, the mind grows taut and strong once more.

## Support for the Exhausted Mind

Commentators say that effort has the function of supporting. It supports the mind when it withers under attack by pain.

Consider an old, dilapidated house on the point of collapse. A slight gust of wind will bring it tumbling down. If you prop it up with two-by-fours, though, the house can continue to stand. Similarly, a mind withered by pain can be supported by courageous effort and can continue the practice with freshness and vigilance. You may have experienced this benefit personally.

Yogis who suffer from chronic ailments may have difficulty practicing in a regular way. Confronting an ailment again and again saps physical and mental energy; it is taxing and discouraging. It is no surprise that yogis who have sicknesses often come to interviews full

of despair and disappointment. They feel they are making
no progress. They merely hit a wall again and again. It all
seems so futile. Little thoughts occur to them, wanting to
give up, wanting to leave the retreat or just stop meditating.
Sometimes I can save this situation with a little discourse
or a word of encouragement. The yogi's face lights up and
he or she is on the road again for a day or two.

It is very important to have encouragement and inspiration, not only from yourself but from someone else who
can help you along, give you a push when you get stuck.

*Courageous Mind: The Story of Cittā*

The manifestation of effort is a bold, brave and courageous
mind. To illustrate this quality, there is a story from the
Buddha's time of a bhikkhuni named Cittā. One day she
reviewed the suffering inherent in mind and body and was
seized by a great spiritual urgency. As a result she renounced the world and took nun's robes, hoping to free
herself from suffering. Unfortunately, she had a chronic
ailment which came in spasms, without warning. One day
she would feel fine, and then suddenly she would fall ill.
She was a determined lady, though. She wanted liberation
and was not one to call it quits. Whenever she was healthy
she would strive intensely, and when she was sick she
continued, though at a lesser pace. Sometimes her practice
was very dynamic and inspired. Then the ailment attacked,
and she would regress.

Her sister bhikkhunīs worried that Cittā would over-
strain herself. They warned her to take care of her health,
to slow down, but Cittā ignored them. She meditated on,
day after day, month after month, year after year. As she
grew older she had to lean on a staff to move around. Her
body was weak and bony, but her mind was robust and
strong.

One day Cittā decided she was sick of putting up with
all this impediment, and made a totally committed decision.
She said to herself, "Today I'm going to do my very best
without considering my body at all. Either I die today or the
kilesas will be vanquished."

Cittā started walking up a hill with her staff. Very mindfully, step by step, she went. Old and thin and feeble, at times she had to get down and crawl. But her mind was persistent and heroic. She was absolutely, totally committed to the Dhamma. Every step she took, every inch she crawled, toward the peak of the hill was made with mindfulness. When she reached the top, she was exhausted, but her mindfulness had not been broken.

Cittā made again her resolution to vanquish the kilesas once and for all or to be vanquished by death. She practiced on as hard as she could, and it seems that on that very day she reached her goal. She was filled with joy and rapture, and when she descended the hill it was with strength and clarity of mind. She was a very different person from the Cittā who had crawled up the hill. Now she was fresh and robust, with a clear and calm expression. The other bhikk-hunīs were astounded to see Cittā like this. They asked her by what miracle she had been transformed. When Cittā explained what had happened to her, the bhikkhunīs were filled with awe and praise.

The Buddha said, "Far better is it to live a day striving in meditation than one hundred years without striving." In business, politics, social affairs and education, we always find that the leaders are people who work hard. Hard work brings you to the peak of any field. This is a fact of life. Effort's role is obvious in meditation as well. Meditation practice takes a great deal of energy. You have to really work to establish continuity of mindfulness and maintain it from moment to moment without a break. In this endeavor there is no room for laziness.

### A Heat that Vaporizes Defilements

The Buddha spoke of energy as a kind of heat, *ātāpa*. When the mind is filled with energy, it becomes hot. This mental temperature has the power to dry up defilements. We can compare the kilesas to moisture; a mind devoid of energy is easily dampened and weighed down by them. If effort is strong, however, the mind can vaporize kilesas before it is even touched by them. Thus, when the mind is energized by effort, mental defilements cannot touch it, or even come near. Unwholesome states cannot attack.

On matter's molecular level, heat appears as increased vibration. A red-hot iron bar is actually vibrating rapidly, and it becomes flexible and workable. This is so in meditation, too. When effort is strong, the increased vibration in the mind is manifested as agility. The energized mind jumps from one object to another with ease and quickness. Contacting phenomena, it heats them up, melting the illusion of solidity, so that passing away is clearly seen.

Sometimes when momentum is strong in practice, effort carries on by itself, just as an iron bar remains red-hot for a long time after it has left the fire. With the kilesas far away, clarity and brightness appear in the mind. The mind is pure and clear in its perception of what is happening. It becomes sharp, and very interested in catching the details of phenomena as they arise. This energetic mindfulness allows the mind to penetrate deeply into the object of observation and to remain there without scattering and dispersing. With mindfulness and concentration established, there is space for clear intuitive perception, wisdom, to arise.

Through diligent effort, then, the wholesome factors of mindfulness, concentration and wisdom arise and strengthen, and bring with them other wholesome, happy states. The mind is clear and sharp, and it begins to enter more deeply into the true nature of reality.

### Disadvantages of Laziness and Delights of Freedom

If instead there is sloppiness and laziness, your attention becomes blunt and noxious states of mind creep in. As you lose focus, you do not care whether you are in a wholesome state of mind or not. You might think your practice can coast along with no help from you. This kind of audacity, a lazy sort of boldness, can undermine you, slow you down. Your mind becomes damp and heavy, full of negative and unwholesome tendencies, like a mildewed horse blanket that has been left out in the rain.

Ordinarily the kilesas pull the mind into their field of sensual pleasures. This is especially true for *rāga*, lust, one aspect of desire. People who are devoid of courageous effort are helpless in rāga's grip. They sink again and again into the field of sensual pleasures. If effort is injected into the mind, though, the mind can free itself from this harmful energy field. The mind becomes very light, like a rocket that has succeeded in entering the weightlessness of outer space. Freed from the heaviness of desire and aversion, the mind fills instead with rapture and calm, as well as other delightful, free states of mind. This kind of delight can only be enjoyed through the fire of one's own efforts.

You may have experienced this freedom personally. Perhaps one day you were meditating while someone was baking cookies nearby. A delicious smell came floating into your nostrils. If you were really mindful, you simply noted this smell as an object. You knew it was pleasant, but no attachment or clinging arose. You weren't compelled to get up from your cushion and ask for one of those cookies. It might have been similar had an unpleasant object come to you. You would have felt no aversion. Confusion and delusion may also have been absent. When you see clearly the nature of mind and matter, unwholesome factors cannot control you.

Food can be one of the most difficult areas for meditators, especially on retreat. Leaving aside the whole problem of greed, yogis often feel strong disgust toward food. When one is really mindful, one can make the shocking discovery that food is quite tasteless on the tongue. As practice deepens, some yogis begin to find food so repulsive that they are unable to eat more than one or two bites. Alternatively, when yogis experience strong rapture, this rapture becomes a nourishment for their minds, such that they entirely lose their appetite. Both of these types of yogis should try to overcome their initial reactions and make a concerted effort to eat sufficient food to maintain their energy. When the body is deprived of physical nutriment it loses strength and stamina, and eventually this undermines the meditation practice.

One may dream of getting the benefits of viriya, but if one does not actually strive for them, it is said that one wallows in disgust. The Pāli word for such a person is *kusīta*. In the world a person who does not work to support him or herself and family will be looked down upon by others. He or she might be called a lazybones or insulted in various ways. The word kusīta refers specifically to someone who is abused verbally. In practice it is the same. At times energy is essential. A yogi who cannot muster the effort to confront a difficult experience, but cringes instead, could be said to be "chickening out." He or she has no courage, no sense of boldness, no bravery at all.

A lazy person lives in misery, lives with suffering. Not only is he or she held in low esteem by others, but also kilesas arise easily when effort is low. Then the mind is assailed by the three kinds of wrong thoughts: thoughts of craving, of destruction and of cruelty. These mental states are oppressive, painful and unpleasant in themselves. A lazy person can easily be pounced upon by sloth and torpor, another unpleasant state. Furthermore, without energy it may be difficult to maintain the basic precepts. One breaks the precepts at one's own expense; one loses the joy and benefit of moral purity.

The work of meditation is seriously undermined by laziness. It robs a yogi of the chance to see into the true nature of things, or to raise his or her mind to greater heights. Therefore, the Buddha said, a lazy person loses many beneficial things.

*Persistence*

For effort to develop to the point of being a factor of enlightenment, it must have the quality of persistence. This means that energy doesn't drop or stagnate. Rather, it continually increases. With persistent effort, the mind is protected from wrong thoughts. There is so much energy that sloth and torpor cannot arise. Yogis feel a sort of durability of precepts, as well as of concentration and insight. They experience the benefit of effort, a mind that is bright and clear and full of strength, active and energetic.

Understanding about good effort is clear just after one has enjoyed a major success in meditation. Perhaps one has watched extremely painful sensations and penetrated them without reacting or becoming oppressed by them. The mind feels a great satisfaction and heroism in its own accomplishment. The yogi realizes for himself or herself that, thanks to effort, the mind has not succumbed to difficulty but has gone beyond it and has emerged victorious.

## Wise Attention is the Cause of Energy

The Buddha was brief in describing how effort or energy arises. It is caused by wise attention, he said, wise reflection on being committed to arousing the three elements of effort.

## Stages of Energy: Leaving the Field of the Kilesas

The Buddha's three elements of effort are launching effort, liberating effort, and persistent effort.

Launching effort is needed at the beginning of a period of practice, particularly on a retreat. At first the mind is overwhelmed by the new situation, and may long for all the things left behind. To get moving on the path of meditation, you reflect on the benefits of your task and then start really putting in the effort to be mindful. When a yogi first starts to practice, only very basic objects are prescribed. You are directed just to watch the primary object and only to attend to other objects when they become distracting. This simple yet fundamental endeavor comprises the first kind of effort, launching effort. It is like the first stage of a rocket which gets the rocket off the ground.

Once you can be mindful of the primary object for some time, you still do not always have smooth sailing. Hindrances come up, or painful sensations, or sleepiness. You find yourself an innocent victim of pain, impatience, greed, drowsiness and doubt. Perhaps you have been enjoying some degree of calm and comfort because you have been able to stay with the primary object, but suddenly difficult objects assault you. At this time the mind has a tendency to become discouraged and lazy. Launching effort is no longer enough. You need an extra boost to face pain and sleepiness, to get above the hindrances.

The second stage of energy, liberating energy, is like the second stage of a rocket which pushes through the earth's atmosphere. Encouragement from a teacher might help here, or you can reflect for yourself on the good reasons to arouse liberating energy. Armed with internal and external encouragements, you now make a concerted effort to observe the pain. If you are able to overcome your difficulty, you will feel very exhilarated; your energy will surge. You will be ready to go for anything that comes into your field of awareness. Perhaps you overcome a back pain, or you look into an attack of drowsiness and see that it vanishes like a little wisp of cloud. The mind grows refreshed, bright and clear. You may feel an energy high. This is the direct experience of liberating energy.

After this the practice may go smoothly, and the mind may feel satisfied. Do not be surprised if the teacher suddenly assigns you extra homework, such as asking you to pay attention to several touch points on the body. This guidance is to encourage persistent energy, the third kind of energy. Persistent energy is necessary to keep deepening your practice, drawing you toward your goal. It is like the third stage of a rocket which gives it the energy to escape altogether from the earth's gravitational field. As you develop persistent energy, you will begin to travel through the stages of insight.

It is easy to forget that the temporary happiness you feel today in practice will pass away when you return to the world, unless you attain some deeper level of peace. You might reflect on this for yourself. Why are you practicing? I feel that the minimum goal is to become a *sotāpanna,* or stream enterer, to reach the first stage of enlightenment, which frees you from rebirth in dangerous and painful lower realms. Whatever your goal is, you should never be complacent until you reach it. For this you need to develop a persistent effort that neither decreases nor stagnates. It grows and grows until it finally brings you to your destination. When effort is well developed in this way, it is called in Pāli *paggahita viriya*.

Finally, at the end of practice, effort achieves a fourth aspect, called fulfilling effort. This is what takes you completely beyond the gravity field of sense pleasures into the freedom of nibbāna. Perhaps you are interested to see what this is like? Well, make an effort and you might find out.

## Eleven More Ways to Arouse Energy

The commentaries list eleven ways to arouse energy.

### 1. Reflecting on States of Misery

The first is to reflect on the fearsomeness of the states of *apāya*, or misery, which you can fall into if you are lazy. The meaning of *apa* is "devoid of." *Aya*, in turn, refers to the wholesome kamma that can bring about happiness – specifically, the kinds of happiness that can be experienced as a human, as a deva, as a brahma, and in nibbāna.

Thus, if you do not practice, you might go into states and realms where you only have the chance to produce unwholesome kamma. There are several realms of unfortunate rebirths. Of these, the easiest for you to observe, and therefore accept, is the animal world. Consider the animals on earth, in the sea, in the air. Can any of them perform wholesome kamma, activities that are free from blame?

Animals live in a haze of delusion. They are covered by a tremendously thick layer of ignorance, of unknowing. Insects, for example, are rather like machines, programmed by their genetic material to carry out certain activities without the slightest capacity for choice, learning, or discernment. Most animals' mental processes are restricted to concerns about mating and survival. In their world, character roles are incredibly simple. You are predator or prey or both. It is a vicious realm where only the fittest survive. Imagine the fear and paranoia there must be in the mind of a being living under such pitiless conditions. Imagine the distress and suffering when one creature dies in the jaws of another. Dying with so much suffering, how can animals gain rebirth in a good life? The quality of the mind at death determines the quality of the next rebirth. How can animals ever escape from their fearful existence?

Do animals have the capacity to be generous? Can they be moral? Can they keep precepts? Not to mention this noble and demanding task of meditation. How can animals ever learn to control and develop their minds to maturity? It is frightening and fearful to contemplate a life where the only option is to behave in unwholesome ways.

Reflecting thus may encourage your effort. "I'm a yogi right now. This is my chance. How can I waste time lazing about? Imagine if my next rebirth was as an animal. I wouldn't ever develop the enlightenment factor of effort. I must not waste time! Now is the time to strive!"

*2. Reflecting on the Benefits of Energy*

A second way to arouse energy is to reflect on energy's benefits, some of which have been described above. You have a precious opportunity to come into contact with the Dhamma, the Buddha's teaching. Having gotten into this incomparable world of Dhamma, you should not waste the opportunity to walk the path that leads to the essence of his teaching! You can attain supramundane states, four successive levels of noble path and fruition, nibbāna itself. Through your own practice, you can conquer suffering.

Even if you do not work to become completely free from all suffering in this lifetime, it would be a great loss not to become at least a sotāpanna, or stream enterer, and thus never again be reborn in a state of misery. Walking this path isn't just for any Dick or Jane, however. A yogi needs a lot of courage and effort. He or she must be an exceptional person. Strive with diligence and you can attain the great goal! You should not waste a chance to walk a path that leads to the essence of the Buddha's teaching. If you reflect in this way, perhaps energy and inspiration will arise, and you will put in more effort in your practice.

*3. Remembering the Noble Ones*

Thirdly, you can remind yourself of the noble persons who have walked this path before you. This path is no dusty byway. Buddhas from time immemorial, the silent Buddhas, the great disciples, the arahants and all the rest of the noble ones, all have walked here. If you want to share this distinguished path, fortify yourself with dignity and be diligent. No room for cowards or the lazy; this is a road for heroes and heroines.

Our ancestors on this path were not just a bunch of misfits who renounced the world to escape from debts and emotional problems. The Buddhas and noble ones were often quite wealthy, and came from loving families. If they had continued their lives as lay persons they would undoubtedly have had a good time. Instead, they saw the emptiness of the worldly life and had the foresight to conceive of a greater happiness and fulfilment, beyond common sensual pleasures. There also have been many men and women whose humble origin, consciousness of oppression by society or a ruler, or battle against ill health has granted them a radical vision – a wish to uproot suffering, rather than to alleviate it only on the worldly level, or to seek revenge for the wrongs done against them. These people joined their more privileged counterparts on the road to liberation. The Buddha said that real nobility depends on inner purity, not on social class. All of the Buddhas and noble disciples possessed a noble spirit of inquiry and a desire for higher and greater happiness, because of which they left home to walk on this path which leads to nibbāna. It is a noble path, not for the wayward or for dropouts.

You might say to yourself: "People of distinction have walked this path, and I must try to live up to their company. I can't be sloppy here. I shall walk with as much care as possible, fearlessly. I have this chance to belong to a great family, the group of distinguished people who walk on this noble path. I should congratulate myself for having the opportunity to do this. People like me have walked on this path and attained the various stages of enlightenment. So I, too, will be able to reach the same attainment."

Through such reflection, effort can arise and lead you to the goal of nibbāna.

## 4. Appreciation for Support

A fourth causative means for arousing effort is respect and appreciation for alms food and the other requisites essential to a renunciate's way of life. For ordained monks and nuns, this means respecting the donations of lay supporters, not only at the moment that the gift is made, but also by having a continuous awareness that the generosity of others makes possible the continuation of one's practice.

Lay yogis also may be dependent on others' support in many ways. Parents and friends may be helping you, either financially or by taking care of your business so that you can participate in intensive retreats. Even if you pay your own way on a retreat, nonetheless many things are provided to support your practice. The building which shelters you is ready-made; water and electricity are taken care of. Food is prepared by volunteers, and your other needs are cared for. You should have a deep respect and appreciation for the service given to you by people who may not owe you anything, people who have good hearts and deep benevolence.

You can say to yourself, "I should practice as hard as possible to live up to the goodness of those people. This is the way to reciprocate and return the goodwill shown by faithful supporters. May their efforts not go to waste. I will use what I am given with mindfulness so that my kilesas will be slowly trimmed and uprooted, so that my benefactors' meritorious deeds will bring about an equally meritorious result."

The Buddha laid down rules of conduct to govern the orders of bhikkhus and bhikkhunīs, monks and nuns. One of these rules was permission to receive what is offered by well-wishing lay supporters. This was not to enable monks and nuns to live a luxurious life. Requisites could be accepted and used in order that monks and nuns might care for their bodies appropriately, giving them the basic right conditions for striving to get rid of the kilesas. Receiving support, they could devote all their time to practicing the threefold training of sīla, samādhi and paññā, eventually gaining liberation from all suffering.

You might reflect that it is only by practicing diligently that you can reciprocate or return the goodwill shown by your supporters. Seen in this way, energetic mindfulness becomes an expression of gratitude for all the help you have received in your meditation practice.

### 5. Receiving a Noble Heritage

The fifth means to arouse energy is reflection on having received a noble heritage. The heritage of a noble person consists of seven nonmaterial qualities: faith or saddhā; morality or sīla; moral shame and moral dread or hiri and *ottappa*, discussed at length in "Chariot to Nibbāna," the last chapter of this book; knowledge of the Dhamma, and generosity – one is very generous in giving up the kilesas, and in giving gifts to others; and lastly, wisdom, which refers to the series of vipassanā insights and finally the wisdom of penetrating into nibbāna.

What is extraordinary about this inheritance is that these seven qualities are nonmaterial and therefore not impermanent. This contrasts with the heritage you may receive from your parents upon their death, which is material and therefore subject to loss, decay and dissolution. Furthermore, material inheritances may be unsatisfying in various ways. Some people quickly squander whatever they receive. Others do not find their new possessions useful. The heritage of a noble one is always beneficial; it protects and ennobles. It follows its heir through the gates of death, and throughout the remainder of his or her samsāric wanderings.

In this world, however, if children are unruly and wayward, their parents may disown them so that the children receive no material inheritance. Similarly in the world of the Dhamma, if one has come into contact with the Buddha's teaching, and then is sloppy and lazy in practice, one will again be denied the seven types of noble heritage. Only a person endowed with enduring and persistent energy will be worthy of this noble inheritance.

Energy is fully developed only when one is able to go through all the levels of insight, up to the culmination of the series in noble path consciousness. This developed energy, or Fulfilling Energy as it is called, is precisely what makes one worthy of the full benefits of the noble heritage.

If you continue to perfect the effort of your practice, these qualities will become permanently yours. Reflecting in this way, you may be inspired to practice more ardently.

### 6. Remembering the Greatness of the Buddha

A sixth reflection which develops energy is considering the greatness and ability of the person who discovered and taught this path to liberation. The Buddha's greatness is demonstrated by the fact that Mother Earth herself trembled on seven occasions during his life. The earth first trembled when the Bodhisatta (Sanskrit: bodhisattva), the future Buddha, was conceived for the last time in his mother's womb. It trembled again when Prince Siddhattha left his palace to take up the homeless life of a renunciate, and then when he attained supreme enlightenment. The earth trembled a fourth time when the Buddha gave his first sermon, a fifth time when he succeeded in overcoming his opponents, a sixth time when he returned from Tāvatimsa Heaven, having given a discourse on *Abhidhamma* to his mother who had been reborn there. The earth trembled for the seventh time when the Buddha attained *parinibbāna*, when he passed from conditioned existence forever at the moment of his physical death.

Think of the depth of compassion, the depth of wisdom the Buddha possessed! There are innumerable stories of his perfections: how long and devotedly the bodhisatta worked toward his goal, how perfectly he attained it, how lovingly he served humanity afterwards. Remember that if you continue to strive, you too can share the magnificent qualities the Buddha had.

Before the Buddha's great enlightenment, beings were engulfed in clouds of delusion and ignorance. The path to liberation had not yet been discovered. Beings groped in the dark. If they sought liberation, they had to invent a practice or follow someone who made a claim to truth that was, in fact, unfounded. In this world a vast array of pursuits have been devised for the goal of attaining happiness. These range from severe self-mortification to limitless indulgence in sense pleasure.

### A Vow to Liberate All Beings

One of the Buddha's previous existences was as a hermit named Sumedha. This was during a previous eon and world system, when the Buddha long previous to this one, Dīpankara, was alive. The hermit Sumedha had a vision of how much beings suffered in darkness prior to the appearance of a *sammā sambuddha*, a fully enlightened Buddha. He saw that beings needed to be led safely across to the other shore; they could not arrive alone. Due to this vision, the hermit renounced his own enlightenment, for which he had a strong potential in that particular existence. He vowed instead to spend incalculable eons, however long it would take, to perfect his own qualities to the level of a sammāsambuddha. This would give him the power to lead many beings to liberation, not just himself.

When this being finally completed his preparations and arrived at his lifetime as the present Buddha, he was truly an extraordinary and outstanding person. Upon his great enlightenment, he was endowed with what are known as "the three accomplishments": the accomplishment of cause, the accomplishment of result, and the accomplishment of service.

He was accomplished by virtue of the cause which led to his enlightenment, that is, the effort he put forth during many existences to perfect his *pāramīs*, the forces of purity in his mind. There are many stories of the bodhisatta's tremendous acts of generosity, compassion and virtue. In lifetime after lifetime, he sacrificed himself for the benefit of others. Thus developed, his purity of mind was the foundation for his attainment under the Bo Tree of enlightenment and omniscient knowledge. That attainment is called the accomplishment of result because it was the natural result of his accomplishment of cause, or the development of very strong powers of purity in his mind. The Buddha's third accomplishment was that of service, helping others through many years of teaching. He was not complacent about his enlightenment, but out of great compassion and loving care for all those beings who were trainable, he set forth after his enlightenment and tirelessly shared the Dhamma with all those beings who were ready for it, until the day of his parinibbāna.

Reflecting on various aspects of the Buddha's three great accomplishments may inspire you to greater effort in your own practice.

### Compassion Leads to Action

Compassion was the bodhisatta Sumedha's sole motivation for sacrificing his own enlightenment in favor of making the incredible effort to become a Buddha. His heart was moved when he saw, with the eye of great compassion, how beings suffered as a result of misguided activities. Thus he vowed to attain the wisdom necessary to guide them as perfectly as possible.

Compassion must lead to action. Furthermore, wisdom is required so that action may bear useful fruit. Wisdom distinguishes the right path from the wrong path. If you have compassion but no wisdom, you may do more harm than good when you try to help. On the other hand, you may have great wisdom, may have become enlightened, but without compassion you will not lift a finger to help others.

Both wisdom and compassion were perfectly fulfilled in the Buddha. Because of his great compassion for suffering beings, the bodhisatta was able to go through his samsāric wanderings with enduring patience. Others insulted and injured him, yet he was able to bear these actions with perseverance and endurance. It is said that if you were to combine the compassion that all the mothers on this planet feel for their children, it would still not come near the Buddha's great compassion. Mothers have a great capacity for forgiveness. It is no easy task to bring up children. Children can be very cruel, and at times they can inflict emotional and physical harm on their mothers. Even when harm is grievous, however, a mother's heart usually has space to forgive her child. In the Buddha's heart this forgiving space was boundless. His capacity for forgiveness was one of the manifestations of his great compassion.

Once upon a time the bodhisatta was born as a monkey. One day he was swinging around in the forest and happened upon a Brahman who had fallen in a crevice. Upon seeing the poor Brahman helpless, the monkey was filled with compassion. This feeling had a great deal of momentum behind it, for by then the bodhisatta had spent many life-times cultivating his pāramī, or perfection, of compassion.

The bodhisatta prepared to leap into the crevice to save the Brahman but he wondered if he had the strength to carry the Brahman out. Wisdom arose in his mind. He decided he should test his capability on a boulder he saw lying nearby. Lifting the boulder and setting it down again, he learned that he would be able to accomplish the rescue.

Down the bodhisatta went and bravely carried the Brahman to safety. Having carried first the boulder and then the Brahman himself, the monkey fell to the ground in exhaustion. Far from being grateful, the Brahman picked up a rock and smashed the monkey's head, so that he could take home the meat for his supper. Awakening to find himself near death, the monkey realized what had happened but did not get angry. This response was due to his perfected quality of forgiveness. He did say to the Brahman, "Is it proper for you to kill me when I've saved your life?"

Then the bodhisatta remembered that the Brahman had lost his way in the forest and would not be able to get home without help. The monkey's compassion knew no bounds. Clenching his teeth, he was determined to lead the Brahman out of the forest even at the risk of his life. A trail of blood fell from his wound as the monkey instructed the Brahman which way to turn. Finally, the Brahman reached the right trail.

If the Buddha had this much compassion and wisdom even as a monkey, you can imagine how much more he had developed these perfections by the time of his enlightenment.

*Full Illumination*

After innumerable existences as a bodhisatta, the Buddha-to-be was born as a human being in his last existence. Having perfected all the pāramīs, he began searc*.ing for the true path to liberation. He endured many trials before he finally discovered the noble path by which he came to see deeply impermanence, unsatisfactoriness and absence of self in all conditioned phenomena. Deepening his practice, he went through the various stages of enlightenment and eventually became an arahant, completely purified of greed, hatred and delusion. Then, the omniscient knowledge he had cultivated arose in him, together with the other knowledges particular to Buddhas. His omniscience meant that if there was anything the Buddha wished to know about, he had only to reflect upon the question, and the answer would come to his mind spontaneously.

As a result of his illumination, the Buddha was now endowed with "The Accomplishment by Virtue of Fruition of Result," as its full title is known. This accomplishment came about because of the fulfilment of certain causes and prerequisites he had cultivated in his previous lives.

Having become a perfectly enlightened Buddha, he did not forget the intention he had resolved upon so many eons ago when he'd been the hermit Sumedha. The very purpose of his working so hard and long was to help other beings cross the ocean of suffering. Now that the Buddha was completely enlightened, you can imagine how much more powerful and effective his great compassion and wisdom had become. Based on these two qualities, he began to preach the Dhamma and continued to do so for forty-five years, until his death. He slept only two hours a night, dedicating the rest of his time to the service of the Dhamma, helping other beings in various ways so that they could benefit and enjoy well-being and happiness. Even on his deathbed he showed the path to Subhadda, a renunciate of another sect, who thereby became the last of many disciples to be enlightened by the Buddha.

The full title of this third accomplishment is "The Accomplishment of Seeing to the Welfare of Other Beings," and it is a natural consequence of the previous two. If the Buddha could become enlightened and totally freed from the kilesas, why did he continue to live in this world? Why did he mingle with people at all? One must understand that he wanted to relieve beings of their suffering and put them on the right path. This was the purest compassion and the deepest wisdom on his part.

The Buddha's perfect wisdom enabled him to distinguish what was beneficial and what was harmful. If one cannot make this crucial distinction, how can one be of any help to other beings? One may be wise indeed, knowing full well what leads to happiness and what to misery, but then, without compassion one might feel quite indifferent to the fates of other beings. Thus it was the Buddha's practical compassion which led him to exhort people to avoid unskilful actions that bring harm and suffering. And it was wisdom that allowed him to be selective, precise and effective in what he admonished people to do. The combination of these two virtues, compassion and wisdom, made the Buddha an unexcelled teacher.

The Buddha had no selfish thoughts of gaining honor, fame or the adulation of many followers. He did not mingle with people as a socialite. He approached beings with the sole intention of pointing out the correct way to them so that they could be enlightened to the extent of their capacities. This was his great compassion. When he had finished this duty, the Buddha would retire to a secluded part of the forest. He did not stay among the crowds, bantering and mixing freely like a common person. He did not introduce his pupils to each other, saying, "Here's my disciple the wealthy merchant; here's the great professor." It is not easy to live a solitary and secluded life. No ordinary worldling can enjoy total seclusion. But then, the Buddha was not ordinary.

### Advice for Spiritual Teachers

This is an important point for anyone aspiring to become a preacher of the Dhamma or a meditation teacher. One should exercise great discretion in relating with students.

If one has any relationship at all with them, one must remember always to be motivated by great compassion, following the footsteps of the Buddha. There is danger in becoming too close and familiar with those who are being helped. If a meditation teacher becomes too close to his or her students, disrespect and irreverence may be the result.

Meditation teachers should also take the Buddha as their model for the proper motivation in sharing the Dhamma with others. One should not be satisfied with becoming a popular or successful Dhamma teacher. One's motivation must be, instead, genuinely benevolent. One must strive to benefit one's students through presenting a technique whose actual practice can tame the behavior of body, speech and mind, thereby bringing true peace and happiness. Teachers must continually examine their own motivations in this regard.

Once I was asked what was the most effective way to teach meditation. I replied, "First and foremost, one should practice until one is dextrous in one's own practice. Then one must gain a sound theoretical knowledge of the scriptures. Finally, one must apply these two, based on a motivation of genuine lovingkindness and compassion. Teaching based on these three factors will doubtless be effective."

In this world many people enjoy fame, honor and success due to uncanny strokes of fate or kamma. They may not really have fulfilled the accomplishment of cause, as the Buddha did. That is, they may not have worked hard, but simply became successful or wealthy by a fluke. Such people are likely to receive a lot of criticism. People might say, "It's a wonder how he or she got into that position, considering how sloppy and lazy he/she is. He/she doesn't deserve such luck."

Other people may work very hard. But perhaps because they are neither intelligent nor gifted, they attain their goal slowly, if at all. They are unable to fulfil the accomplishment of result. People like this are not free from blame either. "Poor old So-and-so. He/she works hard, but does not have much for brains."

Yet another group of people work very hard and become successful. Having fulfilled their ambition, they then rest upon their laurels, so to speak. Unlike the Buddha, who turned his own glorious achievements to the service of humanity, they do not take any further steps by helping society or other beings. Again, these people will be criticized. "Look how selfish he/she is. He/She's got so much property, wealth, and talent, but no compassion or generosity."

In this world it is difficult to be free from blame or criticism. People will always talk behind one another's backs. Some criticisms are merely gossip, and others are deserved, pointing to some real flaw or lack in a person. The Buddha was indeed an exceptional human being in having fulfilled the accomplishments of cause, of result, and of service.

One could write an entire book describing the greatness and perfection of the Buddha, the discoverer and teacher of the path to freedom. Here, I only wish to open the doors for you to contemplate his virtues so that you can develop effort in your practice.

Contemplating the Buddha's greatness, you may be filled with awe and adoration. You may feel deep appreciation for the wonderful opportunity to walk the path which such a great individual discovered and taught. Perhaps you will understand that in order to walk on such a path, you cannot be sloppy, nor sluggish, nor lazy.

May you be inspired. May you be brave, strong and enduring, and may you walk this path to its end.

*7. Remembering the Greatness of Our Lineage*

The seventh reflection that arouses energy is on the greatness of the lineage. We are meditating in accordance with the *Satipaṭṭhāna Sutta*, the Buddha's discourse on the four foundations of mindfulness. Therefore we can all consider ourselves to belong to the noble lineage of Buddhas. You can be proud to call yourself the Buddha's daughter or son.

As you practice vipassanā meditation, you are receiving a transfusion of Dhamma blood. It doesn't matter how far away you are from the Buddha's birthplace, nor how different you may be in terms of race, creed or customs. These differences are quite immaterial. Insofar as we are committed to the threefold training of sīla, samādhi and paññā, we are all members of the same Dhamma family. The Dhamma is our blood, the same that ran through the veins of those noble ones who underwent the same training during the Buddha's time. Practicing diligently, with obedience and respect, we live up to the greatness of that lineage.

The brothers and sisters during the Buddha's time were men and women of great industry and courage. They did not know how to surrender. They only strove on until they were completely free from all suffering. Since we belong to this great lineage, we must never entertain thoughts of giving up.

### 8. Remembering Our Comrades' Greatness

The eighth reflection to generate energy is to reflect on the greatness of our fellow Dhamma farers. The Pāli word is brahmacariya, those who lead the holy life.

Formerly there were bhikkhus or monks, bhikkhunīs or nuns, *sikkhamānās* or probation nuns, and *sāmaṇerīs* and *sāmaṇeras*, female and male novices. In the course of history, the order of Theravada bhikkhunīs died out. Strictly speaking in our own time, the ordained sangha consists of bhikkhus and male novices only, who practice in accordance with the Buddha's rules of conduct. There are also male and female anagārikas, and sīlashin nuns, who, although they take lesser numbers of vows, are still considered to lead the holy life.

No matter. All yogis, formally ordained or not, share virtues of purity, of morality, of concentration and of wisdom. As a yogi you share these virtues with the great disciples of the Buddha's time: the Venerable Sāriputta and the Venerable Mahā Moggallāna, who were the Buddha's right and left hands, as well as the Venerable Mahākassapa. In the bhikkhunī sangha was the Venerable Mahāpajāpati Gotamī and her followers, as well as many other bhikkhunīs who were great and courageous women, strivers for the Dhamma. All these men and women of distinction are our comrades in the holy life. We can read about them and reflect on their greatness, their courage, their commitment. In that reflection we can ask ourselves whether we live up to the same high standard. We may also be inspired to think that we have the support of all these comrades as we make our daily efforts.

*Unwanted, Unloved: The Story of Sonā Therī*

One distinguished elder in the bhikkhunī sangha was named Sonā Therī. Before ordaining, she was married, and she had ten children – a big family by today's standards. One by one they grew up, left the house and settled down with mates of their own. When the last child was married, Sonā's husband decided to become a bhikkhu, so he left for the homeless life. Shortly thereafter, Sonā collected all the property she and her husband had amassed through their marriage and distributed it amongst their children. She asked that each of them support her in turn.

At first she was quite happy, visiting one child after another. She must have been quite old by then, sixty or seventy. But by and by her children began to tire of her presence. They were busy with their own families. "Oh, here comes mother-in-law," they'd say. Sonā noticed their lack of enthusiasm and began to feel depressed. She saw that this was not a noble life for her, being treated as a nuisance, unwanted and unloved. There must be parents in our own time who are familiar with this feeling.

Sonā considered her alternatives. Suicide was not right. She went to a nunnery and begged for ordination, which was granted to her. She was so old by now, alas, that she could not go for alms rounds, nor do the other tasks required of nuns. All she could do was boil water for her companions. However, Sonā was very intelligent. Reflecting on her situation, she said to herself: "Little time is left to me. I must take advantage of this opportunity and practice with diligence. I haven't a moment to lose."

Sonā was so old and frail that the only way she could do her walking meditation was by holding on to the wall that surrounded her nunnery. So she went around in circles, hanging onto the wall. If she did walking meditation in the forest, she chose places where the trees were close together so that she could support herself on them. Through such diligent and persistent effort, through the deep resolution in her heart, she very quickly became an arahant.

We can see that the ingratitude of Sonā's children was a blessing in disguise. After her enlightenment, Sonā Therī used to sing, "Oh, look at this world, how people get caught up in family life and enjoy their worldly happiness. But for me, because I was mistreated by my children, I left my family to lead this life of a renunciate. Now I have reaped the truth of renunciation."

During Sonā Therī's lifetime it was convenient and easy to go to a nunnery and ask to be ordained as a bhikkhunī. Nowadays, however, there is unfortunately no longer that chance for women to become fully ordained, for, as we said, the bhikkhunī order has died out. Do not despair, however. If a woman wants to renounce the world, it still is possible to enter a monastery. Though strictly speaking it is not possible to become a bhikkhunī according to the original Vinaya rules of discipline for the sangha, it is nonetheless still possible to become a bhikkhu or a bhikkhunī according to the suttas, the Buddha's discourses. For this, the only requirement is a sincere practice to purify one's mind according to the Noble Eightfold Path. There is no loss of privileges in this form of bhikkhu-hood; in fact, it may be more appropriate for our times. If everyone simply becomes a bhikkhu, there will be no problems, no inequality.

### 9. Avoiding Lazy People

The ninth way to arouse effort is to avoid the company of lazy persons. There are people who are not interested in mental development, who never try to purify themselves. They just eat, sleep and make merry as much as they want. They are like pythons, who swallow their prey and remain immobile for hours. How will you ever be inspired to put forth energy in the company of such people? You should try to avoid becoming a member of their gang. Avoiding their company is a positive step in developing energy.

### 10. Seeking Energetic Friends

Now you should take another step and choose to associate instead with yogis who are endowed with de-veloped, enduring and persevering energy. This is the tenth way of arousing effort. Most specifically it refers to a yogi in retreat, but in fact, you will be well off spending time with anyone who is totally committed to the Dhamma, enduring and resolute, trying to activate mindfulness from moment to moment, and maintaining a high standard of progressive or persistent energy. People who give top priority to mental health are your best companions. In a retreat you can learn from the people who seem to be model yogis. You can emulate their behavior and practice, and this will lead to your own development. You should allow others' diligence to be contagious. Take in the good energy, and allow yourself to be influenced by it.

### 11. Inclining the Mind toward Developing Energy

The last and best way to arouse energy is persistently to incline the mind toward developing energy. The key to this practice is to adopt a resolute stand. "I will be as mindful as I can at each moment, sitting, standing, walking, going from place to place. I will not allow the mind to space out. I will not allow a moment of mindfulness to be missing." If, on the contrary, you have a careless, self-defeating attitude, your practice will be doomed from the start.

Every moment can be charged with this courageous effort, a very consistent and enduring energy. If a moment of laziness dares to tiptoe in, you will catch it right away and shoo it out! *Kosajja*, laziness, is one of the most undermining and subversive elements in meditation practice. You can eradicate it by effort: courageous, persistent, persevering, enduring effort.

I hope you will arouse energy through any and all of these eleven ways, so that you will make swift progress in the path and eventually attain that consciousness which uproots defilements forever.

## RAPTURE: FOURTH FACTOR OF ENLIGHTENMENT

*Pīti*, or rapture, has the characteristic of happiness, delight and satisfaction. It is in itself a mental state possessing these characteristics. But a further characteristic of rapture is that it can pervade associated mental states, making them delightful and happy and bringing a sense of deep satisfaction.

### Lightness and Agility

Rapture fills the mind and body with lightness and agility. This, according to the classical analysis, is its function. The mind becomes light and energized. The body also feels agile, light and workable. The manifestation of rapture is in actual sensations of lightness in the body. Rapture manifests very clearly through physical sensations.

When rapture occurs, coarse and uncomfortable sensations are replaced with something very soft and gentle, velvet smooth and light. You may feel such a lightness of body that it seems as if you are floating in the air. At times the lightness may be active rather than still. You may feel as if you were being pushed or pulled, swayed and rocked, or as if you are traveling on rough water. You may feel off-balance, but it is nonetheless very pleasant.

### The Five Types of Rapture

There are five types of rapture. The first is called "Lesser Rapture." At the beginning of practice, after the hindrances have been kept at bay for sufficient periods of time, yogis may begin feeling chills and thrills of pleasure, sometimes goosebumps. This is the beginning of rapturous feelings.

The next type is called "Momentary Rapture." It comes in flashes like lightning and is more intense than the first type. The third kind is "Overwhelming Rapture." The classical simile is of someone sitting by the sea and suddenly seeing a huge wave that is coming to engulf her or him. Yogis experience a similar feeling of being swept off the ground. Their hearts thump; they are overwhelmed; they wonder what is happening.

The fourth type of rapture is "Uplifting or Exhilarating Rapture." With this, you feel so light that you might think you are sitting a few feet off the ground. You feel as if you are floating about or flying, rather than walking on the earth.

The fifth type of rapture, "Pervasive Rapture," is the strongest of all. It fills the body, every pore. If you are sitting, you feel fantastically comfortable and you have no desire at all to get up. Instead, there is a great interest in continuing to sit without moving.

The first three types of rapture are called *pāmojja*, or weak rapture. The last two deserve the rightful name of pīti, strong rapture. The first three are causes of, or stepping stones toward, the stronger two.

## Wise Attention Causes Rapture

As with effort, the Buddha said there is only one cause for rapture: wise attention. Specifically, this is wise attention to being effortful in bringing about wholesome rapturous feelings connected with the Buddha, Dhamma and sangha.

## Eleven More Ways to Develop Rapture

The commentaries give eleven ways of arousing rapture.:

### 1. Remembering the virtues of the Buddha

The first way is *buddhānussati*, recollecting the virtues of the Buddha. He has quite a number of virtues, and it might not be necessary for you to go through all of the traditional lists of them before the first hints of rapture begin to appear. For example, the first traditionally listed virtue is the quality of *araha*. This means that the Buddha is worthy of respect by all humans, devas and brahmas, due to the purity he attained by uprooting all kilesas. Think about the purity he achieved in this way, and perhaps some joy will come up in you. You might also recollect the Buddha's three

accomplishments as described in our discussion of courageous effort.

However, reflections and recitation of formulas are not
the only way to recollect the Buddha's virtues. In fact, these
are far less reliable than one's own intuitive insights. When
a yogi attains the insight into arising and passing away,
rapture arises naturally, and so does an appreciation of the
Buddha's virtues. The Buddha himself said, "One who sees
the Dhamma sees me." A yogi who attains insight will
truly be able to appreciate the greatness of the founder of
our lineage. You might say to yourself, "If I am able to
experience such purity of mind, how much greater the
Buddha's purity must have been!"

## 2. Rejoicing in the Dhamma

The second way of arousing rapture is to recollect the
Dhamma and its virtues. The first traditional virtue is
expressed in a phrase: "Well spoken is the Dhamma by the
Buddha, indeed well proclaimed is the Dhamma by the
Buddha." The Buddha taught the Dhamma in the most
effective way, and your present teachers have reliably trans-
mitted it. This is indeed a cause for rejoicing.

The Buddha spoke at length about the threefold training
of sīla, samādhi and paññā. To follow the training, we first
maintain purity of conduct by keeping the precepts. We
try to develop a high level of moral integrity through
taming our actions and speech. This will bring us many
benefits. First, we will be free from self-judgement, self-
blame and remorse. We are free from censure by the wise,
and from punishment by the law.

Next, if we follow the Buddha's instructions, we will
develop concentration. If you are faithful, consistent and
patient, you can experience a mind that is happy and clear,
bright and peaceful. This is *samatha sukha*, the happiness
that comes from concentration and tranquility of mind.
You can even attain the various levels of jhānas or
absorptions, states of consciousness in which the
kilesas are temporarily suppressed and an extraordinary
peace results.

Then, practicing vipassanā, we have the chance to experience a third kind of happiness. As you penetrate deeper into the Dhamma, attaining the stage of insight into the rise and fall of phenomena, you will feel exhilarating rapture. This happiness could be called "Thrilling Happiness." Later on comes the "Happiness of Clarity." And eventually, when you reach the insight called *sankhārupekkhāñana*, the insight into equanimity regarding all formations, you will experience the "Happiness of Equanimity." It is a profound delight, not so agitated and thrilling, but very subtle and balanced.

Thus, true to the promises and guarantees of the Buddha, those who follow the path of practice will be able to experience all these sorts of happiness. If you manage to experience all these kinds of happiness yourself, you can deeply appreciate the truth of the Buddha's words. You too will say, "Well spoken is the Dhamma by the Buddha, indeed well proclaimed is the Dhamma by the Buddha."

Finally, transcending all these kinds of happiness is the ultimate "Happiness of Cessation." Going beyond the happiness of equanimity, a yogi can experience a moment of insight into nibbāna which comes about with the attainment of noble path consciousness. After this, a yogi feels a depth of appreciation for the Buddha's Dhamma that he or she may never have known before. Did the Buddha not say, "If you meditate in this way, you can arrive at the cessation of suffering?" This is true. Many people have experienced it; and when finally you know for yourself, your mind will sing with rapture and gratitude.

### Great Possibilities that Come to Fruition in Practice

Thus, there are three ways of appreciating the fact that the Dhamma is well proclaimed. First, if you think deeply about the great possibilities that lie within meditation practice, your mind will be full of praises for the Dhamma – and of rapture, too, of course. Perhaps you naturally possess great faith, so that whenever you hear a discourse or read about the Dhamma you are filled with rapture and interest. This is the first of three ways of appreciating the

Dhamma. Second, if you enter the practice itself, the promises and guarantees of the Buddha will certainly begin to come true. Sīla and samādhi will improve your life. This teaches you more intimately how well proclaimed the Dhamma is, for it has brought you clarity of mind and a deep, subtle happiness. Third and finally, the greatness of the Dhamma can be seen in the practice of wisdom, which leads eventually to the happiness of nibbāna. At this point profound changes may take place in your life. It is like being reborn. You can imagine the rapture and appreciation you would feel at this point.

### 3. Rejoicing in the Virtues of the Sangha

Recollecting the virtues of the sangha is the third major way of developing rapture listed in the commentaries. The sangha is the group of noble individuals who are totally committed to the Dhamma, striving earnestly and patiently. They follow the path in a straight and correct way and arrive at their respective destinations.

If you have experienced some purity of mind in your practice, you can imagine others feeling the same thing, and perhaps even deeper levels, far beyond what you have known. If you have attained some degree of enlightenment, you will be endowed with unshakable faith in the existence of other noble ones who have traversed this same path with you. Such people are indeed pure and impeccable.

### 4. Considering Your Own Virtue

The fourth way of arousing rapture is to consider the purity of your own conduct. Impeccability of conduct is a powerful virtue which brings a great sense of satisfaction and joy to its possessor. It takes great perseverance to maintain purity. When you review your own efforts in this regard you may feel a deep sense of fulfilment and exhilaration. If you cannot maintain pure conduct, you will be invaded by remorse and self-judgment. You will not be able to concentrate on what you are doing, and thus your practice cannot progress.

Virtue is the foundation of concentration and wisdom. There are many examples of people who have attained enlightenment by turning their mindfulness toward the rapture that arises from their contemplation of the purity of their own sīla. This contemplation can be particularly helpful in an emergency.

### Rapture during an Emergency: The Story of Tissa

There was a young man called Tissa who, upon listening to the Buddha, was struck with a great sense of urgency. He was a very ambitious person, but he felt a deep sense of emptiness in the world and so he turned his ambition toward becoming an arahant. Soon he renounced the worldly life and took the robes of a monk.

Before he ordained, he gave some of his property to his younger brother Cūlatissa, a gift which made his younger brother very prosperous. Unfortunately, Cūlatissa's wife suddenly became very greedy. She was afraid that the bhikkhu might change his mind, disrobe, and come to reclaim his property, which would deplete her own situation. Cūlatissa's wife tried to think of ways to protect her newly-acquired wealth, and finally fell upon the idea of calling some hit men. She promised them a handsome prize if they would kill the bhikkhu.

The thugs agreed, and went in search of this bhikkhu in the forest. Finding him immersed in his practice, they surrounded him and prepared to kill him. The bhikkhu said, "Please wait a while. I haven't finished my job yet."

"How can we wait?" one thug replied. "We've got a job to do as well."

"Just a night or two," the bhikkhu pleaded. "Then you can come back and kill me."

"We don't buy that! You'll run away! Give us a guarantee that you won't."

The bhikkhu had no material possessions beyond his bowl and robe, so he could not leave any deposit with the hit men. Instead, he took a huge boulder and smashed both his thigh bones. Satisfied that he could not escape, the thugs retreated and left him to his striving.

You can imagine what a strong desire the young man had to uproot the kilesas. He was not afraid to die or suffer pain. But he was afraid of the kilesas, which were still very much alive in him. He had his life, but he had not finished his work yet, and he dreaded the thought of dying before he had uprooted the defilements.

Since this young man had renounced the world with such deep faith, he must have been quite diligent in developing his mindfulness. His practice must have been strong enough to face the excruciating pain of smashed thighbones, for he watched that intense pain without giving in. While he watched, he reflected on his own virtue. He asked himself whether he had broken any of the bhikkhu's precepts since the day of his ordination. To his delight, he found that he had been perfectly pure, without committing a single offense. This realization filled him with satisfaction and rapture.

The pain of his fractured limbs subsided, and intense rapture became the most prominent object in the young man's mind. He turned his mindfulness toward it, and noted rapture, happiness and joy. As he was noting in this way, his insight matured and speeded up. Suddenly he broke through: he experienced the Four Noble Truths and became an arahant in a short space of time.

The moral of this story is that one should build a good foundation in sīla. Without sīla, sitting meditation is no more than an invitation to aches and pains. Build up your foundation! If your sīla is powerful, your meditative efforts will prove very fruitful.

*5. Remembering Your Own Generosity*

The fifth way of arousing rapture is to recollect one's own generosity. If one can perform an act of charity without any selfish motivation at all, but rather wishing for the welfare and happiness of others, or wishing for liberation from suffering, then that act will be full of merit. Not only that, but the act brings great happiness and gladness into your mind. Motivation is crucial in determining whether generosity is beneficial. It should not be motivated by ulterior selfishness.

*Gifts in Times of Scarcity*

Generosity is not only financial. It can also mean simply encouraging a friend who is in need of support. It is most important to be generous in times of scarcity, and these can also be the most satisfying time to share the little that one has.

There is a story of a king in Sri Lanka in the old days. It seems that one day he was retreating hastily from a battle, carrying only the barest of provisions. While he was going through the forest he chanced upon a bhikkhu making alms rounds. The bhikkhu was an arahant, it seems. The king gave part of his food to that monk, even though he only had enough for himself, his horse and his attendant. Much later, when he recalled all the gifts he had given in his life, some of which had been splendid and precious, this was the one he cherished most.

Another story on this subject is set in the Mahāsī Sāsana Yeiktha, a center in Rangoon. Some years ago, when the center still was in a slow process of development, some of the yogis could not afford to pay for their food and accommodations. People were poor at that time. But these yogis were making good progress, and it was a great pity to see them leaving the center only because they could not afford to stay. So the meditation teachers got together and supported those yogis who had strong potential. Indeed, these students made tremendous progress. When the yogis succeeded in attaining their goals, the teachers were filled with joy and rapture.

*6. Considering the Virtues of the Gods*

The sixth way to bring rapture is to think of the virtues of the devas and brahmas, beings in the higher realms. While these beings were still in the human realm, they had great faith in kamma. They believed that good actions will bring a reward, and harm will bring harmful consequences. So, they tried to practice what was good and refrain from unskilful actions. Some of them even meditated. The positive force of these beings' actions resulted in their rebirth in higher planes, where life is more pleasant than it is in our human world. Those who gained absorption in the jhānas were reborn in the brahma world, with lifespans lasting eons. Thus, when we think of the virtues of super-human beings, we actually consider the faith, charity, effort and perseverance which they developed in the human world. It is easy to compare them with ourselves. If we can find ourselves on a par with the devas and brahmas, we can be filled with satisfaction and joy.

### 7. Reflecting on Perfect Peace

The seventh way of arousing rapture is to reflect on the peace of the cessation of kilesas. In the ultimate sense, this means reflecting on nibbāna. If you have experienced this depth of peace, you can bring up a lot of rapture upon recollecting it.

If you have not yet experienced nibbāna yourself, you can reflect on the coolness of deep concentration or jhāna. The peace of deep concentration is far superior to worldly pleasures. There are people whose skill at absorption is so strong that even when they are not actually practicing concentration, their minds are never invaded by the kilesas. Thus, for sixty or seventy years they may live in peace. To think about this degree of coolness and clarity can bring about extraordinary joy.

If you have not experienced jhāna, then you can remember times in your practice when the mind felt pure and clean. When the kilesas are put aside for some time, tranquility and coolness naturally fill the mind. You may find yourself comparing this with the happiness you may have enjoyed in this world. You will see that worldly happiness is quite coarse and gross in comparison with the happiness of practice. Unlike the rapture of coolness that arises from purity of mind, there is something burning about worldly pleasures. Comparing thus, you may be filled with rapture.

### 8-9. Avoiding Coarse People, Seeking Refined Friends

The eighth and ninth ways of arousing rapture are related. They are to avoid rough and coarse persons, persons overwhelmed by anger and lacking in *mettā*, or loving kindness; and to seek out refined persons who have mettā in their hearts. In this world there are many people who are so overwhelmed by anger that they cannot appreciate the difference between wholesome and unwholesome activities. They do not know the benefit or appropriateness of paying respect to persons worthy of respect, nor of learning about the Dhamma, nor of actually meditating. They may be hot-tempered, easily victimized by anger and aversion. Their lives may be filled with rough and distasteful activities. Living with such a person, you can imagine, might not be a very rapturous experience.

Other people have a deep considerateness and loving care for other beings. The warmth and love of their hearts is manifested in actions and speech. Refined individuals like these carry out their relationships in a subtle, sweet way. Gaining their company is very fulfilling. One is surrounded by an aura of love and warmth, which leads to the arising of rapture.

### 10. Reflecting on the Suttas

The tenth way of arousing rapture is reflecting on the suttas. Some suttas describe the virtues of the Buddha. If you are a person with a lot of faith, reflecting on one of these suttas can give you great joy and happiness. The *Satipaṭṭhāna Sutta*, among others, talks about the benefits one can enjoy through practicing the Dhamma. Others contain inspiring stories of the sangha, the community of noble ones. Reading or reflecting on these suttas can fill one with inspiration, which leads to rapture and happiness.

### 11. Inclining the Mind

Finally, if you firmly and consistently incline the mind toward developing rapture, your aim will be fulfilled. You must understand that rapture arises when the mind is relatively clean of kilesas. So, to reach rapture, you must put in energy to be mindful from moment to moment so that concentration arises and the kilesas are kept at bay. You must be fully committed to the task of arousing firm mindfulness in each moment, whether you are sitting or lying down, walking, standing or doing other activities.

TRANQUILITY: FIFTH FACTOR OF ENLIGHTENMENT

Most people's minds are in a state of agitation all the time. Their minds run here and there, flapping like flags in a strong wind, scattering like a pile of ashes into which a stone is tossed. There is no coolness or calmness, no silence, no peace. This restlessness or dissipation of mind might properly be called the waves of mind, reminiscent of the water's surface when wind is blowing. Ripples or waves of mind become apparent when restlessness occurs.

Even if this scattered mind becomes concentrated, the concentration still is associated with restlessness, as when one sick member of the family affects all the others with feverishness and unrest. So, too, restlessness has a strong effect on other simultaneously occurring mental states. When restlessness is present, it is not possible for true happiness to be reached.

When the mind is scattered, it is difficult to control our behavior. We begin to act according to our whims and fancies without considering properly whether an action is wholesome or not. Because of this unthinking mind, we may find ourselves performing unskilful actions or saying unskillful things. Such speech and action can lead to remorse, self-judgement and even more agitation. "I was wrong. I shouldn't have said that. If only I'd thought about it before I did it." When the mind is assaulted by remorse and regret, it will not be able to gain happiness.

The enlightenment factor of tranquility arises in the absence of restlessness and remorse. The Pāli word for it is *passaddhi*, which means cool calmness. Coolness and calmness of mind can only occur when mental agitation or activity have been silenced.

In the world today, people feel a lot of mental suffering. Many resort to drugs, tranquilizers and sleeping pills to bring calm and enjoyment to their minds. Often young people experiment with drugs to get through a period in their lives when they feel great agitation. Unfortunately they sometimes find drugs so enjoyable that they end up addicted, which is a terrible pity.

The tranquil peace that comes from meditation is far superior to anything drugs or any other external substances can provide. Of course, the goal of meditation is much higher than just peace, but peace and tranquility are nonetheless benefits of walking the straight, correct path of the Dhamma.

## Calming the Mind and Body

The characteristic of passaddhi is to calm the mind and body, to silence and tranquilize agitation.

## Extracting Heat from the Mind

Its function is to extract or suppress the heat of the mind which arises due to restlessness, dissipation or remorse. When the mind is assaulted by these harmful states, it becomes hot, as if on fire. Tranquility of mind extinguishes that heat and replaces it with the characteristic of coolness and ease.

## Nonagitation

The manifestation of passaddhi is nonagitation of body and mind. As a yogi you can easily observe how this state of mind brings about great calm and tranquility, physical and mental.

Surely you are familiar with the absence of tranquility. There is always an urge to move, to get up and do something. The body twitches, the mind darts nervously back and forth. When all of this ceases, there are no ripples in the mind, just a smooth and calm state. Movements become gentle, smooth and graceful. You can sit with hardly a flutter of movement.

This factor of enlightenment follows invariably upon the arising of the previous one, rapture. The strongest rapture, pervasive rapture, is most particularly associated with strong tranquility. After pervasive rapture has filled the whole body, one feels unwilling to move at all, not to mention to disturb one's mental stillness.

It is said that the Buddha spent the first forty-nine days after his liberation enjoying the fruits of enlightenment. He maintained certain postures for seven days each, at seven different places, enjoying the fruits of enlightenment by going in and out of fruition attainments. By virtue of his pervasive *Dhamma pīti* or Dhamma rapture, his whole body was permeated with satisfaction for all of that time, so that he did not want to move and could not even fully close his eyelids. His eyes remained fully opened or half opened. You, too, may experience how the eyes fly open involuntarily when strong rapture arises. You may try to close them, but they fly open again. Eventually you may decide to continue your practice with your eyes open. If you have such experiences, perhaps you can appreciate how much greater was the Buddha's happiness and Dhamma rapture.

## Wise Attention Brings Tranquility

According to the Buddha the way to arouse tranquility is through wise attention. More specifically, this is wise attention directed toward activating wholesome thoughts, wholesome mental states and, more importantly, meditative mental states, so that tranquility and rapture will arise.

## Seven More Ways of Developing Tranquility

For their part, the commentators point out seven ways of arousing tranquility.

### 1. Proper food

The first way is to take sensible and nutritious food – food that satisfies the twin principles of necessity and suitability. Nutrition is very important, as you know. One's diet need not be elaborate, but it should provide for the body's physical needs. If your food is not nutritious enough, your physical strength will not be sufficient for you to make progress in meditation. Food should also be suitable, which means appropriate for you personally. If certain foods cause digestive upheavals, or if you really dislike them, you will not be able to practice. You will not feel well and you will constantly be pining for foods you would prefer to have.

We might draw a good lesson from the Buddha's time. A particular rich merchant and a laywoman were the leaders and organizers of most of the religious occasions in the area where the Buddha was teaching. Somehow things never seemed to work quite right unless these two were involved in planning and organizing a retreat or other event. Their secret of success was holding to the principles of necessity and suitability. They always took the trouble to find out what was needed by the monks, nuns or yogis who were invited to receive food donations. The man and woman also found out what was suitable. Perhaps you can remember having food you needed and longed for, food which also was suitable, so that after eating it you found your mind became calm and concentrated.

### 2. Good Climate

The second way to arouse tranquility is to meditate in an environment where the weather is good, so that you find it comfortable and convenient to meditate. Everyone has preferences. No matter what we prefer, however, it is possible to adapt to different climates by the use of fans and heaters, or lighter and heavier clothing.

### 3. A Comfortable Posture

A third way to cultivate tranquility is to adopt a comfortable posture. We generally sit and walk in vipassanā practice. These are the two best postures for beginners. Comfortable does not mean luxurious! Lying down or sitting in a chair with a backrest might be considered luxurious postures unless you have a physical ailment that makes them necessary. When you sit unsupported, or when you walk, you need a certain degree of physical effort to keep from falling over. In the luxurious postures this effort is missing, and it is easier to doze off. The mind becomes very relaxed and comfortable, and in no time you might disturb the air with snores.

### 4. Neither Overenthusiasm nor Sloppiness

The fourth way to arouse tranquility is to maintain a balanced effort in practice. You should be neither overenthusiastic nor sloppy. If you push yourself too hard, you will miss the object and become tired. If you are lazy, you will not move very far ahead. Overzealous people may be likened to people who are in a big hurry to reach the top of a mountain. They climb very quickly, but because the mountain is steep, they must stop frequently to rest. In the end it takes them a long time to get to the top of the mountain. Lazy, sloppy types, on the other hand, will be like snails crawling far behind.

### 5-6. Avoiding Louts, Choosing Calm and Kind Friends

Avoiding bad-tempered, rough or cruel people can also aid tranquility. It is obvious that if your companions are hot-tempered, always angry with you and scolding you, you will never arrive at peace of mind. It is also evident that you will become more tranquil by associating with people who are calm and quiet in body and in mind.

### 7. Inclining the Mind toward Peacefulness

Last, if you constantly incline your mind toward practice, hoping to achieve tranquility and peace, you can realize this aim. If you are vigilant in activating mindfulness, the enlightenment factor of tranquility will arise in you quite naturally.

### CONCENTRATION: SIXTH FACTOR OF ENLIGHTENMENT

Concentration is that factor of mind which lands on the object of observation, which pricks into it, penetrates into it and stays there. The Pāli word for it is samādhi.

### Nonagitation

The characteristic of samādhi is nondispersal, nondissipation, nonscatteredness. This means that the mind sticks with the object of observation, sinks into it, and remains still and calm, right there.

### Fixed Concentration and Moving Concentration

There are two types of samādhi. One is continuous samādhi, which is the concentration gained while meditating on a single object. This is the type of concentration gained in pure tranquility meditation, where the one requirement is for the mind to stay put on one object to the total exclusion of all other objects. Those who follow the path of continuous concentration are able to experience it especially when they gain absorption into the jhānas.

Vipassanā practice, however, is aimed toward the development of wisdom and the completion of the various stages of insight. Insight, of course, refers to basic intuitive understandings such as the distinction between mind and matter, the intuitive comprehension of their interrelationship by virtue of cause and effect, and the direct perception of the impermanence, unsatisfactoriness and selflessness of all physical and mental phenomena. These are basic insights, and there are others which one must traverse before attaining the path and fruition consciousness which have nibbāna or the cessation of all suffering as their object.

In vipassanā practice, the field of awareness of objects is crucially important. The field of vipassanā objects are mental and physical phenomena, those things which are directly perceptible without resorting to the thinking process. In other words, as we practice vipassanā we observe many different objects, with the goal of gaining insight into their nature. Momentary concentration, the second type, is most important in vipassanā practice. Vipassanā objects are arising and passing away all the time, and momentary concentration arises in each moment with each object. In spite of its momentary nature, such samādhi can arise from moment to moment without breaks in between. If it does so, momentary concentration shares with continuous concentration the power to tranquilize the mind and keep the kilesas at bay.

## Gathering the Mind

Let us say you are sitting, watching the rise and fall of the abdomen. As you make the effort to be mindful of the rising and falling processes, you are being with the moment. With each moment of energy and effort you expend in cultivating awareness, there is a corresponding mental activity of penetration. It is as though the mind were stuck fast onto the object of observation. You drop, or fall, into the object. Not only is the mind one-pointed and penetrating into the object, not only does the mind remain still for that moment in that object, but this mental factor of samādhi has the power to gather together the other mental factors which arise simultaneously with that moment of consciousness. Concentration is a factor which collects the mind together; this is its function. It keeps all the mental factors in a group so that they do not scatter or disperse. Thus, the mind remains firmly embedded in the object.

*Peace and Stillness*

There is an analogy here with parents and children. Good parents want their children to grow up to be well-mannered and morally responsible adults. Toward this goal, they exercise some degree of control over their offspring. Kids are not yet mature, and they lack the wisdom of discretion. So parents must make sure they do not run out and mix with the naughty children of the neighborhood. Mental factors are like children in this respect. Just as children who lack parental guidance may act in ways that harm themselves and others, so too the uncontrolled mind will suffer from bad influences. The kilesas are always loitering nearby. If the mind is not contained, it can easily mix with delinquents like desire, aversion, anger, or delusion. Then the mind becomes wild and ill-mannered, which manifests in bodily behavior as well as in speech. The mind, like a child, may resent discipline at first. By and by, however, it will become more and more tame and civilized and tranquil, and more remote from attacks by the kilesas. The concentrated mind becomes more and more still, more and more quiet, more and more peaceful. This sense of peace and stillness is the manifestation of concentration.

Children, too, can be tamed if they are properly cared for. They may have a wild nature at first, but eventually, as they mature, they will understand why they should avoid bad people. They will even begin to be grateful for the care and control their parents gave to them. Perhaps they even observe that some childhood friend whose parents lacked vigilance has grown up to be a criminal. When they are old enough to go out into the world, they will be able to discriminate for themselves what sort of people to choose as friends, and whom to stay away from. As they grow older and more mature, this upbringing of theirs causes their continued development and prosperity.

### Concentration Permits Wisdom to Arise

Concentration is the proximate cause for the unfolding of wisdom. This fact is very important. Once the mind is quiet and still, there is space for wisdom to arise. There can be comprehension of the true nature of mind and matter. Perhaps there will be an intuitive insight into how mind and matter can be differentiated, and how they are related by cause and effect. Step by step, wisdom will penetrate into more and more profound levels of truth. One will see clearly the characteristics of impermanence, suffering and absence of self; and finally insight is gained into the cessation of suffering. When this illumination happens, a person will never be able to become a grossly evil person again, no matter what environment he or she may be in.

### Parents and Children

Parents or potential parents should perhaps prick up their ears here. It is very important for parents to control their own minds by concentration. Eventually they should complete the various levels of insight. Such parents can be very skillful in bringing up children, because they can differentiate clearly between wholesome and unwholesome activities. They will be able to instruct their children likewise, most particularly by setting a good example. Parents who do not control their minds, who are given to ill-mannered behavior, cannot help their children develop goodness and intelligence.

Some of my students in Burma have been parents. When they started meditation, they only considered their children's worldly welfare with respect to education and earning a livelihood in this world. Then these parents came to our meditation center and practiced. They had deep practice. When they returned to their children, they had new attitudes and plans. They now felt that it was more important for their children to learn to control their minds and develop good hearts than just to gain success in the world. When the children came of age, their parents urged them to practice meditation. In fact, when I asked the parents if there was a difference between children born before and after meditation experiences, the parents replied, "Oh, certainly. Those who were born after we completed our meditation practice are more obedient and consid-erate. They have good hearts compared with the other children."

### Steady Attention Causes Concentration

The Buddha said that continuous wise attention, aimed toward the development of concentration was the cause of concentration. Preceding concentration causes successive concentration to arise.

### Eleven More Ways to Arouse Concentration

The commentaries describe eleven more ways to arouse concentration.

### 1. Cleanliness

The first is purity of the internal and external bases, of the body and the environment. This influence has been discussed under the second factor of enlightenment, investigation (see page 103).

### 2. A Balanced Mind

The second cause of concentration is balancing the controlling faculties, wisdom and faith on the one hand, energy and concentration on the other. I have devoted a chapter to this balancing (see page 29).

### 3. Clear Mental Image

The third cause is more relevant to jhāna practice than to strict vipassanā, and so I will mention it only briefly. It is to be skillful in the concentration object, meaning to maintain a clear mental image as is practiced in tranquility meditation.

### 4. Uplifting the Discouraged Mind

The fourth cause is to uplift the mind when it becomes heavy, depressed or discouraged. You have doubtless taken a lot of bumps and tumbles in your practice. At these times you should try to uplift your mind, perhaps applying techniques for arousing energy, rapture or insight. Uplifting the discouraged mind is also one of the teacher's jobs. When a yogi comes to interviews with a long and sullen face, the teacher knows how to inspire him or her.

### 5. Calming the Overenthusiastic Mind

At times it is also necessary to put down the excited mind. This is the fifth cause leading to the development of concentration. At times yogis have fascinating experiences in their meditation practice. They become excited and active; their energy overflows. At these times the teacher should not be encouraging. He or she should speak in such a way as to put yogis in their proper place, one might say. A teacher might also help to activate the fifth factor of enlightenment, tranquility, by the means discussed in the previous section. Or the teacher may instruct yogis to take it easy, just settle back and watch without trying too hard.

### 6. Cheering the Mind that is Withered by Pain

If the mind is shrunken and withered by pain, it may need to be made happy. This is the sixth means. A yogi may feel depressed by the environment, or by a recurrence of an old health problem. At this time the mind needs to be uplifted and cleared so that it becomes bright and sharp again. You might try to liven it up in various ways. Or the teacher also can cheer you up, not by telling jokes, but by encouraging talk.

### 7. Continuous Balanced Awareness

The seventh way to arouse samādhi is to continue balanced awareness at all times. Sometimes as the practice really deepens, you seem to be making no effort, but you are still mindful of objects as they arise and pass. At such times you should try not to interfere, even if this comfortable speed feels too slow for you and you want to step on the gas. You may want to realize the Dhamma very quickly. If you do try to speed up, you will upset the mind's equilibrium, and your awareness will become blunt. On the other hand, everything is so nice and smooth that you might relax too much. This, too, brings regression in practice. When there is effortless effort, you should cruise along, yet nonetheless keep up with the momentum that is present.

*8-9. Avoiding the Distracted, Choosing Friends who are Focused*

You should avoid people who are unconcentrated, and keep company with people who are concentrated – the eighth and ninth arousers of concentration. People who are neither calm nor peaceful, who have never developed any kind of concentration, carry a lot of agitation within them. Children born to such parents may also lack peace of mind.

In Burma there is a concept closely related to the current Western notion of "good vibes." There are many cases of people who have never meditated before, but when they come into the meditation center as visitors, they begin to feel very tranquilized and peaceful. They get the vibrations of yogis who are working seriously. Some visitors decide to come and practice. This seems very natural.

In the Buddha's time there was a king named Ajātasattu who had killed his father to gain the throne. He spent many, many sleepless nights after committing this evil deed. Finally he decided to consult the Buddha. He went through the forest and came upon a group of monks listening with peaceful concentration to a discourse of the Buddha. It is said that all his remorse and agitation disappeared, and he was filled with calm and tranquility such as he had not felt in a long time.

*10. Reflecting on the Peace of Absorption*

The tenth method is to reflect on the peace and tranquilty of the jhānic absorptions. This is relevant for yogis who have meditated in this way and attained pure tranquility. Remembering the method they used to attain jhāna, they can briefly use it in the present moment to attain concentration of mind. Those who have not yet attained the jhānas perhaps can recall some of the times when momentary concentration was very strong, when there was a feeling of peace and one-pointedness. By remembering the feeling of liberation from hindrances and the peace of mind that comes from continually activating momentary concentration, concentration could again arise.

### 11. Inclining the Mind

The eleventh and last cause for concentration is to incline the mind persistently toward developing concentration. Everything depends on the effort expended in each moment. If you try to be concentrated, you will succeed.

## EQUANIMITY: SEVENTH ENLIGHTENMENT FACTOR

Perhaps the United Nations should be given a new name. If it were called the Organization of Equanimities, delegates might be reminded of the state of mind that is essential at the negotiating table, especially when facing a hot problem. Any decision maker must be able to remain unbiased in the face of difficult problems.

The Pāli word *upekkhā*, usually translated as equanimity, actually refers to the balancing of energy. It is that state of mind which is in the center, inclining neither to one extreme nor to the other. It can be cultivated in ordinary life, with its daily processes of decision, as well as in meditation.

### Mediating the Internal Contest

In meditation various states of mind compete. Faith tries to overwhelm its complement, intelligence or wisdom, and vice versa. It is the same with effort and concentration. It is common knowledge among meditators that a balance in these two pairs of mental states is essential to maintain progress and direction in practice.

At the beginning of a retreat you may be very enthusiastic and ambitious. Immediately upon sitting down, you pounce on the rising and falling or any other object that arises in your field of awareness. Due to excess effort, your mind is likely to overshoot the object of meditation or to slip off it. This missing of the mark may upset you, for you will feel that you are doing your best and yet not succeeding.

Perhaps you discover your folly and are able to slip into the rhythm of what is happening. As you watch the rising and falling, the mind fits into these processes and goes along with them. In time it becomes easy, and you begin to relax a bit. Effort seems pointless, but if you are not careful, sloth and torpor will creep in and overwhelm you.

At times a yogi may be quite successful in distinguishing mind and matter and seeing their connection. She or he gets a flavor of the Dhamma and finds this quite exciting. Filled with faith, the yogi begins to want to tell friends and parents about the wonderful truth she or he has just discovered. Due to faith, imagination and planning run wild. With so much thinking and feeling going on, the practice grinds to a halt. This succession of events is symptomatic of excessive faith.

Another yogi might have the same intuitive insight, but instead of wanting to spread the Dhamma, he or she begins to interpret the experience. You might say this type of yogi makes a mountain out of a molehill. Every little thing he or she perceives is interpreted in light of the meditation literature which this yogi has read. A string of reflections and thoughts arises, again blocking the practice. Such are the symptoms of excess of intelligence.

Many yogis have a great tendency to reason and check out what they hear before they accept it. They take pride in their quality of discrimination. When they come to meditate, they are always testing in an intellectual way the validity of what they are doing, verifying the practice against their intellectual understanding. If they remain caught in this pattern, such yogis will always be plagued by doubt. Rotating endlessly on doubt's merry-go-round, they will never move forward.

Having heard of a method of practice, or having practiced a method and found it basically effective, then one should surrender oneself totally to the instructions given. Only then can swift progress be made. Yogis are like soldiers fighting a battle. They are on the front lines, and have no time to squabble or question orders. Every order that comes from the top must be obeyed without question; only then can the battle be won. Of course, I am not suggesting you surrender totally, with blind faith.

Up to the time when the arising and passing of phenomena can be seen lucidly and sharply, any yogi's practice will be variable and shaky, for faith and wisdom, energy and concentration are not yet in balance. If, however, the hurdles of imbalance are overcome and the yogi can simply watch the rapid arising and passing of phenomena, the imbalances between energy and concentration, faith and wisdom will be rectified. At this point, we say the yogi is endowed with the state of equanimity, which is the balancing of these four factors. It may seem that the noting or mindfulness is effortlessly carrying on by itself.

The mind that is balanced is like a carriage being pulled by two horses of equal strength and stamina. When both are running, driving the carriage is easy. The driver just lets the horses do the work. But if one horse is fast and the other is an old nag, the driver will have hard work. To avoid landing in the ditch, he or she will constantly have to make efforts to slow down the fast horse and speed up the nag. Similarly in meditation practice, at first there is no equilibrium among mental states, and the yogi is constantly careening from enthusiasm to doubt, from overexertion to laziness. As the practice continues, however, the enlightenment factor of equanimity arises, and then mindfulness seems to go along by itself. At this time we can experience a great comfort. To jump forward into a modern metaphor, we become drivers of a luxury automobile, going along an untrafficked freeway with the car on cruise control.

*Faith Balanced with Intelligence, Energy Balanced with Concentration*

The characteristic of equanimity is the balancing of corresponding mental states so that one does not overwhelm the other. It creates a balance between faith and intelligence, energy and concentration.

### Neither Excess nor Lack

The function of equanimity as a factor of enlightenment is to fill in where there is a lack and to reduce where there is excess. Equanimity arrests the mind before it falls into extremes of excess or lack. When upekkhā is strong, there is total balance, no inclination at all toward excess in any direction. The yogi does not need to make an effort to be mindful.

### A Good Driver Just Lets the Horses Pull

It seems as if mindfulness is taking care of everything, like the driver of the carriage who settles back and lets the horses do the work of pulling. This state of ease and balance is the manifestation of equanimity.

When I was a child, I heard people talking about how to carry two baskets on the ends of a bamboo pole. This is common in Burma. The pole is carried over one shoulder, with a loaded basket on the front end and another in back. When you first start off, you have to exert a lot of effort, and the load feels burdensome. But after ten or fifteen steps, the pole begins rocking up and down to the rhythm of your walking. You and the pole and the baskets move along in a relaxed way, so that you hardly feel the load. I could not believe this at first, but now that I have meditated, I know that it is quite possible.

### Continuous Mindfulness Causes Equanimity

According to the Buddha the way to bring about equanimity is wise attention: to be continually mindful from moment to moment, without a break, based on the intention to develop equanimity. One moment of equanimity causes a succeeding moment of equanimity to arise. Once equanimity is activated, it will be the cause for equanimity to continue and to deepen. It can bring one to deep levels of practice beyond the insight into the arising and passing away of phenomena.

Equanimity does not arise easily in the minds of beginning yogis. Though these yogis may be diligent in trying to be mindful from moment to moment, equanimity comes and goes. The mind will be well balanced for a little while and then it will go off again. Step by step equanimity is strengthened. The intervals when it is present grow more prolonged and frequent. Eventually, equanimity becomes strong enough to qualify as a factor of enlightenment.

## Five More Ways to Develop Equanimity

There are five ways to arouse equanimity discussed in the commentaries.

### 1. Balanced Emotion toward All Living Things

The first and foremost is to have an equanimous attitude toward all living beings. These are your loved ones, including animals. We can have a lot of attachment and desire associated with people we love, and also with our pets. Sometimes we can be what we call "crazy" about someone. This experience does not contribute to equanimity, which is a state of balance.

To prepare the ground for equanimity to arise, one should try to cultivate an attitude of nonattachment and equanimity toward the people and animals we love. As worldly people, it may be necessary to have a certain amount of attachment in relationships, but excessive attachment is destructive to us as well as to loved ones. We begin to worry too much over their welfare. Especially in retreat, we should try to put aside such excessive concern and worry for the welfare of our friends.

One reflection that can develop nonattachment is to regard all beings as the heirs of their own kamma. People reap the rewards of good kamma and suffer the consequences of unwholesome acts. They created this kamma under their own volition, and no one can prevent their experiencing the consequences. On the ultimate level, there is nothing you or anybody else can do to save them. If you think in this way, you may worry less about your loved ones.

You also can gain equanimity about beings by reflecting on ultimate reality. Perhaps you can tell yourself that, ultimately speaking, there is only mind and matter. Where is that person you are so wildly in love with? There is only *nāma* and *rūpa*, mind and body, arising and passing away from moment to moment. Which moment are you in love with? You may be able to drive some sense into your heart this way.

One might worry that reflections like this could turn into unfeeling indifference and lead us to abandon a mate or a dear person. This is not the case. Equanimity is not insensitivity, indifference or apathy. It is simply nonpreferential. Under its influence, one does not push aside the things one dislikes nor grasp at things one prefers. The mind rests in an attitude of balance and acceptance of things as they are. When equanimity, this factor of enlightenment, is present, one abandons both attachment to beings and dislike for them. The texts tell us that equanimity is the cause for the cleansing and purification of one who has deep tendencies toward lust or desire, which is the opposite of equanimity.

### 2. Balanced Emotion toward Inanimate Things

The second way of developing this factor of enlightenment is to adopt an attitude of balance toward inanimate things: property, clothing, the latest fad on the market. Clothing, for example, will be ripped and stained someday. It will decay and perish because it is impermanent, like everything else. Furthermore, we do not even own it, not in the ultimate sense. Everything is nonself; there is no one to own anything. To develop balance and to cut down attachment, it is helpful to look at material things as transient. You might say to yourself, "I'm going to make use of this for a short time. It's not going to last forever."

People who get caught up in fads may be compelled to buy each new product that appears on the market. Once this gadget has been bought, another more sophisticated model will soon appear. Such persons throw away the old one and buy a new one. This behavior does not reflect equanimity.

### 3. Avoiding People Who "Go Crazy"

The third method for developing equanimity as an enlightenment factor is avoiding the company of people who tend to be crazy about people and things. These people have a deep possessiveness, clinging to what they think belongs to them, both people and things. Some people find it difficult to see another person enjoying or using their property.

There is the case of an elder who had a great attachment to pets. It seems that in his monastery he bred a lot of dogs and cats. One day this elder came to the center in Rangoon to do a retreat. When he was meditating, he was practicing under favorable circumstances, but his practice was not very deep. Finally I had an idea and asked him if he had any pets in his monastery. He brightened up and said, "Oh yes, I have so many dogs and cats. Ever since I came here I've been thinking about whether they have enough food to eat and how they're doing." I asked him to forget about the animals and concentrate on meditation, and quite soon he was making good progress.

Please do not allow overattachment to loved ones, or even pets, to prevent you from attending meditation retreats which will allow you to deepen your practice and to develop equanimity as a factor of enlightenment.

### 4. Choosing Friends who Stay Cool

As a fourth method of arousing upekkhā, you should choose friends who have no great attachment to beings or possessions. This method of developing equanimity is simply the converse of the preceding one. In choosing such a friend, if you happen to pick the elder I described just now, it could be a bit of a problem.

## 5. Inclining the Mind toward Balance

The fifth and last cause for this factor of enlightenment to arise is constantly to incline your mind toward the cultivation of equanimity. When your mind is inclined in this way, it will not wander off to thoughts of your dogs and cats at home, or of your loved ones. It will only become more balanced and harmonious.

Equanimity is of tremendous importance both in the practice and in everyday life. Generally we get either swept away by pleasant and enticing objects, or worked up into a great state of agitation when confronted by unpleasant, undesirable objects. This wild alternation of contraries is nearly universal among human beings. When we lack the ability to stay balanced and unfaltering, we are easily swept into extremes of craving or aversion.

The scriptures say that when the mind indulges in sensual objects, it becomes agitated. This is the usual state of affairs in the world, as we can observe. In their quest for happiness, people mistake excitement of the mind for real happiness. They never have the chance to experience the greater joy that comes with peace and tranquility.

### THE FACTORS OF ENLIGHTENMENT DEVELOPED: HEALING INTO THE DEATHLESS

All of the factors of enlightenment bring extraordinary benefits. Once fully developed, they have the power to bring samsāric suffering to an end. So the scriptures tell us. This means that the perpetual, cyclical birth and death of beings who are composed of mental and physical phenomena can come to a complete stop.

The factors of enlightenment also have the capacity to pulverize Māra's ten armies, the destructive inner forces which keep us bound on the wheel of suffering and rebirth. For this reason, Buddhas and enlightened ones develop the factors of enlightenment and are thus able to transcend this realm of sensual pleasures as well as the realms of subtle form and all the formless realms.

You may ask where one goes after being liberated from these three types of realms. It cannot be said there is another birth of any kind, for with nibbāna comes cessation of birth and death. Birth brings inevitable life, aging, sickness and eventual death – all the aspects of suffering. To be free from all suffering is to be free from birth. Nor will death be able to happen. Nibbāna is free from birth and also from death.

When fully developed, these factors of enlightenment bring the yogi to attain nibbāna. In this they are comparable to strong, effective medicine. They confer the strength of mind necessary to withstand the ups and downs of life. Moreover, they often cure physical and mental diseases.

There is no guarantee that if you meditate you will be able to cure every disease. However, it is possible that the development of enlightenment factors can bring healing to sicknesses, even those which appear incurable.

*Purifying Our Mental Illnesses*

Mental disease is the disease of greed, hatred, delusion, jealousy, miserliness, conceit and so forth. When these forces arise, they make the mind unclear and clouded. This clouded mind will produce physical phenomena which reflect its clouded state. Instead of having a clear and bright complexion, when your mind is clouded by negativity, you will look dull, unhappy and unhealthy, much as if you had been breathing polluted air.

However, if you are energetically trying to activate a penetrative mindfulness from moment to moment on the object of observation, very naturally the mind will stay on this object without scattering or dissipating. Samādhi or concentration is present at this time. After a due period, the mind will be cleansed of the hindrances or negative tendencies. Now wisdom will begin to unfold. When insights arise, the mind becomes even purer, as if it were breathing clean air again after returning from the hustle and bustle of a city.

Mindfulness, energy and investigation lead to concentration and insights which arise in successive stages. Each

new insight is like another breath of fresh air to the mind.
The stage of insight into the arising and passing away of
phenomena is the beginning of good, deep practice. The
factor of equanimity begins to stabilize the mind, and
mindfulness becomes deeper and deeper. The arising and
passing away of objects will be perfectly clear, and there will
be no doubt about the true nature of what can be directly
experienced.

Sudden upsurges of energy may make the practice seem
effortless at this point. Yogis may understand that there is
no one present even to make an effort. Joy and rapture
arise as the yogi perceives directly his or her own purity
of mind, as well as the secret of reality unfolding from
moment to moment. Tremendous joy is followed by tranquil peace and a mind that is free from doubts and worries.
In this peaceful space it is possible to see more and more
clearly. Concentration can also deepen when there is no
disturbance.

At this deep level of practice, one can truly experience
a balanced mind, a mind that is not swept away by  pleasant sensations, even though extreme rapture and joy may
be present. Nor do unpleasant objects agitate the mind.
Yogis feel no dislike for pain nor attachment to pleasure.

### Effects on the Body

The seven factors of enlightenment naturally affect the body
as well as the mind, for these two are intricately connected.
When the mind is really pure and suffused with the factors
of enlightenment, this has a tremendous effect on the
circulatory system. New blood being produced is extremely
pure. It permeates the various organs and sense organs,
clearing them. The body becomes luminous, and perceptions are heightened. Visual objects will be extremely bril-
liant and clear. Some yogis may perceive so much light
emanating from their bodies that their entire rooms may
be lit up at night. The mind, too, is filled with light. There
is bright faith, as well as the verified faith of believing in
your own unmediated experience of what is happening.
The mind becomes light and agile, as does the body, which

sometimes feels as if it is floating in the air. Often the body may become quite imperceptible, and yogis can sit for many hours without feeling any pain at all.

## Miraculous Cures

Old diseases, incurable ailments, are affected by the strength of the enlightenment factors, especially at the deeper levels of practice. At the center in Rangoon, it is a common occurrence for so-called miraculous cures to occur. Entire books could be written just listing the cases. Here I will merely mention two outstanding ones.

## A Case of Tuberculosis

Once there was a man who had been suffering from tuberculosis for many years. Having sought treatment from various doctors and traditional Burmese herbalists, and having spent time in the TB ward of Rangoon General Hospital, still he was not cured. Downhearted and desperate, he felt certain that the only path open to him led toward death. As a last resort, he applied to meditate at the center but concealed his poor state of health lest he be refused admittance on the grounds that other yogis' health would be endangered.

Within two weeks of practice, his chronic symptoms came to the surface with a vengeance, exacerbated by the painful sensations that normally come during a certain period of practicing the Dhamma. His pain was so excruciating, agonizing and exhausting that he could not sleep at all but lay awake all night coughing.

One night I was in my cottage and I heard the terrible coughing sounds that came from his quarters. Taking some Burmese herbal cough medicine, I went to him expecting to help alleviate some recently contracted flu or cold. Instead, the man was sprawled in his room, so exhausted that he could not say a word to me. His spittoon was nearly filled with blood he had coughed up. I asked if he wanted medicine, and when at last he was able to speak, he confessed his medical condition. My first thought was to wonder whether I had breathed any of his germs.

The man went on, apologizing for having brought this infectious condition into the retreat center, but begging for permission to continue his practice. "If I leave there is only one path for me and that is the path of death," he said. These words touched my heart. I quickly began to encourage and inspire him to continue the practice. After making quarantine arrangements to prevent his tuberculosis from spreading all over the center, I continued to instruct him.

Within a month the man had overcome his tuberculosis through his fantastic progress in meditation. He left the center completely cured. Three years later he reappeared as a robust and healthy monk. I asked him how he felt now. Had his TB or coughing fits recurred? "No," said the man. "The TB has never returned. As for coughing, at times my throat itches, but if I am mindful of this sensation immediately, I don't begin to cough. The Dhamma is fantastic, miraculous. Having drunk the medicine of Dhamma, I am completely cured."

### A Woman's High Blood Pressure

Another case happened about twenty years ago. This was a woman who lived in the center compound. She was related to one of the staff members. For a long time she had suffered from high blood pressure and had sought treatment and drugs from doctors. Sometimes she came to me and I would encourage her to meditate, saying that even if she died in the course of the practice, she would enjoy a lot of happiness in her next rebirth. She always had an excuse, though, and continued to take refuge in her doctors.

Finally I gave her a scolding. "Many people come from long distances, even from foreign countries, to taste the Dhamma in this retreat center. Their practice is deep and they experience many fantastic things. You live here and yet you haven't meditated to any level of satisfaction at all. You remind me of the fierce-looking stone lion which guards the foot of a stupa. Those lions, you know, always have their backs to the stupa so that they can never pay it any respect."

The woman was quite hurt by this scolding and agreed to try meditation. Within a short time she had reached the stage of great pain. The pain of her illness, combined with the pain of the Dhamma, gave her a really tough time. She could hardly eat or sleep. Eventually her family members, who also lived at the center, began to become alarmed at her condition. They begged her to return to their quarters so that they could take care of her. I was opposed to this and exhorted her to continue her practice rather than to listen to them.

Her family members came to her again and again, and I for my part insisted that she continue. It was quite a battle for this woman, but she persisted with her meditation. She was very tough. She had a new surge of inspiration and resolved to see her practice through to the end, even if she died.

The woman's pain was fantastically severe. She felt as if her brain was going to fall apart. The veins in her head throbbed, pounded and hammered. She endured all of it with patience, simply watching the pain. Soon a great heat began to emanate from her body. She emanated and radiated a great fire. Finally she overcame all these sensations and everything became still and calm. She had won the battle. Her high blood pressure was completely cured, and she never again had to take medicines for that disease.

### Other Diseases – and Don't Forget Liberation!

I have witnessed cures of impacted intestines, uterine fibroids, heart disease, cancer and more. There is no guarantee of this outcome, though I hope the stories are inspiring to you. Nonetheless, if a yogi is ardent, persistent, heroic and courageous in trying to be mindful of painful sensations that arise from diseases or old injuries, he or she may find a miraculous recovery from these troubles. Persistent effort carries a great possibility.

Satipatthāna meditation is perhaps especially useful for cancer patients. Cancer is terrible. There is so much suffering both in the body and in the mind. One who is versed in satipatthāna meditation can lighten his or her burden by being mindful of pain, no matter how dire. He or she can die a peaceful death, perfectly and impeccably mindful of just the pain. This kind of death is good and noble.

May you make full use of the knowledge you have gained through this exposition on the seven factors of enlightenment. May you cultivate each factor, starting from mindfulness and finishing with equanimity, so that you can become a fully liberated being.

# 5  The Vipassanā Jhānas

SOFTENING THE RIGID MIND

The Buddha said, "Indeed with meditation, one can develop knowledge and wisdom as grounded and as vast as the earth." The quality of such wisdom permeates the mind, making it expansive and vast. In the absence of meditation, however, the mind becomes narrow and rigid under the constant assault of kilesas. Each moment we are unmindful, the kilesas penetrate into the mind, making it tight, tense and agitated.

The objects that bombard us at the six sense doors are sometimes good and sometimes bad, sometimes pleasant, sometimes unpleasant. A pleasant visual object presents itself: the unguarded mind will naturally fill with craving and clinging, closing tightly around that object. Seized by this tension and agitation, the mind begins to scheme of ways to get that very pleasant object. From this plan to grasp the object, speech and physical movements may develop.

If the mind is unguarded and an unpleasant object appears, aversion will naturally arise. Again, the mind will become agitated. Some manifestation might be seen: a bright face twisted into a scowl, harsh and dreadful words, or even acts of violence.

In the face of objects neither pleasant nor unpleasant, if the mind is unguarded, delusion will cloud the mind, stopping it from seeing what is true. At this moment, too, there is tension and hardness of mind.

It would be foolish to think that we can eliminate pleasant, unpleasant and neutral objects from our lives. What is important is to maintain a wholesome relationship with them. Perhaps one could stuff one's ears with cotton wool, blindfold oneself and grope about while maintaining a meditative state of mind. But obviously one could not block one's nostrils or anesthetize one's tongue, nor cut off the sensitivity of the body to heat, cold and other sensations. Sitting in meditation, we try to concentrate on the primary object. But we will still hear sounds, and strong sensations may arise in other parts of the body. Despite our best effort, our practice could slip for a few moments, and our thinking mind could run completely wild.

## The Power of Restraint

The practice of restraint is an effective way of preventing this assault by kilesas. Restraint does not mean becoming dead and numb. It means guarding each sense door so that the mind does not run out through it into fantasies and thoughts, plans and schemes. Mindfulness is actually the cause for restraint to arise. When we are mindful in each moment, the mind is held back from falling into a state where greed, hatred and delusion may erupt. If we are vigilant, eventually the mind will become somewhat tamed and content not to escape into danger of ambush by kilesas.

We have to be on our toes. As soon as we come into contact with an object, we note it immediately for what it is. We want to be sure that in seeing is only the seeing, in hearing only the hearing, in touch only the touch, in taste only the taste, and in thinking, just the thought. Each of these processes should be clear and simple, not burdened with a lot of extra rumination, not clotted with kilesas. If we are able to be really mindful, objects will arise and pass without further thoughts or reactions, just the process in itself. No matter what kind of objects we are forced to encounter, we will be safe from desire or aversion.

There was a great king in the Buddha's time who was once very curious as to how monks could keep their precepts. Young monks, he observed, remained chaste even in the vigor of their prime, when lust easily arises. He asked a senior monk about this. The monk said, "When young monks come across a girl younger than they are, they consider her as their younger sister. When they come across a woman of the same age or slightly older, they consider her their elder sister. When they come across a woman older than that, they consider her their mother. If she is advanced in age, they consider her their grandmother."

The king was not satisfied. He said, "But the mind is very quick, and even if you make yourself think in those ways, lust may already have arisen."

The elder tried again. "If a monk comes across a woman, if he is unmindful and begins to admire her features, her body, then naturally lust will arise. But if he should look at a woman by dissecting her into pieces, in terms of the thirty-two parts of the body – hair, teeth, nails and so forth – and if he reflects on the repulsiveness of these parts, he will be filled with disgust and not desire her at all." This meditation on the body was given by the Lord Buddha.

The king then asked, "What if a monk has more imagination than concentration?" On the subject of imagination, I would like to interpolate another story here.

Somewhere on the premises of a certain meditation center there is a little closet in which a skeleton is hung. The skeleton is for people to come and look at, reflecting upon the imminence of death, and perhaps also on bones as a repulsive body part. Under its bony feet is a small sign that says, "Sixteen-year-old girl."

Possessed of wise attention, one visitor might say, "Oh, that poor girl, only sixteen but she had to die. I too will die one day." Spiritual urgency might arise, and this person might try to do more good deeds, or practice meditation with greater ardor. Another visitor might reflect on the repulsiveness of the bones, and see that there is nothing to the body, just bones, this frame.

Along comes a young and imaginative man. Standing in front of the skeleton, his eyes fall on the placard that says what it once was. He says to himself, "What a pity! How beautiful she must have been before she died." He looks at the skull and starts to flesh it out with a beautiful face, adding nice hair and a very nice neck. His eyes travel slowly downward, filling out each part of the body. He is filled with craving by the image he has called up, an image perhaps not so different from the creations of a taxidermist.

Let us return now to the story of the king. The older monk replied, "All the young monks practice mindfulness. They activate restraint of their senses, so that they are guarded at each sense door. Their minds are not wild. They don't fantasize about the things they see."

The king was impressed. He said, "Yes, that must be very true. I can testify from my own experience that when I go to my harem without mindfulness, I get into a lot of trouble. But if I am mindful I have no problems."

I hope these tales illustrate the importance of sense restraint.

### Intensive Restraint for Retreats

During an intensive meditation retreat, the value of restraint cannot be overestimated.

The scriptures give four practical guidelines for restraint during intensive practice.

First, a yogi must act like a blind person even though he or she may possess complete sight. The yogi should go about with lowered eyelids, incuriously, to keep the mind from scattering.

Second, the yogi must act like a deaf person, not reflecting, commenting upon, nor judging the sounds he or she may hear. A yogi should pretend not quite to understand sounds and should not listen for them.

Third, though a yogi may have a great deal of learning, may have read a tremendous amount about meditation and tried fifteen techniques, during actual practice he or she should put away all this knowledge. Keep it under lock and key, maybe even under the bed! A yogi should act like an ignorant person who does not know much and does not talk about the few things he or she does know.

Fourth, a yogi should act like a hospital patient, frail and sick, by slowing down and moving very mindfully.

There ought also to be a fifth principle. Even though a yogi is very much alive, he or she should behave like a dead person with respect to painful sensations. As you know, a corpse can be chopped to pieces like a log without feeling anything at all. If pain arises during meditation, a yogi should summon all of his or her courage and energy simply to look it in the face. He or she should make a heroic effort to penetrate and understand the pain, without shifting posture or letting aversion take over the mind.

In each moment we try to be mindful and present with whatever is arising. We try to note "seeing, seeing" at the moment of seeing; "hearing, hearing" at the moment of hearing, and so forth. Real effort is being made to note. There is also accuracy of mind, a precise aim that enables the mind to hit its target of observation. Mindfulness also is present, penetrating deeply into the object. And with mindfulness comes right concentration, which keeps the mind collected, not strained or dissipated.

## How Wisdom Softens the Mind

Right effort, right aim, right mindfulness, right concentration: all these are factors of the Noble Eightfold Path. When they are present in the mind, the kilesas have no chance to arise. The kilesas, which make the mind so hard and rigid and agitated, are dispelled when one is with the moment, and so the mind has a chance to soften.

With continuous noting the mind gradually becomes more able to penetrate into the true nature of things. There comes the insight that everything is made up of just mind and matter, and the mind experiences a huge sense of relief. No one is there, just mind and matter, with no one creating them. If we can further see how these phenomena are conditioned, the mind will be free of doubts.

A yogi full of doubt is difficult to work with, rigid and tough and tense. No matter how much the teacher might try to convince him or her of what is beneficial in the practice, the effort will be in vain. If such a yogi can be persuaded to practice at least enough to gain insight into cause and effect, however, there will be no more problem. This insight clears the mind of doubt and makes it soft. The yogi will no longer wonder whether these phenomena of mind and matter might be created by some external force, another being invisible or supreme.

As we go deeper and deeper into the moment, the mind becomes softer and more relaxed as the tensions of the kilesas loosen. Observing the fleeting nature of mental and physical phenomena, one gains insight into their impermanence. As a side effect of this process, one is freed from pride and conceit. If one sees clearly the tremendous oppression brought about by phenomena, one gains insight into their suffering nature and thereby is freed from craving. If one sees the absence of self in all phenomena, realizing that the process of mind and matter is empty and not at all related to one's wishes, one can be freed from the wrong view that there is some permanent entity called the self.

This is only the beginning. The deeper we penetrate into the true nature of reality, the more our mind becomes flexible, pliable, workable, dextrous. If one attains the first path consciousness, the first experience of nibbāna, certain kilesas will never make the mind tense and rigid again.

I hope that you may be continuous and active in mindfulness, so that you can develop that vast and expansive wisdom, as grounded as Mother Earth, the basis for all that exists on this planet.

BLOWING OUT SUFFERING

*Neither Wandering nor Stopping: A Riddle from the Buddha*

As a teacher I observe that many yogis' minds seem prone to wander, unaware of what is present here and now. Because I would like to help you understand the nature of the wandering mind, I will give you the following riddle. The Buddha said, "One should not allow the mind to wander without. Neither should one allow the mind to stop within. A bhikkhu who is able to be mindful in that way will eventually be able to extinguish all suffering."

First of all I would like to say that all of you who sincerely practice may consider yourselves bhikkhus. Those of you who want to be free from suffering may be eager to apply this advice. However, it may be hard to know in which direction to make one's leap. What is meant by wandering without, and how can we ensure that the mind will not do it? Perhaps we believe that the task is not so difficult. We have all experienced wandering mind, and we could just use force to prevent it. But if we do not let the mind wander outside, then it must have to stay inside, and the Buddha just told us not to do that!

You have probably noticed that the mind occurs within you. If you focus your attention on the present moment, where is your mind? If it is not outside, then it must be inside. What can you do now? Should you take a tranquilizer and forget this whole problem? Would even this be against the Buddha's advice not to let the mind stop within?

Ah, but the Buddha promised that if we follow these instructions, we can escape from rebirth and its consequences – old age, diseases and death – all the things that happen against our wishes! He made this very pithy statement and then retired to his *Gandhakuṭi*, or fragrant chamber, leaving most of his listeners bewildered.

Looking around for help, people finally selected the Venerable Kaccāyana to explain the discourse. He was an arahant and was famous for explicating the very short discourses which the Buddha sometimes gave.

### Solving the Buddha's Riddle

Unravelling this discourse is a challenging and rewarding intellectual exercise. I suggest you begin by asking yourself what would happen to your mind if you did not keep it under control. How would it respond to objects?

If the mind comes into contact with a pleasant, desirable, tempting object, it naturally fills with greed. This is the moment we say it has wandered off. When it touches a disgusting, painful object, it fills with aversion. Again it becomes a wandering mind. The mind veiled in delusion, unable to see what is happening, is also a mind that has run away. So the Buddha was actually instructing his disciples not to allow the mental factors of greed, aversion and delusion to arise.

The experiences of seeing, hearing, tasting, touching and smelling: are these to be considered part of the wandering mind as well?

## The Sensing Process with and without Mindfulness

All the sensing processes occur through a series of consciousnesses which are neither wholesome nor unwholesome. Immediately after this series, however, if mindfulness does not intervene, there will occur a second, and perhaps a third or fourth and further series of consciousnesses accompanied by greed, hatred and delusion. The point of vipassanā practice is to sharpen mindfulness until it can catch the bare sensing process at the end of the amoral series of consciousnesses, and forestall the arising of further series accompanied by greed, hatred and delusion. If a mind can make this interception, we say that it is not wandering. The wandering mind is the mind that has been polluted by kilesas as it reflects on what has happened or what is happening.

Practically speaking, if we begin to reflect upon the characteristics of the object – "Oh, what a gorgeous color" – we know the mind has wandered off. If, on the other hand, we activate precise and penetrative mindfulness and diligent effort at the moment of seeing that colored object, we have the chance to understand the seeing process for what it really is. This is the chance to develop wisdom. We can see the relationship of mind to matter, the conditionality that relates them, and the characteristics of impermanence, suffering and absence of self they share.

You might like to try an experiment right now. Direct your attention to the rise and fall of the abdomen. If the mind makes an effort to be precisely aware of these movements, actually to feel them from beginning to end, it will be freed of greed, hatred and delusion. There are no thoughts of pleasurable objects, nor aversion to unpleasant objects, nor deluded confusion about what is going on.

CRASH!

Sound suddenly becomes predominant. At this moment, we leave behind the rising and falling movements. Even so, we do not consider that the mind has wandered if we are able to recognize immediately that this is a sound, and note it as "hearing, hearing," without getting carried away by reflections about what caused the sound and so forth. There is no greed, no hatred or delusion in the mind.

It is another matter if the mind is drawn away by a familiar tune, and we begin to remember the last time we heard it and what the singer's name is. Even during a sitting some yogis wriggle and tap their fingers when they remember songs from the past. They certainly suffer from wandering mind.

Once there was a yogi who was having a very interesting and powerful sitting. She was sitting nice and quiet when suddenly a neighboring yogi noisily got up from the cushion. She heard bones creak and clothing rustle. Immediately our yogi began to think, "Inconsiderate! How can he get up like that in the middle of the hour, when I'm trying to meditate!" She worked herself into quite a rage. That might be called "The Great Mind Wandering." Most yogis, of course, work very conscientiously to avoid this state by being mindful of objects at the moment of occurrence, so as not to be caught by the wandering mind. This is exactly what the Venerable Kaccāyana said to do.

### Jhāna

There are yet deeper aspects to this business of not wandering. The mind that is not wandering is the mind that is penetratively mindful of what is happening. The word "penetrative" is not used casually. It refers to a jhānic factor that must arise in the mind. Jhāna is usually translated as "absorption." Actually, it refers to the quality of mind that is able to stick to an object and observe it.

Imagine you find something in the mud and you want to pick it up. If you take a sharp instrument and stick it into that thing, it will penetrate the object so that you can lift it out of the mud. If you were uncertain what that object was, you can look at it closely now. The same goes for the food on your plate. The way your fork pierces a morsel illustrates this jhānic factor.

## Samatha Jhāna

There are two types of jhāna, *samatha jhāna* and *vipassanā jhāna*. Some of you may have read about the samatha jhānas and wonder why I am talking about them in the context of vipassanā. Samatha jhāna is pure concentration, fixed awareness of a single object – a mental image, for example, such as a colored disk or a light. The mind is fixed on this object without wavering or moving elsewhere. Eventually the mind develops a very peaceful, tranquil, concentrated state and becomes absorbed in the object. Different levels of absorption are described in the texts, each level having specific qualities.

## Vipassanā Jhāna

On the other hand, vipassanā jhāna allows the mind to move freely from object to object, staying focused on the characteristics of impermanence, suffering and absence of self that are common to all objects. Vipassanā jhāna also includes the mind which can stay focused and fixed upon the bliss of nibbāna. Rather than the tranquility and absorption which are the goal of samatha jhāna practitioners, the most important results of vipassanā jhāna are insight and wisdom.

Vipassanā jhāna is the focusing of the mind on *paramattha dhammas*. Usually these are spoken of as "ultimate realities," but actually they are just the things we can experience directly through the six sense doors without conceptualization. Most of them are *saṅkhāra paramattha dhamma,* or conditioned ultimate realities: mental and physical phenomena which are changing all the time. Nibbāna is also a paramattha dhamma, but of course it is not conditioned.

Breathing is a good example of a conditioned process. The sensations you feel at the abdomen are conditioned ultimate realities, saṅkhāra paramattha dhamma, caused by your intention to breathe. The whole purpose of concentrating one's attention on the abdomen is to penetrate the actual quality and nature of what is happening there. When you are aware of movement, tension, tautness, heat or cold, you have begun to develop vipassanā jhāna.

Mindfulness at the respective sense doors follows the same principle. If there is diligent effort and penetrative awareness, focusing on what is happening in any particular sense process, the mind will understand the true nature of what is happening. The sensing processes will be understood in individual characteristics as well as common ones.

According to the fourfold way of reckoning, which admits of four levels of jhāna, the first jhāna possesses five factors which we will describe below. All of them are important in vipassanā practice.

## The Five Jhānic Factors

The first of them is called *vitakka*. It is the factor of aiming, accurately directing the mind toward an object. It also has the aspect of establishing the mind on the object, so that the mind stays there.

The second factor is *vicāra* (pronounced "vichara"), generally translated as "investigation" or "reflection." After vitakka has brought the mind to the object and placed it firmly there, vicāra continues to rub the mind onto the object. You can experience this yourself when observing rising and falling. First you make the effort to be precise in aiming the mind at the rising process. Then your mind reaches the object and it does not slip off. It impinges on the object, rubs against it.

As you are mindful in an intuitive and accurate way from moment to moment, the mind gets more and more pure. The hindrances of desire, aversion, sloth, restlessness and doubt weaken and disappear. The mind becomes crystal clear and calm. This state of clarity results from the presence of the two jhānic factors we just discussed. It is called *viveka*, which means seclusion. The consciousness is secluded, far away from the hindrances. This viveka is not a jhānic factor. It is merely a descriptive term for this secluded state of consciousness.

The third jhānic factor is *pīti*, rapture, a delighted interest in what is occurring. This factor may manifest physically as gooseflesh, as feelings of being dropped suddenly as if in an elevator, or as feelings of rising off the ground. The fourth jhānic factor, *sukha*, happiness or comfort, comes on the heels of the third. One feels very satisfied with the practice. Because both the third and the fourth jhānic factors come about as a result of seclusion from the hindrances, they are called *vivekaja pīti sukha*, meaning the rapture, joy and happiness born out of seclusion.

Think of this sequence as a causal chain. Seclusion of mind comes about because of the presence of the first two jhānic factors. If the mind is accurately aimed at the object, if it hits it and rubs it, after some time the mind will become secluded. Because this mind is secluded from the hindrances, one becomes happy, joyous and comfortable.

When these first four jhānic factors are present, the mind automatically becomes calm and peaceful, able to concentrate on what is happening without getting scattered or dispersed. This one-pointedness of mind is the fifth jhānic factor, samādhi, or concentration.

### Access to the First Vipassanā Jhāna Requires Insight into Mind and Matter

It is not sufficient to have all five factors present for one to say one has attained the first vipassanā jhāna. The mind must also come to penetrate into the Dhamma a little bit, enough to see the interrelationship of mind and matter. At this time we say that access to the first vipassanā jhāna has occurred.

A yogi whose mind is composed of these five jhānic factors will experience a new accuracy of mindfulness, a new level of success in sticking with the object. Intense rapture, happiness and comfort in the body may also arise. This could be the occasion for him or her to gloat over the wondrousness of the meditation practice. "Oh wow, I'm getting really precise and accurate. I even feel like I'm floating in the air!" You might recognize this reflection as a moment of attachment.

*Stopping Within*

Anyone can get caught up in rapture, happiness and comfort. This attachment to what is happening within us is a manifestation of a special kind of craving, a craving not connected with ordinary, worldly sensual pleasures. Rather, such craving comes directly out of one's meditation practice. When one is unable to be aware of this craving when it arises, it will interfere with one's practice. Rather than directly noting, one wallows in the pleasant phenomena unmindfully, or thinks about the further delights that might ensue from one's practice. Now we can understand the Buddha's mystifying admonition, for this attachment to the pleasant results of meditation is what he meant by stopping within.

It seems we have explicated this very short sutta instructing us to avoid wandering without as well as stopping within. There is still a bit more to discuss, however, to deepen our understanding.

*Threefold Seclusion*

The sutta implies that one should avoid certain things when one practices meditation. One avoids contact with *kāma* or sensual pleasures and with unwholesome dhammas. One avoids these two things precisely by practicing threefold seclusion: *kāya viveka*, seclusion of the body; *citta viveka*, seclusion of mind; and *upadhi viveka*, which comes as a result of the first two and is a state where defilements and hindrances are very far away and weak.

Kāya viveka actually refers to seclusion not from a physical body, but from the "body" of objects related to sensual pleasures. This means simply the objects of the senses considered as a group: sounds, visual objects, smells, tastes and tactile objects.

Seclusion from unwholesome dhammas comes under the category of citta viveka: seclusion of the mind from the various hindrances which obstruct the growth of concentration and insight. In a practical way, this citta viveka simply means activating mindfulness moment to moment.

A yogi who can maintain continuity of mindfulness moment to moment has activated citta viveka.

These two types of viveka do not come without an effort. For kāya viveka, we must remove ourselves from an environment of sensual pleasures, taking the opportunity to practice in a place conducive to peace of mind. This removal is not in itself sufficient, of course. To acquire citta viveka, we become mindful of all the objects that arise at the six sense doors.

To be mindful, one must direct the mind toward an object. The effort to be mindful is instrumental in bringing a sense of accuracy in the mind. This aim, this effort toward accuracy in placing the mind squarely on the meditation object, is the first jhānic factor, vitakka.

So, you must have aiming. You try to observe the rising and falling of the abdomen. Eventually the mind hits the bull's-eye, clearly noticing sensations of hardness, tension, movement. It begins to impinge and rub against the object. This is vicāra, as we said before. After the mind has been rubbing against its object for some time, it will become engrossed and absorbed into it. When you stay with the rise and fall of the abdomen, fewer thoughts arise. You may even go for some time without having a single thought. Clearly, the mind is free from objects of sense pleasure and also from kilesas which are caused by these objects. Kāya viveka and citta viveka are therefore present. With continued practice, effort and continuity, the kilesas will fade into extreme remoteness. At last you have the third type of seclusion, *upadhi viveka*.

## A Special Kind of Happiness

With upadhi viveka, the mind becomes soft and subtle, light and buoyant, dextrous and flexible. A special kind of happiness, *nekkhamma sukha* arises, the happiness and comfort that come from being free from sensual objects as well as from the unwholesome kilesas which react to those objects. So, in place of ordinary apparent happiness, this liberating comfort appears. Does it seem strange that in relinquishing the comfort of the senses, one gains a very comfortable state of being liberated from the very senses we have relinquished? This is the true renunciation of sense pleasures.

Seclusion of the mind from unwholesome dhammas actually means seclusion of the mind from all kilesas. There is no opportunity for kilesas to arise because the immediate cause of kilesas, namely sense objects, have been given up. Now the word jhāna, the state of being absorbed, takes on a whole new meaning. As a result of the jhānic factors of vitakka, aim, and vicāra, rubbing, sensual pleasures have been given up and the kilesas put away. Not only does jhāna allow absorption, but it also removes kilesas. It burns them away as if it were fire.

## The Relationship of Vitakka and Vicāra

In the development of jhānic states, these two factors of vitakka and vicāra, accurate aim and impingement, are absolutely important. The two of them have a close relationship which is much discussed in the scriptures. Below are two examples.

Imagine that you have a brass cup that is covered with dirt and stains. You take brass polish and put it on a rag. Holding the cup in one hand, you use the other hand to rub the rag against its surface. Working diligently and carefully, soon you will have a shiny cup.

In the same way, a yogi must hold his or her mind in the particular place where the primary object is occurring, the abdomen. He or she keeps applying mindfulness at that place, rubbing it until the stains and pollution of the kilesas disappear. Then he or she will be able to penetrate into the true nature of what is happening at that spot. He or she will comprehend the process of rising and falling. Of course, if other objects become more prominent than the primary object, a yogi must note them, applying vitakka and vicāra toward the new phenomena.

Holding the mug with one hand is analogous to vitakka, while the polishing action is analogous to vicāra. Imagine what would happen if this yogi only held on to the mug and did not polish it. It would remain as dirty as before.

If he or she tried to polish it without holding it steady, it would again be impossible to do a good job. This illustrates the interdependency of the two factors.

The second example is that of a compass, the kind used in geometry. As you know, a compass has two arms, a pointed one and another which holds the pencil. You must firmly place your mind on the object of meditation, as if your mind were the pointed end of the compass; and then you must rotate the mind, so to speak, until it can see the object as a whole and very clearly. A perfect circle will result. Again, the placing of the pointed end is analogous to vitakka, and the rotation to vicāra.

### Direct, Intuitive Knowledge

Sometimes vicāra is translated into English as "investigation" or "sustained thought." This is very misleading. People in the West have been educated since kindergarten to use their intellects, always to seek the whys and wherefores. Unfortunately, this kind of investigation is inappropriate for meditation. Intellectual learning and knowledge is only one of two kinds. The other means of knowledge and learning is direct and intuitive. In meditation one examines the ultimate realities, or paramattha dhammas, directly. One must actually experience them, without thinking about them. This is the only way to attain insight and wisdom relating to things as they really are, the natural state of affairs. One may understand a lot intellectually about ultimate reality. One may have read a great deal, but without experiencing reality directly, there can be no insight.

The reason why the samatha jhānas can grant tranquility, but do not lead directly to wisdom is that they have concepts as their objects, rather than objects which can be directly experienced without thinking. The vipassanā jhānas lead to wisdom, because they consist of direct, sustained contact with the ultimate realities.

Say you have an apple in front of you and you have heard someone say that it is a very juicy, sweet and delicious apple. Perhaps instead you come across this same apple and you think, "Boy, that looks like a really juicy apple. I bet it will be very sweet." You can think, you can bet, but until you take a bite you will not experience the taste of that fruit. So too with meditation. You may vividly imagine what a certain experience is like, but you have not experienced the real thing until you have actually made the effort to practice in the right way. Then you will have your own insight. There is no arguing with the taste of an apple.

## HINDRANCES AND ANTIDOTES

Just as darkness engulfs a room in the middle of the night when there is no candle, so the darkness of delusion and ignorance arises in the human mind when it is not properly attuned to the object of meditation. This darkness is not empty and uneventful, though. On the contrary, in each moment of ignorance the mind is continually seeking and grasping after desirable sights, sounds, thoughts, smells, tastes and sensations. Beings in this condition spend all their waking hours seeking, grasping and clinging. They are so enmeshed that it is difficult for them to appreciate the possibility of another sort of happiness beyond those sensual pleasures which are so familiar. Talk of meditation, the practical method of achieving a higher happiness, will be unintelligible to them.

Vipassanā practice is a full and continuous attention to the object. This involves two aspects of concentration, vitakka and vicāra: aiming and rubbing, discussed above. These two jhānic factors keep the mind absorbed in the object of noting. If they are absent, the mind will stray. Bombarded by sense objects and kilesas, especially the kilesas of longing for sensual objects, the mind will be engulfed by delusion and ignorance. There will be no light, no chance for the remaining three jhānic factors to assemble with the first two to create the environment of peace, clarity and joy where insight blossoms.

*The Five Hindrances*

The five specific ways in which the mind strays from its object are called the five hindrances. Of the seemingly endless variety of kilesas, the hindrances represent the five major types. They are labeled "hindrances" because each of them has a particular power to obstruct and impede our practice.

As long as the mind is seduced by temptations of the senses, it cannot remain steadily observing a meditation object. Drawn away time and again, it will never travel that path of practice which leads beyond ordinary happiness. Thus, *kāmacchanda,* or sensual desire, is the first and greatest hindrance to our practice.

For an object to be distracting in an unpleasant way is another frequent occurrence. Upon contact with an unpleasant object, the mind fills with *vyāpāda,* aversion or anger. This too leads the mind away from the object, and so also away from the direction of true happiness.

At other times alertness and vigilance vanish. The mind becomes drowsy, unworkable and sluggish. Once again, it cannot stay with the object. This is called thina middha, sloth and torpor. It is third on the list of hindrances.

Sometimes the mind becomes very frivolous and dissipated, flirting with one object and then another. This is called *uddhacca kukkucca,* restlessness and worry. The mind cannot stay one-pointed on its object but is scattered and dissipated, full of memories of past deeds, remorse and regret, worry and agitation.

The fifth and last major hindrance is *vicikicchā,* skeptical doubt and criticism. Surely you have experienced times when you have doubted yourself, the method of practice or your teachers. You may compare this practice to others you have done or heard about, and you become completely paralyzed, like a traveler at a crossroads who, unsure of the right way, cannot decide which path to take.

The presence of hindrances means that rapture, comfort, one-pointedness of mind, right aim and continuity are lacking. These five wholesome factors are the factors of the first jhāna; they are integral parts of successful vipassanā practice. Each jhānic factor is the antidote for a specific hindrance, and each hindrance is the enemy of a jhānic factor.

### Concentration: The Antidote for Sense Desire

In this sensual world the hindrance of sense desire is chiefly responsible for keeping us in darkness. Concentration, one-pointedness, is its antidote. When your mind is concentrated on the object of meditation, it does not attach itself to other thoughts, nor does it desire pleasant sights and sounds. Pleasurable objects lose their power over the mind. Dispersion and dissipation cannot occur.

### Rapture: The Antidote for Aversion

As concentration takes the mind to more subtle levels, deep interest arises. Rapture and joy fill one's being. This development frees the mind from the second hindrance, for anger cannot coexist with joy. Thus, the scriptures say that joy and rapture are the antidotes to anger.

### Happiness or Comfort: The Antidote for Restlessness

Now, with meditation well developed, a great sense of comfort can begin to arise. The mind watches unpleasant sensations peacefully, without aversion. There is ease in the mind, even if the objects are difficult. Sometimes pain even disappears under the influence of mindfulness, leaving behind a sense of physical release. With this physical and mental comfort, the mind is content to remain with the object. It does not fly about. Comfort is the antidote for restlessness and anxiety.

### Aim: The Antidote for Sloth and Torpor

The jhānic factor of vitakka or aim has the specific power to open and refresh the mind. It makes the mind alive and open. Thus, when the mind is continually and diligently trying to be accurate in aiming at the object, sloth and torpor do not arise. A mind attacked by drowsiness is a mind that has been constricted and withered. Vitakka is the antidote to thina middha.

*Continuous Attention or Rubbing: The Antidote for Doubt*

If aim is good, it follows that the mind will hit its target of observation. This impinging or rubbing against the object is the jhānic factor of vicāra, which has the function of continuity, keeping the mind stuck to its object of observation. Continuous attention is the opposite of doubt, for doubt is indecision. The doubting mind cannot fix itself on any particular object; instead it runs here and there considering possibilities. Obviously, when vicāra is present the mind cannot slip from the object and behave in this manner.

Immature wisdom also contributes to the spreading of doubt. Without a certain depth and maturity of practice, it is obvious that very profound Dhamma will be obscure to us. Beginning yogis may wonder about things they have heard about but never experienced. But the more they try to think such things through, the less they will understand. Frustration and continued thinking eventually lead to criticism. For this vicious cycle continuous attention is again the antidote. A mind firmly stuck to its object uses all its power to observe; it does not generate critical thoughts.

COMPREHENDING THE NATURE OF THIS WORLD

When you can keep your attention on the rising and falling from the very beginning of its occurrence to the very end, developing that penetrative, accurate mindfulness from moment to moment in an unbroken and continuous manner, then you may come to notice that you can see clearly with your mind's eye the entire rising process. From its beginning, through the middle, to the end, there is not a single gap. The experience is utterly clear to you.

You now begin to move through the progression of insights that is only available through vipassanā meditation, direct observation of mind and body. First you make the subtle distinction between the mental and physical elements constituting the rising and falling processes. Sensations are material objects, distinct from the consciousness that perceives them. As you observe more carefully, you begin to see how mind and matter are mutually connected, causally linked. An intention in the mind causes the appearance of a series of physical objects constituting a movement. Your mind starts to appreciate how mind and matter come into being and disappear. The fact of arising and vanishing comes into crystal focus. It becomes obvious that all objects in your field of consciousness have the nature to come and go. Sounds begin and then they end. Sensations in the body arise and then dissolve. Nothing lasts.

At this point in practice, there begins to be a strong presence of all five factors of the first jhāna, discussed above. Aiming and impinging, vitakka and vicāra, have strengthened. Concentration, rapture and comfort join them. The first vipassanā jhāna is said to be complete, and vipassanāñāṇa or vipassanā insight knowledge can begin to arise.

Vipassanā insight knowledge is concerned specifically with the three general characteristics of conditioned phenomena: *anicca* (pronounced "anicha"), or impermanence; *dukkha* (pronounced duke-ka) unsatisfactoriness or suffering; and *anatta* or absence of an abiding self.

## Anicca: Impermanence

As you watch objects come and go, you will begin to appreciate their momentary nature, their impermanence. This knowledge of anicca is direct, first-hand; you feel its truth anywhere you place your attention. During the moment your mind is in contact with the object, you see clearly how the object dissolves. A great sense of satisfaction arises. You feel a deep interest in your meditation, and rejoice at having discovered this fact and truth about the universe.

Even simple and general observation tells us that the whole body is anicca, or impermanent. Therefore the term anicca refers to the whole body. Looking closer, we see that all phenomena which occur at the six sense doors are anicca; they are impermanent things. We can also understand anicca to mean all the impermanent things comprising mind and matter, mental and physical phenomena. There is no object we can find in this conditioned world that is not anicca.

The fact of arising and falling away is *anicca lakkhaṇa*, the characteristic or sign of impermanence. It is precisely in the arising and passing that anicca can be recognized. *Aniccā-nupassanā-ñāṇa* is the intuitive comprehension which realizes the fact of impermanence; it occurs in the very moment of noting a particular object and watching it dissolve. It is important to make this point, that *aniccā-nupassanā-ñāṇa* only can occur in the precise moment when one sees the passing away of a phenomenon. In the absence of such immediate seeing, then, it is impossible to understand impermanence.

Would one be justified in saying that one has had an insight into impermanence through reading about the impermanent state of things? Can one say an insight has occurred at the moment when one's teacher says that all things pass away? Or can one deeply understand impermanence through deductive or inductive reasoning? The answer to these questions is a firm "No." True insight only occurs in the presence of a nonthinking, bare awareness of the passing away of phenomena in the present moment.

Say you are watching the rising and falling of the abdomen. In the moment of rising, you may be aware of tautness, tenseness, expansion and movement. If you can follow the rising process from beginning to end, and the ending of these sensations is clear to you, it is possible for *aniccā-nupassanā-ñāṇa* to occur. All sensations that can be felt at the abdomen or anywhere else are anicca, impermanent things. Their characteristics, of having appeared at the beginning of the rising process and having disappeared at the end, constitute anicca lakkhaṇa. The realization that they are impermanent can only occur in a moment when one is observing their disappearance.

Impermanence is not confined to one's abdomen. Everything that occurs in seeing, hearing, smelling, tasting, thinking, touching – all the sensations of the body, heat and cold and hardness and pain – and all of one's miscellaneous activities – bending, turning, reaching out, walking – all these things are impermanent. If you can see the vanishing of any of these objects, you will be involved in aniccanupassana-ñāṇa. You will lose the illusion of permanence. *Māna* or conceit also will be absent. In fact, during times when you are mindfully aware of impermanence, your general level of conceit will progressively diminish.

### Dukkha: Suffering or Unsatisfactoriness

The second characteristic of conditioned reality is dukkha, suffering or unsatisfactoriness. It can be discussed under the same three categories: dukkha, *dukkha lakkhaṇa* and *dukkhā-nupassanā-ñāṇa*.

During your observation of anicca, very naturally the factor of suffering will also become apparent. As phenomena arise and pass, you will realize that nothing is dependable and there is nothing fixed to cling to. Everything is in flux, and this is unsatisfactory. Phenomena provide no refuge. Dukkha itself is actually a kind of synonym for impermanence, referring to all impermanent things. Whatever is impermanent also is suffering.

At this point of development in meditation practice, painful sensations can become very interesting. One can observe them for some time without reacting. One sees that they are not solid at all; they do not actually last more than the briefest instant. The illusion of continuity begins to crumble. A pain in the back: one sees fiery heat transform itself into pressure, and then into throbbing. The throbbing changes its texture, its shape and intensity moment by moment. Finally, a climax occurs. The mind is able to see the breakup and disintegration of that pain. Pain vanishes from the field of consciousness.

Conquering the pain, one is filled with joy and exhilaration. The body feels cool, calm, comfortable, yet one is not deluded into thinking that suffering has been abolished. The unsatisfying nature of sensations becomes ever more clear. One begins to see this body as a mass of painful and unsatisfactory phenomena, dancing without respite to impermanence's tune.

The characteristic of dukkha, or dukkha lakkhaṇa, is oppression by impermanence. Precisely because all objects arise and pass away from moment to moment, we live in a highly oppressive situation. Once arising has occurred, there is no way to prevent passing away.

Dukkhā-nupassanā-ñāna, the insight that comprehends suffering, also occurs at the moment when one is contemplating the passing away of phenomena, but it has a different flavor from aniccā-nupassanā-ñāna. One is suddenly seized by a great realization that none of these objects is dependable. There is no refuge in them; they are fearsome things.

Again it is important to understand that the appreciation of suffering we gain through reading books, or through our own reasoning and reflection, does not constitute the real thing. Dukkhā-nupassanā-ñāna only occurs when the mind is present with bare awareness, watching the arising and passing away of phenomena, and understanding that their impermanence is fearful, fearsome, undesirable and bad.

The true realization that suffering is inherent in all phenomena can be very powerful. It eliminates the deluded view that these things are pleasurable. When such an illusion vanishes, craving cannot arise.

### Anatta: The Absence of Self

Automatically now, one appreciates anatta, that no one is behind these processes. Moment to moment, phenomena occur; this is a natural process with which one is not identified. This wisdom relating to the absence of self in things, *anattā-nupassanā-ñāna*, also is based on two preceding aspects, anatta itself and *anatta lakhana*.

Anatta refers to all impermanent phenomena which possess no self-essence – in other words, every single element of mind and matter. The only difference from anicca and dukkha is that a different aspect is being highlighted.

The characteristic of anatta, anatta lakkhana, is seeing that an object does not arise or pass according to one's wishes. All the mental and physical phenomena that occur in us come and go of their own accord, responding to their own natural laws. Their occurrence is beyond our control.

We can see this in a general way by observing the weather. At times it is extremely hot, at other times freezing cold. At times it is wet, at other times dry. Some climates are fickle, such that one does not know what will happen next. In no climate can one adjust the temperature to suit one's comfort. Weather is subject to its own natural laws, just like the elements that constitute our minds and bodies. When we fall ill, suffer, and eventually die, are these processes not contrary to our wishes?

While conscientiously watching all the mental and physical phenomena arising and passing away within, one may be struck by the fact that no one is in control of the process. Such an insight comes quite naturally. It is not affected or manipulated in any way. Nor does it come from reflection. It simply occurs when one is present, observing the passing away of phenomena. This is called anattā-nupassanā-ñāṇa.

When one is unable to see the momentary arising and passing away of phenomena, one is easily misled to think that there is a self, an individual unchanging entity behind the process of body and mind. With clear awareness, this false view is momentarily eliminated.

*Verified Knowledge by Comprehension: The Fulfillment of the First Vipassanā Jhāna*

When awareness is clear, especially when the passing away of things is noticeable, one can appreciate intuitively the characteristics of impermanence, of suffering, or of absence of self that are inherent in all phenomena. The intuitive understanding of all three of these characteristics is included in a particular stage of insight, *sammasanañāṇa*, meaning the insight that arises out of verification. Often this term is translated as "verified knowledge by comprehension." One comprehends or verifies the three characteristics through a personal experience of seeing the disappearance of phenomena.

Though it is very commonly used, the word "insight" may not be an appropriate translation of the Pāli word vipassanā. The word vipassanā has two parts, *vi* and *passanā*. *Vi* refers to various modes, and *passanā* is seeing. Thus, one meaning of vipassanā is "seeing through various modes."

These various modes, of course, are those of impermanence, suffering and absence of self. A more complete translation of vipassanā now becomes "Seeing through the modes of impermanence, suffering, and absence of self."

Another synonym for vipassanāñāna is *paccakkha-ñāna*. Paccakkha here refers to direct experiential perception. Because true vipassanāñāna only arises when one is mindful, because it occurs intuitively rather than from reasoning, it is called a direct experiential insight, paccakkha-ñāna.

As vipassanāñāna recurs in one's practice, the mind is led into a natural and spontaneous reflection that impermanence, suffering and nonselfness are not only manifest in the present situation. One realizes by deduction that these three qualities have also manifested throughout the past and will continue to prevail in the future. Other beings and objects are constituted of the same elements as oneself, all impermanent, unsatisfactory and empty of self-nature. This reflection is called deductive knowledge, and it is a further aspect of the jhānic factors of vitakka and vicāra, manifesting in this case on the thinking level.

At this stage the first vipassanā jhāna is considered to be fully developed, and the stage of practice called "verified knowledge by comprehension," sammasanañāna, is fulfilled. One has a deep and clear appreciation of the three general characteristics of conditioned phenomena: anicca, dukkha and anatta. One has reached the deductive conclusion that in this world there never has been, nor will there ever be, a situation that is not pervaded by these three aspects.

Deduction and reflection tend to be present in the first vipassanā jhāna. They are harmless unless they begin to take over one's mind. Especially in the case of a person who is highly intellectual, who has a vivid imagination or is philosophically bent, too much reflection can get in the way of personal and direct experience. It can actually put a stop to insight.

If one is this kind of person and finds one's practice somewhat undermined, one can console oneself with the knowledge that this is not wrong thinking. In this instance, reflection is connected with the Dhamma rather than with greed or aversion. Despite this fact, of course, one should make the effort to return to bare observation, simply experiencing phenomena.

*Wholesome and Unwholesome Vitakka*

The word vitakka, used for the jhānic factor of accurate aim, includes this reflection on a thinking level, directing one's attention toward a thought. There are wholesome and unwholesome kinds of vitakka.

Directing one's attention toward sense pleasures is said to be unwholesome vitakka. Its wholesome counterpart is vitakka connected with renunciation. Vitakka connected with aversion and aggression is unwholesome. Vitakka connected with nonaversion and with nonviolence is wholesome.

When deductive knowledge of anicca, dukkha and anatta arises as explained above, the vitakka connected with sensual pleasures is absent. In the series of thoughts that come out of direct personal insight, some desire may be present, but it probably will not be concerned with the pleasures of this world – fame, sex, wealth, property. More likely one will feel a very wholesome desire to renounce the world or to be generous or to spread the Dhamma. Though these thoughts constitute vitakka or reflection, they are connected with nongreed or renunciation.

Vitakka connected with anger is an aggressive state of mind, in which one desires that another person suffer harm and misfortune. Rooted in anger, it has a destructive quality behind it. Nonaversion or nonhatred refers to the lovely quality of mettā, loving kindness. In contrast to the aggressive, destructive quality of hatred, mettā wishes the welfare and happiness of others. When one has tasted the flavor of the Dhamma through personal experiences as mentioned above, it is not unusual to want to share it with loved ones. You want others to have the same experience. This kind of thought is connected with metta, for it wishes the well-being of others.

The last path of vitakka is connected with causing harm. It has two branches: cruel thought and noncruel thought. A cruel thought contains the desire to harm, oppress, torture or torment or kill other beings. It is another very destructive quality of the mind rooted in hatred. Noncruelty, on the other hand, is the quality of compassion or *karuṇā*, wanting to help others and to relieve them of any suffering or distress they may feel. One who has strong compassion will not only feel it emotionally, but will also seek ways and means to relieve the suffering of others.

## Vicāra as Reflective Knowledge

If such reflective thoughts recur again and again, this process takes the name of vicāra. This is the same word used for the more sustained, rubbing aspect of focused attention. Here it means repeated reflection on the thinking level. First one experiences a direct intuitive insight; and afterwards, deductive knowledge arises concerning the insight. Deductive knowledge is spicy and enjoyable, but in excess it develops into long trains of thought which interrupt the process of direct observation. These may be very noble thoughts – of renunciation, metta and compassion – but nonetheless one is caught by them and carried away. At this time insight cannot occur.

May you strongly generate those two very important mental factors, vitakka and vicāra, in your practice. May you aim the mind carefully and rub the object thoroughly until you see it clearly and penetrate its true nature. May you not be sidetracked even by wonderful thoughts. Thus you will go through the various stages of insight and eventually realize nibbāna.

### REACHING THE HIGHER VIPASSANĀ JHĀNAS

The first vipassanā jhāna operates up to the point where a yogi attains the insight into the rapid arising and passing away of phenomena. Experiencing this insight and going beyond it, a yogi grows up, as it were.

### The Second Vipassanā Jhāna

He or she leaves behind the childhood of reflective thinking and enters the maturity of simple, bare attention.

Now the meditator's mind becomes lucid and sharp. He or she is able to follow the very fast rate at which phenomena appear and disappear from moment to moment. Because of the continuity and sharpness of mindfulness, there is little discursive thinking. Nor is there doubt about the impermanent, momentary nature of mind and matter. At this time, the practice seems effortless. In the absence of effortful application and reflective thought, there is space for joy and rapture. This nonthinking, bare attention is called the second vipassanā jhāna.

In the first vipassanā jhāna, then, the mind is congested with effort and discursive thinking. It is only when the second vipassanā jhāna arises at the beginning of insight into the arising and passing away of phenomena that clarity, rapture, faith and great comfort begin to predominate.

### The Danger of Faith, Calm, Rapture and Happiness

The mind is able to become more precise, and concentration deepens. This deepened concentration leads to the clear, verified faith that arises from personal experience. It also brings believing faith, faith that if one continues the practice one will gain the benefits promised by the Buddha and by one's teachers. Rapture, mental and physical comfort also become strong at this stage. When yogis attain the second vipassanā jhāna there is a strong likelihood that they will become attached to these extraordinarily pleasant states of mind. They experience the deepest happiness of their lives. Some may even believe they have become enlightened. In such a case, the prospect of further progress grows dim. Yogis will have done what the Buddha called "stopping within," which I discussed earlier.

If you have extraordinary experiences, please make it a point to note and label them. Be clearly aware that rapture, faith, tranquility and so forth are no more than mental states. If while noting them you realize that you are attached to them, cut the attachment immediately and return your attention to the primary object at the abdomen. Only then will your progress continue, and it will bring you even sweeter fruit.

Meditation teachers have to be tactful in dealing with students who are in this stage of practice. The students are so excited by their experiences that they tend to rebel if the teacher is too deflating. Instead, one might gently say, "Your practice is not bad. These are natural things which arise in practice, but there are many other experiences which are much better than what you have now. So why don't you note all these things so you can experience the better ones?"

Paying heed to these instructions, the yogi returns to sitting and carefully notes the lights, faith, rapture, happiness, tranquility and comfort. It dawns on him or her that this simple noting actually is the correct path of practice.

Thus oriented, he or she can proceed with great confidence.

### The Arising of the Third Vipassanā Jhāna

Rapture will gradually fade, but mindfulness and concentration will continue to deepen. Then insight into the true nature of what is happening will become very strong. At this point, the enlightenment factor of upekkhā, equanimity, becomes predominant. The mind remains unshaken by pleasant objects as well as unpleasant ones, and a deep sense of comfort arises in the body and mind. Yogis can sit for long hours without pain, and their bodies become pure, light and robust. This is the third vipassanā jhāna, whose two jhānic factors are comfort and one-pointedness of mind. The third jhāna arises at a more mature stage of the insight into arising and passing away.

The transition from the second jhāna to the third is a critical turning point in practice. Human beings have a natural attachment to thrills and excitement which agitate the mind. Rapture is one of these agitating pleasures; it creates ripples in the mind. It is rather adolescent, though. So when you experience it, be certain to increase your vigilance and note as meticulously as you can. As long as a yogi remains attached to rapture, he or she will not move forward into the more mature, subtle happiness that comes with peace and comfort.

### The Climax of Happiness

The scriptures illustrate this transition with the story of a mother cow who is suckling her calf. It is important to wean the calf early, so that the cow's milk can be used by human beings. If the calf is not weaned, it will constantly drink up all the cow's milk. This calf is like the second jhāna which feeds and thrives on pīti or rapture. The mother cow might be the third jhāna, and the person who is able to drink the sweet, fresh milk is like a yogi who has successfully gone beyond his or her attachment to rapture.

The happiness or comfort that can be tasted in this third vipassanā jhāna is said in the scriptures to be the peak or climax of happiness that can be experienced in vipassanā practice. It is the sweetest. Nevertheless, the yogi can dwell in it with equanimity and without attachment.

To continue noting precisely remains crucial, lest the comforts of mind and body, the sharpness and clarity of insight, give rise to a subtle attachment. If you feel that your insight is fantastic, sharp and clear, you should note this. However, attachment is less likely to arise, since a comprehensive, panoramic mindfulness is present which notes each object easily and without slipping.

### Dissolution of Phenomena: The Comfort Disappears

The third jhāna is called the climax of happiness because there is no more happiness in the next jhāna. As you note phenomena, you will gradually pass beyond the stage of insight into arising and passing away into the stage of dissolution of phenomena. At this point the beginnings and the middles of objects are no longer clear. Instead the mind perceives continuous dissolution of phenomena, which disappear as soon as they are noted. Often it seems as if there is no body at all, only bare phenomena dissolving away continuously.

Yogis tend to get distraught and upset, not only because they feel a lack of comfort, but also because the rapid disappearance of phenomena can be quite disconcerting. Before you can note an object, it is gone, leaving empty space. The next phenomenon behaves in the same way.

Concepts become indistinct. Up to now, the yogi may have seen phenomena clearly, but the mental factor of perception, or recognition, was still mixed in. Thus he or she was able to see both the ultimate, nonconceptual reality of objects and also the concept of form: body, arm, leg, head, abdomen and so forth. At the dissolution stage of insight, concepts fall away. You may be unable to tell where the phenomena are located; there is only disappearance.

"What happened?" you may cry. "I was doing so well, and now my practice is falling apart. It's out of control. I can't note a single thing." Self-judgment, dissatisfaction, fill your mind. Obviously there is no comfort.

Eventually it is possible to gain ease in this new space. You can just coolly settle back and watch the continual flow of phenomena. This stage of insight is called "insight into dissolution of phenomena." It has an interesting quality. There is no more physical or mental happiness or ease, nor are there outright discomforts or pains in the body at this time. The feeling in the mind is rather neutral, too.

## The Appearance of the Fourth Vipassanā Jhāna

During the maturation of insight into the arising and passing away of phenomena, the rapture of the second jhāna gave way to the third jhāna factor of comfort. The outrageous pleasure of rapture was replaced by milder and subtler feelings of comfort and peace. As comfort disappears in the dissolution stage of insight, it still does not incur mental displeasure. Now the third jhāna gives way to the fourth, whose characteristic jhāna factors are equanimity and one-pointedness of mind.

*Insight into Equanimity Regarding All Formations*

With a mind that is neither pleased nor displeased, comfortable nor uncomfortable, upekkhā or equanimity arises. Upekkhā has a tremendous power to balance the mind. In this particular aspect, it is known as *tatramajjhattatā*. In this environment of balance, mindfulness can become perfectly pure, keen and sharp. Subtle aspects of phenomena can be seen with incredible and uninterrupted clarity as particles and tiny vibrations. In fact, tatramajjhattatā is present in each of the jhānas from the beginning. Yet in the first, second and third jhānas, it is hidden by more assertive qualities, like the moon in daylight which cannot compete with the sun.

*Summary of the Four Vipassanā Jhānas*

In the first jhāna, balance is quite undeveloped. Predominant instead are vitakka and vicāra, aiming and rubbing, or initial application and sustained application. As discussed above, the vitakka and vicāra of the first jhāna often include large amounts of discursive thinking.

In the second jhāna, the thrills and chills of rapture overshadow equanimity. Come the third jhāna, there is the sweetest happiness and comfort, so that balance has no chance to show itself. When comfort evaporates, however, bringing about that feeling which is neither pleasant nor unpleasant, then balance has a chance to shine. In just this way, when dusk sets in and darkness begins to thicken, the moon reigns splendidly over all the sky.

After the insight into dissolution come successive insights into fear, disgust, and wanting to be liberated. Equanimity is not strongly shown until the stage of insight known as "equanimity regarding all formations."

This is a deep level of practice where things begin to move very smoothly. Mindfulness is so agile now that it picks up the objects before the mind can begin to be perturbed by pleasantness or unpleasantness. There is no chance for attachment or aversion to arise. Objects which normally are very unpleasant lose their influence completely, as do thrilling and exciting objects. Because this is true at all six sense doors, the kind of equanimity now present is known as "six-limbed equanimity."

A great subtlety of awareness is another feature of this time in practice. The rising and falling process becomes a vibration. It breaks into particles and may eventually disappear. If this happens, you should try to look at the sitting posture as a whole and perhaps some touch points such as buttocks and knees. These, too, may disappear, leaving behind no perception of the body whatsoever. Sickness and pains disappear, for no physical phenomena remain to be perceived, no itches left to scratch. What remains is only the consciousness which knows the absence of physical phenomena. At such a time, this consciousness itself should be taken as the object of knowing. As you note, "knowing, knowing," even that consciousness can begin to flicker and reappear. Yet, at the same time, there will be clarity of mind and extreme sharpness.

This state of extreme mental balance is said to be like the mind of an arahant, which remains unshakable in the face of any object capable of arising in the field of consciousness. However, even if you have attained this stage of practice, you still are not an arahant. You are only experiencing a mind similar to an arahant's during this particular moment of mindfulness.

Each of the four vipassanā jhānas is characterized by a distinct type of happiness. In the first vipassanā jhāna, one can experience the happiness of seclusion. The hindrances are kept away, and so the mind is remote and secluded from them.

In the second jhāna, one experiences the happiness of concentration. Good concentration brings happiness in the form of rapture and comfort. As rapture is abandoned, the happiness of the third jhāna is simply known as the happiness of equanimity.

Finally in the fourth jhāna, we experience the purity of mindfulness due to equanimity.

The fourth type is the best happiness, of course. Like the first three, however, it still occurs in the realm of conditioned phenomena. Only if the yogi transcends this realm can he or she experience the ultimate happiness, the happiness of real peace. This is called *santisukha* in Pāli. It occurs when the objects of meditation and all other mental and physical phenomena, as well as the noting mind itself, come to a complete stop.

I hope that you will be able to taste all four kinds of happiness that arise through the vipassanā jhānas, and also that you will go on to taste the highest happiness, the happiness of nibbāna.

ON NIBBĀNA

*Confusion about Nibbāna*

There has been a lot of discussion about the nibbānic experience. Whole books have been written about it. Some people think that nibbānic happiness refers to a special sort of physical or mental state. Some believe it exists in one's body. Others say that when mind and matter are extinguished, what remains behind is the essence of eternal bliss.

Some may be filled with doubt. They say, "If nibbāna is the extinguishing of mind and matter, how can there be anything left to experience?" It is hard to think of happiness that is not experienced through the senses. This entire discussion, moreover, will be Greek to people who have no experience of meditation.

In fact, only a person who has experienced nibbāna for herself or himself will be able to speak of it with conviction. Nonetheless, there are also inferential ways to speak of it, which will seem quite familiar to anyone whose practice has deepened to the extent of having had the nibbānic experience.

Some people think that nibbāna is some special kind of mind or matter, but this is not so. There are four kinds of what are called in Pāli the paramattha dhammas, which we mentioned above, the realities that can be experienced directly without any conceptualization or thinking. These four are material phenomena, two kinds of mental phenomena – consciousness itself, plus the other mental factors that occur with each moment of consciousness – and nibbāna. Thus nibbāna is defined as being different from matter and also from mind.

A second mistaken notion is that nibbāna is what is left behind when mind and matter are extinguished. Nibbāna is the source of ultimate reality, and it is classified as an external phenomenon rather than an internal one. As such, it has nothing to do with anything that might remain in one's body after the mind and body process has been extinguished.

Nibbāna cannot be experienced in the same way that, say, visual objects or sounds can be experienced, through the senses. It is not a sensual object. Therefore it cannot be included in any category of sensate (or sense-based) pleasures, no matter how extraordinary. It is nonsensate happiness, not based on the senses.

Arguments about the nature of nibbāna have been going on since the Buddha's time. It seems there was an abbot of a monastery who was discussing nibbānic bliss before an audience of bhikkhus. One of the bhikkhus stood up and said, "If there is no sensation in nibbāna, how can there be bliss?"

The elder answered, "My friend, it is precisely because there is no sensation in nibbāna that it is so blissful." This answer is almost like a riddle. I wonder what you think the answer is. If you cannot find an answer, I will be happy to give one to you.

### Disadvantages of the Senses

First, we must talk about sensate pleasure. It is fleeting. Happiness is here one moment and gone the next. Is it really so enjoyable to go around hunting for something so ephemeral, which is changing all the time?

Look at the amount of trouble you have to go through to get all those novel experiences you think will bring happiness. Some people have such strong desire for pleasure that they will even break the law, commit atrocious crimes and cause others to suffer just so they can experience these fleeting sense-based pleasures. They may not understand how much suffering they themselves will have to endure in the future as a consequence of the unwholesome acts they have committed. Even ordinary people who are not criminals may become aware that a disproportionate amount of suffering is necessary to bring together a few moments of happiness, so much that it really is not worth it.

Once one has begun to practice meditation, sources of happiness become available that are more refined, more enjoyable, than mere sense pleasures. As we have seen, each of the vipassanā jhānas brings its own kind of joy. The first jhāna brings the happiness of seclusion; the second, the happiness of concentration, which consists of intense rapture and joy. The third jhāna brings a refined contentment, which educates the mind to understand that the happiness of rapture and joy actually is rather coarse. Last and deepest, the happiness of equanimity that is discovered in the fourth vipassanā jhāna has the nature of stillness and peace. All these four are known as *nekkhamma sukha*, the happiness of renunciation.

However, the peace and happiness to be found in nibbāna is superior to both the happiness of renunciation as well as that of sense pleasures. It also is quite distinct from all of them in nature. The happiness of nibbāna occurs upon the cessation of mind and matter. It is the peace of the extinction of suffering. It is independent of contact with the six kinds of sense objects. In fact, it arises because there is no contact at all with sense objects.

People whose idea of happiness is to take a vacation, go on a picnic and swim in a lake, people who use their free time just to attend parties or barbecues, these people may not understand how happiness could arise when there is no experience at all. As far as they are concerned, there can be beauty only when they have eyes to see it, a lovely object to look at, and the consciousness to be aware of sight, and similarly with the other senses. They might say, "If there is fragrance but no nose and no consciousness of smell, where can I find delight?" They may find it impossible to imagine how anyone could contrive of such a horrid thing as nibbāna. They might reason that nibbāna is a kind of secret death, something really horrendous. Human beings become intensely frightened at the prospect of annihilation.

Other people doubt that nibbāna can exist. They say, "This is a poet's dream." Or they say, "If nibbāna is nothing, how can it be better than a beautiful experience?"

### Indescribable Bliss: A Sleeping Millionaire

Let us imagine that there is a multi-millionaire or million-airess who has available to him or her all the imaginable sense pleasures. One day this person is having a nice, sound sleep. While he or she is sleeping, the chef has been at work, cooking an array of delicious food and arranging it on the table. Everything is quite in order in the full splendor of the millionaire's mansion.

Now the chef becomes impatient. The food is getting cold and the chef wants the owner of the house to come down and eat. Let us say that the chef sends the butler to wake up the millionaire. What do you think? Will the millionaire leap joyfully from bed and come down to eat, or does the butler run the risk of being clobbered?

When this millionaire is in a deep, sound sleep, he or she is blissfully oblivious to the surroundings. No matter how beautiful the bedroom, he or she does not see it. No matter how beautiful the music that is piped throughout the house, he or she is deaf to it. Fine fragrance may waft through the air, but he or she is oblivious to it. He or she is not eating, that is clear. And no matter how comfortable and luxurious the bed may be, he or she is completely unaware of the sensation of lying upon it.

You can see that there is a certain happiness in sound sleep which is not connected with sensate objects. Anyone, rich or poor, may wake up from sound sleep and feel wonderful. One may gather, then, that some sort of happiness exists in that sleep. Though it is difficult to describe, it cannot be denied. In the same way, the noble ones who have touched the fulfilment of Dhamma know of a kind of happiness that can neither be denied nor fully described, but which we know by deductive reasoning actually exists.

Supposing it were possible to have deep, sound sleep forever. Would you want it? If one does not like the kind of happiness that comes with sound sleep, it may be difficult to have a preference for nibbāna. If one does not want the happiness of nonexperience, one is still attached to the pleasure of the senses. This attachment is due to craving. It is said that craving actually is the root cause of sense objects.

### The Root of All Trouble

Suffering will always follow craving. If we care to look closely at the situation on this planet, it will not be difficult to see that all the problems in this world are rooted in the desire for sense-based pleasures. It is on account of the continual need to experience these pleasures that families are formed. Members of the family have to go out and toil through the day and night to get money to support themselves. It is on account of the need for pleasure that quarrels occur within the family, that neighbors do not get along well, that towns and cities are at loggerheads, that states have conflict, that nations go to war. It is on account of sense-based pleasures that all these hosts of problems plague our world, that people have gone beyond their humanness into great cruelty and inhumanity.

### Singing the Praises of Nonexperience

People may say, "We are born as human beings. Our heritage is the whole field of sense pleasures. What is the point of practicing for nibbāna which is the annihilation of all these pleasures?"

To such people one might ask a simple question. Would you be prepared to sit down and watch the same movie again and again and again throughout the day? How long can you listen to the sweet voice of your loved one without interruption? What happened to the joy that you got from listening to that sweet voice? Sense pleasures are not so special that we do not need a rest from them sometimes.

The happiness of nonexperience or nonsensate experience far exceeds the happiness that comes through sense pleasures. It is much more refined, much more subtle, much more desirable.

In fact, deep sleep is not exactly the same as nibbāna! In sleep, what is occurring is the life continuum, a very subtle state of consciousness with a very subtle object. It is because of the subtlety of the object that sleep seems to be nonexperience. In fact, the nonsensate happiness of nibbāna is a thousand times greater than what is experienced in the deepest sleep.

Due to their great appreciation for nonexperience, non-returners and arahants continually resort to *nirodha samāpatti*, the great cessation attainment, whereby neither matter, mind, mental factors, nor even that most subtle form of matter, mind-borne matter, occur. When the non-returners and arahants emerge from this state, they sing the praises of nonexperience.

Here is part of their song: "How wonderful it is to have this suffering of mind and matter extinguished in nibbāna. When all sorts of suffering connected with mind and matter are extinguished, one can deduce that the opposite will occur, that there is happiness. So in the absence of suffering we noble ones rejoice, so blissful is nibbāna. Happy is nibbāna as it is free from suffering."

### The Nibbāna of the Buddhas

Who was it that showed us the path to this great happiness? The Lord Buddha. This is a nibbāna which has been pro-claimed by all enlightened Buddhas. In Pāli, the Buddha is called *sammā sambuddha*. *Sammā* means perfectly, correctly, rightly, and the Buddha is unique in that he understood the true nature of things as they really are. The truth is true, yet what is known of it may be incorrect and wrong. The Buddha made no such mistakes. The prefix *sam-* means personal, by oneself; and Buddha means enlightened. The Buddha was enlightened by his own efforts. He did not receive his attainment from superbeings, nor did he depend on any other person. So, the nibbāna we are talking about is the one proclaimed by the sammā sambuddha, the per-fectly self-enlightened one.

*Freedom from Sorrow*

Another characteristic of nibbāna is that it is free from sorrow. Most of you are familiar with sorrow. Imagine how wonderful it would be to be free from it. Nibbāna is called *virāga* in Pāli. This means free from dust and pollution. Dust as we normally know it makes things dirty and unpleasant. It may damage clothing and health. Far more lethal is the pollution of the kilesas! How often our minds are bombarded by this constant stream of greed, hatred, delusion, pride, conceit, jealousy, miserliness. In such a state, how can one expect the mind to be clean, pure and clear? In contrast, nibbāna is completely free of the kilesas.

*Perfect Security*

*Khema* or security is another characteristic of nibbāna. In this world we are constantly confronted by dangers. Danger of accident, danger of enemies harming us, danger of poison. In this age of advanced science, we live in constant fear of the weapons of war that have been invented. We would be completely helpless if a war occurred in which nuclear weapons are used. There is no escape from any of this except in nibbāna, which is totally free from all dangers, totally secure.

In the scriptures the nonsensate happiness of nibbāna is called that sort of happiness which is not mixed with kilesas. For people who experience sensate happiness, there is always some degree of greed involved. It is like food which you cook: if you add no spices, it will taste flat and not at all delicious. With spices, though, you can enjoy your food. It is the same with sensate happiness: unless there is greed, lust and desire you will not enjoy an object. Precisely because nibbāna is not mixed with other things, it is called *pārisuddhi sukha*, meaning pristine and pure.

In order for us to experience this pristine happiness, we must first of all cultivate sīla, samādhi and paññā. Continuous effort to purify action, speech and mind will bring your mind to the point where it can enjoy nibbāna. I hope you will be able to work in this direction and attain pristine happiness in due course.

# 6  *Chariot to Nibbāna*

Once, when the Buddha was staying in the Jeta Grove near the ancient city of Sāvatthī in India, he was visited in the wee hours of the night by a deva, come down from the heaven realms with a retinue of a thousand companions.

Although the deva's radiance filled the entire grove, he was nonetheless visibly distraught. He paid his respects to the Buddha and then launched into the following lament:

"O Lord Buddha," he cried, "deva-land is so noisy! It's full of racket from all these devas. They look like *petas* (unhappy ghosts) to me, frolicking in their own land. Confusing it is to be in such a place. Please show me a way out!"

This was an odd speech for a deva to make. The heaven realms are characterized by delight. Their residents, elegant and musically inclined, hardly resemble petas who live in extreme misery and suffering. Some petas are said to have gigantic bellies and pinhole mouths, so that they feel a constant, terrible hunger which they cannot satisfy.

Using his psychic powers, the Buddha investigated the deva's past. He learned that only recently this deva had been a human being, a practitioner of the Dhamma. As a young man he had had such faith in the Buddha's doctrine that he left home to become a bhikkhu. After the required five years under a teacher, he had mastered the rules of conduct and community life and had become self-sufficient in his meditation practice. Then he retired to a forest alone. Because of his tremendous wish to become an arahant, the bhikkhu's practice was extremely strenuous. So as to devote as much time as possible to meditation, he slept not at all and hardly ate. Alas, he damaged his health. Gas accumulated in his belly, causing bloating and knifelike pains. Nonetheless the bhikkhu practiced on single-mindedly, without adjusting his habits. The pains grew worse and worse, until one day, in the middle of a walking meditation, they cut off his life.

The bhikkhu was instantly reborn in the Heaven of the Thirty-Three Gods, one of several deva realms. Suddenly, as if from a dream, he awoke dressed in golden finery and standing at the gates of a glittering mansion. Inside that celestial palace were a thousand devas, dressed up and waiting for him to arrive. He was to be their master. They were delighted to see him appear at the gate! Shouting in glee, they brought out their instruments to entertain him.

Amidst all this, our poor hero had no chance to notice that he had died and been reborn. Thinking that all these celestial beings were no more than lay devotees come to pay him respects, the new deva lowered his eyes to the ground, and modestly pulled up a corner of his golden outfit to cover his shoulder. From these gestures, the devas guessed his situation and cried, "You're in deva-land now. This isn't the time to meditate. It's time to have fun and frolic. Come on, let's dance!"

Our hero barely heard them, for he was practicing sense restraint. Finally some of the devas went into the mansion and brought out a full-length mirror. Aghast, the new deva saw he was a monk no more. There was no place in the entire heaven realm quiet enough to practice. He was trapped.

In dismay he thought, "When I left my home and took robes, I wanted only the highest bliss, arahantship. I'm like the boxer who enters a competition hoping for a gold medal and is given a cabbage instead!"

The ex-bhikkhu was afraid even to set foot inside the gate of his mansion. He knew his strength of mind would not last against these pleasures, far more intense than those of our human world. Suddenly he realized that as a deva he had the power to visit the human realm where the Buddha was teaching. This realization cheered him up.

"I can get celestial riches anytime," he thought. "But the opportunity to meet a Buddha is truly rare." Without a second thought he flew off, followed by his thousand companions.

Finding the Buddha in the Jeta Grove, the deva approached him and asked for help. The Buddha, impressed by his commitment to practice, gave the following instructions:

> O deva, straight is the path you have trodden. It will lead you to that safe haven, free from fear, which is your goal. You shall ride in a chariot that is perfectly silent. Its two wheels are mental and physical effort. Conscience is its back rest. Mindfulness is the armor that surrounds this chariot, and right view is the charioteer. Anyone, woman or man, possessing such a chariot and driving it well, shall have no doubt of reaching nibbāna.

### What is Wrong with a Continuous Party?

This story of the bhikkhu-deva is outlined in the collection of Pāli suttas known as the *Saṁyutta Nikāya*. It illustrates many things about meditation practice. We will examine it step by step. But perhaps the first question you will ask is, "Why would anyone complain about rebirth in a heaven realm?" After all, deva-land is a continuous party, where everyone has a gorgeous, long-lasting body and is surrounded by sensual pleasures.

It may be unnecessary to die and be reborn to understand the deva's reaction. There are heaven realms right on this planet. Is true and permanent happiness to be found in any of them? The United States, for example, is a very advanced country materially. There, a vast array of sense pleasures is available. You can see people intoxicated, drowning, in luxury and pleasure. Ask yourself whether such people think of looking deeper, of making an effort to seek the truth about existence? Are they truly happy?

When he had been a human being, our deva had had utter faith in the Buddha's teaching that the highest bliss is the freedom that comes through Dhamma practice. In search of this happiness beyond the senses, he renounced worldly enjoyments and devoted himself to the life of a bhikkhu. He strove ardently to become an arahant. In fact, he strove too ardently and brought on his own premature death. Suddenly he found himself back at square one – surrounded by the sensual pleasures he had tried to leave behind. Can you understand his feeling of disappointment?

Actually death is nothing very novel. It is just a shift of consciousness. There is no intervening consciousness between the awareness of death and rebirth-consciousness. Unlike humans, moreover, birth for devas is spontaneous and painless.

Therefore, the yogi lost no momentum in his practice between one life and the other. Here again, it is not surprising that he would complain about the noise in devaland. If you have ever practiced deeply, you know how disruptive and painful sound can be at times, either in a sudden burst or as a sustained barrage. Imagine you have just reached a place of quiet and calm in your sitting, and the telephone rings. Instantly your whole hour of samādhi can go to pieces. If this experience has ever happened to you, you might understand this yogi's outburst comparing devas to the unhappy ghosts. When that phone rings, I wonder what sort of curse arises in you, even if a friend is calling!

In the original Pāli, this sutta contains a play on words. The deva had found himself in a heavenly pleasure grove called Nandana Vana, famous for its beauty. In his speech to the Buddha, he renamed it Mohana, from the word *moha*, delusion – a place that creates chaos and confusion in the mind.

### The Way of Renunciation

From a yogi's point of view, surely you can also appreciate the distracting quality of intense pleasure. Perhaps your goal is not arahantship, as this yogi's was – or perhaps it is. Whatever results you expect from your meditation practice, surely you value the concentration and tranquility that meditation brings. To achieve these goals, a certain amount of renunciation is necessary. Each time we sit down to meditate, even for one hour, we renounce the possibility of seeking out an hour's worth of pleasure and distraction. But we find some measure of relief from distraction itself, the suffering of the mind which chases after pleasant feelings. If we go to a longer retreat, we leave behind our home, our loved ones and our pastimes. Yet many of us find these sacrifices worthwhile.

Though he complained of the heavenly conditions, the bhikkhu-deva was not really looking down on the devas' way of life. Much more, he was disappointed in himself for not achieving his goal. It is as if you took a job in hopes of earning $1,000. You work hard, industriously and meticulously, but at the end of the day your task remains unfinished, and you are paid only $50. This would be a letdown. Not that you would despise the $50, but you feel disappointed at not meeting the goal you set for yourself. So, too, this yogi was angry with himself and compared himself to the boxer who had won a cabbage instead of a gold medal. His deva companions understood and were not insulted in the least. In fact, they were intrigued enough to follow him to the earthly realm, where they, too, benefitted from the Buddha's instructions.

If you are well established in Dhamma, your interest in meditation will follow you wherever you go, even into devaland. If not, you will shortly become entangled in the pleasures offered by whatever environment you may inhabit, and that will be the end of your career as a Dhamma pilgrim.

## Establishing Oneself in Practice

Let us investigate how this yogi became established in his practice. Before going alone into the forest, he was dependent on a teacher for five years and lived in community with other bhikkhus. He served the teacher in large and small ways, received meditation instruction, and perfected the Vinaya rules of morality. Each year he sat a three-month Rains retreat and afterwards participated in the traditional ceremony where monks discuss each other's faults in a spirit of loving-kindness and compassion, so that each can correct his own shortcomings.

This man's background is significant for all of us as yogis. Like him, all yogis should strive to fully understand the mechanics of observing the precepts, until purity of conduct is a full and natural part of our lives. We must also be aware of our responsibilities to each other as we live together in this world. We must learn to communicate in ways that are helpful and loving. As for meditation, until we have a high degree of skill, completing the whole series of vipassanā insights, it is also necessary for us to depend on a reliable and competent teacher.

## Distinguishing the Essential from the Superfluous

This bhikkhu had a great virtue: total commitment to the Dhamma, to realizing the truth. For him all else was secondary. Extremely careful to distinguish the essential from the superfluous, he avoided external activities and spent as much time as possible trying to be mindful.

It is good for all of us to limit our responsibilities so that we have more hours for meditation. When at times this is impossible, we can remember the tale of Mother Cow. As you know, cattle are forever busy munching grass; they eat all day. Now, Mother Cow has a pretty young calf who is also quite frisky and mischievous. If she grazes on without a thought for her calf, the calf will surely run off and get into trouble. But if she neglects her own needs and only watches the calf, she will have to graze all night. So, Mother Cow keeps an eye on the calf and grazes at the same time. A yogi who has a job or a task to do should imitate her. Do your work, but keep an eye on the Dhamma. Make sure your mind does not wander off too far!

We know that this bhikkhu was an industrious and ardent yogi. During his waking hours he tried his best to be mindful, as all of us know should be done. The Buddha allowed monks to sleep four hours, through the middle watch of the night. But this bhikkhu's sense of urgency was such that he put his bed aside and did not even think of sleeping. Furthermore, he ate almost nothing, content with his exercise of persistent energy.

I do not suggest that you should stop eating and sleeping. I would like you simply to appreciate his level of commitment. During an intensive meditation retreat it is advisable to sleep as the Buddha instructed, four hours, if one can manage this. More is necessary in daily life, but still it is not good to dull oneself with too much lying in bed. As for food, you should eat to your satisfaction, so that you have sufficient strength for your daily activities and for meditation practice, but not so much that you feel bloated and sleepy. The story of this bhikkhu points out the need to eat, for health, at least a sufficiency of food.

A person who dies in the process of meditation, or while giving a discourse on the Dhamma, can be regarded as a hero or heroine fallen in battle. Our bhikkhu was doing his walking meditation when he was struck down by the sharp knife of wind in his system. He woke up in devaland. And so might you, if you die while meditating, even if you are not enlightened.

Even from a fortunate rebirth, you may wish for an escape route, a way to perfect freedom and safety. During his visit to the heaven realm, the bhikkhu-deva was frightened by his own capacity for desire. If he so much as set foot in the gate of his palace, he realized that his moral precepts might begin to erode. Enlightenment was still his first priority, and for this he needed to keep his virtue intact. He fled to Jeta Grove and blurted out his question.

## The Buddha's Progressive Instructions

The Buddha's response was unusually succinct. Generally he instructed people step by step, beginning with morality, progressing through the right view of kamma and concentration, before he began with insight practice. To illustrate this order of teaching, he once gave the example of an art master. Approached by a neophyte who wants to paint, the master does not just hand out a brush. The first lesson is stretching a canvas. Just as an artist cannot paint in empty air, so it is futile to begin vipassanā practice without a basis in morality and understanding of the law of kamma. Without these two things, there will be no surface, as it were, to receive concentration and wisdom. In some meditation centers, morality and kamma are ignored. Not much can result from meditation under these circumstances.

The Buddha also tailored his instructions to his listeners' backgrounds or propensities. He saw that this unusual deva had been a mature bhikkhu and meditation practitioner, and that he had not broken his moral precepts during that abbreviated stop in the Heaven of the Thirty-Three Gods.

There is a Pāli word, *kāraka*, meaning a dutiful and industrious person. Our bhikkhu had been one of these. He was not a yogi by name only; not a philosopher or a dreamer, lost in ideas and fantasies; nor a sluggard, gazing blankly at whatever objects arose. On the contrary, he was ardent and sincere. The bhikkhu walked the path with total commitment. His profound faith and confidence in the practice supported a capacity for sustained effort. Moment to moment, he tried to put into practice the instructions he had received. One might regard him as a veteran.

## The Direct Route to Freedom

The Buddha gave this committed one a veteran's instructions. "Straight is the path you have trodden," he said. "It will lead you to that safe haven, free from fear, that is your goal." The path in question, of course, was the Noble Eightfold Path. This deva had already begun walking on it, and the Buddha was giving him the go-ahead to continue. Aware, moreover, that the deva wanted to be an arahant in this very life, the Buddha was offering the straight path, straight vipassanā.

The Noble Eightfold Path is very straight indeed. It has no sidetracks. It neither curves, nor bends, nor wriggles. It just leads straight on toward nibbāna.

*The Ten Types of Crooked Behavior*

We can better understand this virtue of straightness by examining its opposite. It is said that there are ten types of unwholesome, or crooked, behavior. A person untamed with respect to these ten actions of body, speech and mind, is seen as crooked in the eyes of the wise. He or she is not honest, not straight, lacks moral integrity.

Crooked bodily behavior is of three kinds. The first is connected with feelings of hatred and aggression. If one lacks mettā and karuṇā, love and compassion, one can easily succumb to such feelings and translate them into actions on a physical level. One might kill, harm or otherwise oppress other beings. Crooked behavior can also stem from greed, which, uncontrolled, leads to stealing or deceitful acquisition of another's property. Sex is the third area of bodily crookedness. A person attacked by lust, interested only in his or her own gratification, may commit sexual misconduct without consideration for another's feelings.

There are four kinds of crooked speech. First, one can lie. Second, one can speak words that cause disharmony, instigating the breakup of friendships or communities. Third, one can speak hurtfully, coarsely and crudely, obscenely. Frivolous chatter is the fourth kind of crooked speech.

On the level of the mind, three types of crookedness are listed. One might think about harming other people. One might covet their property. Or, one can have a wrong view of the law of kamma. Not accepting the law of kamma, believing inconsequential the good or evil one does, is considered an unwholesome attitude. In Buddhism, thinking is considered a form of behavior. Thoughts are very important, since actions proceed from them. Not believing in kamma can lead to acting irresponsibly, creating the conditions for one's own suffering and that of others.

There are other kinds of mental behavior that are unwholesome though not included in this list, such as sloth and torpor, restlessness, and all the myriad subtle permutations of the kilesas. A person subject to these forces is considered to possess a crooked mind.

*Dangers of Walking a Crooked Path*

One who is not free from these inner and outer forms of unwholesome behavior is said to walk a crooked path. He or she cannot expect to arrive at any safe place. He or she is constantly exposed to many kinds of danger.

There is the danger of self-judgment, remorse and regret. One may find a justification for a particular unwholesome action, word or thought, or one might be unaware at first that it is unskillful. Later reflection brings a flood of remorse. One berates oneself, "That was really a stupid thing to do." Remorse is painful, and it is not a feeling anyone else imposes on you. By walking the crooked path, you brought its suffering on yourself. Such an eventuality is fearsome anytime, but it is truly dreadful on one's deathbed. Just prior to death, an uncontrollable stream of consciousness arises, a recollection of one's life and actions. If you have many virtuous and generous actions to remember, your heart will be filled with warmth and calm, and you can die in peace. If you have not been careful in your morality, remorse and regret will overwhelm you. You will think, "Life is so short, and I misused my time. I failed to make full use of the chance to live up to the highest standard of humanity." By then it will be too late to mend your ways. Your death will be a painful one. Some people suffer so greatly at this time that they weep and cry out as they die.

Self-judgment is not the only danger for a person choosing the crooked path. He or she must also contend with the blame and censure of the wise. Good-hearted people do not offer their friendship to the untrustworthy or the violent, nor hold them in high esteem. Unwholesome people end up as misfits, unable to live in society.

Somewhere along the crooked path, you may find yourself crossing swords with the law. If you break the law, the law gets even with you. The police nab you and you will be forced to pay for your misdeeds, with a fine, or a jail sentence, or perhaps even capital punishment, depending on the crime. The world at this present age is filled with violence. Many, many people break the law out of greed, out of hatred, and out of delusion. They do so not just once, but over and over again. There is no limit to the depth to which a person can sink. We read about rampages of killing. When the law finally catches up with such criminals, they may have to pay with their lives. Thus, it is said that one who walks on the crooked path is in danger of punishment.

Of course, if you are intelligent you might get away with a crime and even commit it by legal means. One may indeed avoid punishment at the hands of external authorities, but there is no escape from the self-punishment discussed above. The honest knowledge that you have done wrong is very painful. You are always your own best witness; you can never hide from yourself. Nor is there escape from miserable rebirths, as an animal, in hell realms, as a hungry ghost. Once an act has been committed, kamma has the potential to bear fruit. If the fruit does not ripen in this life, it will follow you until sometime in the future. The crooked path leads to all these kinds of danger.

### The Noble Eightfold Path

No crookedness exists in the Noble Eightfold Path. With its three divisions – morality, concentration, and wisdom – it brings integration, straightness, to every aspect of a human life.

### The Morality Group of the Noble Eightfold Path

*Sammā-vācā* or right speech – literally, thorough or perfect speech, according to the meaning of the prefix sammā – is the first member of what is known as the morality group of the Noble Eightfold Path. This means truthful words, of course. Yet there are further criteria to be met. One's speech should lead to harmony among beings. It should be kind rather than hurtful, pleasant, sweet to the ear and beneficial, not frivolous. Practicing right speech, we are freed from the four types of unwholesome behavior through speech, which were discussed above.

Right action, called *sammākammanta* in Pāli, is the second factor of the morality group. Right action involves restraint.

We must refrain from the three types of immoral behavior manifested through the body: taking life, stealing, and sexual misconduct. The last member of the morality group, *sammā-ājīva* is right livelihood. One's livelihood should be decent, legal and free from any sort of blemish. One should not practice a crooked occupation.

Eliminating crookedness in these three areas, one can easily keep at bay the grossest forms of the kilesas. Kilesas are our enemies. They should be considered and recognized as such. Free from enemies, one is free from danger.

## The Concentration Group of the Noble Eightfold Path

The concentration or samādhi group is the next division of the Noble Eightfold Path. It contains three factors: *right effort*, *right mindfulness* and *right concentration*.

This segment should be familiar to you if you have followed the meditation instructions. When you try to focus attention on the abdomen, this is right effort. It has the power to push aside the kilesas. When right effort is put forth, mindfulness is efficiently activated and will be able to observe the object. Mindfulness, too, acts as a protector. Effort moves the kilesas out of the way, and mindfulness closes the door on them. Now the mind can become focused. Moment to moment it remains with the object: collected, unscattered, calm. This is right concentration.

With these three factors present, we say the samādhi group is well developed. At this time, mental defilement, mental crookedness, is kept at a distance. This samādhi group is directly opposed to crookedness of mind.

## The Wisdom Group of the Noble Eightfold Path

Moment to moment, your mind can become pure and peaceful through your own effort. In one minute you can have sixty moments of a mind free from crookedness. In two minutes you can have one hundred twenty moments. Think how many moments of peace you could activate during an hour, or even an entire day. Every second counts!

In each such moment, you will see that the mind falls directly onto its target, the object of meditation. This is *right aim,* a factor of the Noble Eightfold Path's wisdom group. When the mind is accurately aimed, it sees the object clearly: wisdom will arise. Wisdom's clear seeing, or knowing of phenomena as they really are, constitutes another Noble Eightfold Path factor, *right view.*

If the mind falls precisely on the target, wisdom will arise perceiving the mechanism of conditionality, the cause-and-effect relationship which links mental to physical phenomena. If the mind falls on impermanence, the mind will clearly perceive and know impermanence for what it is. Thus, right aim and right view are linked.

This right view, resulting from right aim, has the power to uproot the seed of the crooked mind. The seed of the crooked mind refers to extremely subtle, latent defilements, which can only be uprooted in wisdom's presence. This is very special. It can only happen in the moment, in a way that is real and practical, not by one's imagination.

Perhaps now you can better appreciate why the Buddha said the path was straight. Crookedness of body, speech and mind are overcome by this threefold training of sīla, samādhi and paññā found in the Noble Eightfold Path. Walking straight along this path, one transcends crookedness and is free from many dangers.

*Nibbāna as Haven and the Path as Haven*

The Buddha further promised the bhikkhu-deva that this straight path leads to a safe haven. The word "haven" is discussed at length in the commentary on this sutta. It actually means nibbāna, where not a single danger, nothing fearful, remains. Old age and death are conquered; the burden of suffering falls. A person who reaches nibbāna is completely protected and can therefore be called "The Fearless," the one without danger.

In order to reach this safe haven of nibbāna we must walk the mundane portion of the Noble Eightfold Path – mundane in the sense that it is not beyond this world. You cannot reach nibbāna except by this route; nibbāna is its culmination.

We talked about the three sections of the path itself: sīla, samādhi and paññā. When one is pure in sīla or conduct, one is free from remorse and from censure by the wise, from punishment by the law, from rebirth in states of woe. If the second group is accomplished, one can be free from the danger of obsessive defilements, those negative tendencies which arise in our hearts and oppress us inwardly. Insight knowledge, arising in the wake of mindfulness and concentration, has the power to overcome latent or subtle kilesas. So even before arriving at the perfect safety of nibbāna, one is protected from fearful things while walking the Noble Eightfold Path. Therefore, this path itself is a haven.

### Kilesas, Kamma and Results: The Vicious Cycle of Samsāra

Kilesas are responsible for the perils of the world. Ignorance, craving and clinging are kilesas. Based on ignorance, dominated by craving, one makes kamma and then must live with the results. Due to our past kammic activities in a sensate realm, we were reborn on this planet, in the body and mind we now possess. That is to say, our present life is the effect of a previous cause. This body and mind, in turn, become the objects of craving and clinging. Craving and clinging create kamma, the conditions to be reborn again – again to crave and cling to bodies and minds. Kilesas, kamma and results are the three elements of a vicious cycle. It is the cycle of samsāra, beginningless. Without meditation practice, it could be endless also.

If not for *avijjā*, ignorance, the cycle could not exist. We suffer first from the ignorance of simply not knowing, not seeing clearly. On top of that is the ignorance of delusion. If we have not practiced deeply, we don't perceive the true characteristics of reality: impermanence, suffering and absence of self. Obscured is the fleeting nature of body and mind, mere phenomena arising and vanishing moment to moment. Disguised is the tremendous suffering we undergo, oppressed by arising and passing away. We do not see that no one controls this process, that no one is behind it, no one at home. If we deeply understood these three characteristics of mind and body, we would neither crave nor cling.

Then, because of delusion, we add illusory elements to reality. We falsely perceive mind and matter as permanent and unchanging. We find joy in possessing this body and mind. And we assume that a permanent self or "I" is in charge of the mind-body process.

These two types of ignorance cause the arising of craving and clinging. Clinging, *upādāna*, is just a solidified form of *taṇhā*, or craving. Desiring pleasant sights, sounds, smells, tastes, touch sensations and thoughts, we crave new objects to come to us. If we get what we want, we cling to it and refuse to let go. This creates the kamma that keeps us bound on the wheel of rebirths.

### Breaking the Cycle of Samsāra

Of course, there are various sorts of kamma. Unwholesome kamma brings about unwholesome results, and it perpetuates our existence in samsāra. While walking on the preliminary part of the Noble Eightfold Path, one need not worry about the negative repercussions of one's actions, since one is avoiding unwholesome deeds. Sīla protects the yogi from suffering in the future. Wholesome kamma brings about happy results even as it, too, propels us through renewed rounds of existence. But during meditation, perpetuating kamma is no longer being created. Simply watching things come and go is wholesome, and more: it does not bring about continual existence in samsāra. In its purest sense, meditation does not produce resultants, called *vipāka* in Pāli. When awareness is precise enough, it prevents the arising of craving, and therefore also the arising of successive links to existence, kamma, birth, old age, and death.

Moment by moment, vipassanā practice breaks through the vicious three-part cycle of kilesas, kamma and results. When effort, mindfulness and stable concentration are activated, precise aim allows consciousness to penetrate into the true nature of existence. One sees things as they are. The light of wisdom dispels the darkness of ignorance. In the absence of ignorance, how will craving arise? If we see clearly the impermanence, suffering, and insubstantiality of things, craving will not arise, and clinging cannot follow. Thus, it is said that not knowing, one clings; but knowing, one is free from clinging. Free from clinging, one creates no kamma, and therefore no results.

Ignorance leads to craving and to clinging both to existence and to the wrong view of the self. Walking the Noble Eightfold Path, you kill the causes of ignorance. If these are absent, even for a moment, there is freedom. The vicious cycle has been shattered. This is the haven of which the Buddha spoke. Free from ignorance, from the dangers of the kilesas, from fearsome kammic activities that may cause suffering in the future, you can enjoy safety and security as long as you are mindful.

Perhaps you feel that this body and mind are so dreadful that you want to get rid of them. Well, you would not be doing yourself any favors by committing suicide. If you really want to be free, you must behave intelligently. It is said that only if the effects are observed can the causes be destroyed. This is not destruction in an active sense. Rather, it is an absence of perpetuating force. Mindfulness destroys the causes that result in a similar mind and body in the future. When the mind is focused with right mindfulness, concentration and aim – watching each object that arises, at its moment of occurrence, at each of the six sense doors – at that moment the kilesas cannot infiltrate. They are quite unable to arise. Since the kilesas are the cause of kamma and rebirth, you sever a link in samsāric existence. There can be no effect in the future if there is no cause now.

Following this Noble Eightfold Path, going through the various stages of vipassanā insight, one eventually arrives at the haven of nibbāna, free from all dangers. There are four stages of nibbānic attainment. In each one, particular kilesas are uprooted forever. The ultimate haven is reached at the final stage of enlightenment, arahantship, when the mind is completely purified.

*Stream Entry: The First Experience of Nibbāna*

At the first experience of nibbāna, the moment of attaining the *sotāpatti magga*, the path consciousness of the stream winner, the three cycles which are connected to states of misery are shattered. One can never again be reborn as an animal, a hungry ghost, or in hell. The kilesas which cause these rebirths are uprooted. One never again performs the kinds of kammic activities that cause rebirth in such states, and past kamma that might have led to such rebirth is rendered ineffective.

At the higher levels of enlightenment, more and more kilesas are uprooted. In the end, at the attainment of the path consciousness of an arahant, there is a total obliteration of kilesas, kamma and resultant. An arahant will never be plagued by these again, and at death will enter the haven of parinibbāna, a nibbāna from which one never reenters samsāra.

You may be encouraged to know that even with the lowest level of enlightenment, you will be free from following a wrong spiritual practice or a crooked path of any kind. This it says in the *Visuddhi Magga*, Buddhaghosa's great work from the fifth century CE, known in English as *The Path of Purification*. As a corollary, you will also be free from self-blame, from censure by the wise; from danger of punishment and of falling into states of misery.

*The Perfectly Silent Chariot*

A worldling who has not yet attained the state of a stream entrant is likened to a traveler undertaking a perilous journey. Many dangers await one who wishes to cross the desert, jungle or forest. He or she must be well equipped. Among the essentials for such a journey is a good and reliable vehicle. The Buddha offered the deva a magnificent option. "You shall ride," he said, "in a chariot that is perfectly silent."

One can imagine that the deva would have found a quiet ride attractive after his recent experiences among the heavenly musicians. But there is additional meaning here.

Most vehicles are noisy. The primitive carts and carriages used in the Buddha's time creaked noisily, especially if they were poorly greased, or were badly made, or carried a heavy load of passengers. Modern cars and trucks still make quite a racket. The chariot the Buddha offered, however, was no ordinary vehicle. It is so well made that it moves without a sound, no matter how many thousands or millions or billions of beings ride upon it. This chariot can carry all of them safely across the ocean, the desert, through the jungle of samsāra. It is the chariot of vipassanā practice, of the Noble Eightfold Path.

When the Buddha was alive, millions of beings became enlightened by simply listening to his discourses. A thousand, or a hundred thousand, or a million beings might be listening to a single discourse. All these beings would cross together at once on the chariot.

The chariot may never creak, but its passengers often make a lot of noise, especially those who reach the farther shore, the safe haven of nibbāna. They cry out in praise and exaltation: "How wonderful is this chariot! I've used it and it works! It brought me to enlightenment."

These are the noble ones, the stream entrants, the once returners, the nonreturners and arahants – those who have attained the four degrees of enlightenment. They sing the chariot's praises in various ways. "My mind has changed completely. It's filled with faith and crystal clarity and spaciousness. Much wisdom can unfold within me. My heart is strong and stable, it faces the vicissitudes of life with resilience."

The noble ones who have been able to enter the jhānas will also sing the praises of this vehicle, as will once returners and arahants who enter into the absorption of cessation. They can experience cessation of mind, mental factors, and all mind-borne phenomena. Arising from such states, they are full of joy and praise for the vehicle.

Normally when a person dies, people grieve and cry out in deep sorrow. There is lamenting, wailing, sadness to see a being leave this world. For an arahant who has uprooted all the imaginable kilesas, however, death is something to look forward to. "At last this mass of suffering can be discarded. This is my last life. I'll have no more confrontation with suffering but only bliss in the haven of nibbāna," he or she can say.

The preciousness of an arahant may be beyond your ability to conceive. But you can know for yourself how an arahant might feel. Look at your own practice. You may have been able to overcome the basic hindrances – craving, aversion, sloth and torpor, restlessness, and doubt – and can see clearly the nature of the object. You may have seen the distinction between mind and matter, or the momentary arising and passing of phenomena. The stage of seeing arising and passing is one of freedom and exhilaration. This joy, this clarity of mind, is the fruit of the practice.

The Buddha said, "For one who has retired to a retreat, for one who has attained the jhānas, there is a joy which arises in him or her which far surpasses the happiness that can be experienced through sensual pleasures either of this human world, or of the world of the devas."

The jhānas here can equally refer either to fixed concentration, or to very deep levels of moment-to-moment concentration developed during the course of insight practice. As we discussed earlier, the latter are called the vipassanā jhānas.

## An Incomparable Flavor

A yogi who can maintain continuous mindfulness will experience deep joy in the practice. There is a flavor of the Dhamma you may not have tasted before. It is incomparable. The first time you taste it you will be filled with wonder. "How wonderful the Dhamma is. It's fantastic. I can't believe how much calm, rapture and joy arise in me." You are filled with faith and confidence, with satisfaction and fulfillment. Your mind starts to think of sharing this experience with others. You may even get ambitious and plan your evangelical campaign. This is the noise in your mind, your song of praise for the ride on the silent chariot.

Another noise is somewhat less enthusiastic. It is the screeching of yogis who ride the chariot without grace or pleasure. They may manage to hang on, but just barely. These are the yogis who do not practice diligently. In vipassanā practice, a puny effort brings measly results. Slack yogis will never get to taste the flavor of the Dhamma. They may hear of others' success. They may see others sitting still and straight, presumably enjoying deep concentration and insight, but they themselves will be swamped by distractions and hindrances. Doubts will creep into their minds: doubts about the teacher, the method, and the chariot itself. "This is a lousy chariot. It won't get me anywhere. The ride is bumpy, and it makes a lot of noise."

Sometimes one might even hear a desperate wail coming from the chariot's direction. This is the cry of yogis who have faith in the practice and are trying hard, but who for one reason or another cannot make as much progress as they wish. They begin to lose confidence. They doubt whether they can reach their goal.

## The More You Lose Your Way, the More Rice You Will Get

In Burma there is a saying to encourage these people. "The more the anagārika loses his way, the more rice he or she gets." An anagārika is a kind of renunciate that exists in Buddhist countries. Such a person takes eight or ten precepts, puts on a white coat and shaves his or her head. Having renounced the world, anagārikas live in monasteries, maintaining the compound and aiding the monks in various ways. One of their duties is to go into town every few days and ask for donations. In Burma, donations often come in the form of uncooked rice. The anagārika goes through the streets shouldering a bamboo pole that has a basket hanging from each end.

Perhaps he or she is unfamiliar with the village byways and, when it is time to go home, cannot find the way back to the monastery. The poor renunciate bumps into this dead end, turns around in an alley, gets stuck in that back lane. And all the while people think this is part of the rounds and keep making donations. By the time the anagārika finds the way home, he or she has a big pile of loot.

Those of you who get lost and sidetracked now and then can reflect that you will end up with a really big bag of Dhamma.

### *"Its Two Wheels are Mental and Physical Effort"*

As the Buddha described it, this noble chariot has two wheels. In those days that was the way carts were made, so this metaphor was accessible to listeners of his time. He explained that one wheel was physical effort and the other was mental effort.

In meditation as in any other pursuit, effort is crucial. We must be hardworking and industrious in order to succeed. If our effort is persevering, we can become a hero or heroine, a courageous person. Courageous effort is precisely what is needed in meditation.

Physical effort is the effort to maintain the body in its postures: to sit, to stand, to walk, to lie down. Mental effort is that without which meditation would not exist. It is the energy one puts forth to be mindful and to concentrate, making sure that the kilesas are kept at a remote distance.

The two wheels of effort together carry the vehicle of practice. In walking meditation, you must lift your leg, push it forward and then place your foot on the ground. Doing this again and again constitutes the act of walking. When you walk meditatively, physical effort creates the movement, while mental effort evokes a continuous and unbroken mindfulness of the movement. Physical exertion, in regulated quantities, contributes to wakefulness and energy of mind.

One cannot fail to notice that effort is basic to the Buddha's vehicle design. Just as it is necessary for a worldly chariot's two wheels to be firmly affixed, so too mental and physical effort must always be engaged to move this chariot of the Noble Eightfold Path. We will not get anywhere if we do not actually make the physical effort to sit in meditation; nor if we fail, while sitting, to keep the mind penetrative, continuous and accurate in noting. If the twin wheels of effort are kept moving, however, the vehicle will roll on straight ahead.

A significant effort is required simply to maintain the physical postures. If you are sitting, you must exert yourself not to fall over. If you are walking, you must move your legs. We try to balance the four major postures, to balance energy and create conditions for good health. In a retreat situation especially, we must have sufficient hours of sitting, walking and, secondarily, standing and lying down. Sleeping hours should be limited.

If postures are not rightly maintained, laziness results. In sitting, you may seek out something to lean against. You might decide that walking is too tiring, or that some relaxing hobby might be preferable to meditation. As you might guess, none of these ideas are recommended.

Similarly with mental effort. It is not good to slacken. One must assume from the very beginning that it will be necessary to put forth a persistent and continuous mental effort. Tell yourself that you are not going to entertain any gaps in mindfulness, you are just going to be as continuous as possible. Such an attitude is very useful. It opens your mind to the possibility of actually realizing your goal.

Some yogis have a peculiar distaste for walking meditation. Considering it a tiring waste of time, they only do it because the teacher tells them to. On the contrary, due to the strong dual effort it requires, walking meditation is essential to keep the wheels of effort rolling. With proper attention to walking, you can arrive at your destination in ease and comfort.

When mental effort is present from moment to moment, it bars the kilesas from entering. They are kept at bay, they are put aside, they are rejected by the mind.

Some yogis are sporadic in their application of effort. They do it in spurts. This approach can be very disorienting. The energy built up in one burst of mindfulness is all in vain, for in the next few moments of mindlessness the kilesas have a field day. Then, when such yogis start being mindful again, they have to start back at square one. Trying and resting, trying and resting, they do not build a momentum – they do not progress.

Maybe you should do some soul-searching. Be honest. Are you truly being mindful? Are you truly and sincerely activating that persevering, persistent effort to be mindful from moment to moment throughout your waking hours?

## The Virtues of Ardency

One who keeps the wheel of mental effort turning continuously is said to possess ardent energy. The Buddha praised such a person, saying, "One who possesses ardent energy lives in comfort." Why so? Ardent effort keeps the kilesas at bay. This creates a cool and calm, enjoyable mental atmosphere, free from greedy, cruel, destructive thoughts, all of which are painful.

There is no end to the virtues of ardent effort. The Buddha said, "Better to live one day with ardent effort than a hundred years without it." I hope that you gain sufficient inspiration from this discussion to set your wheels turning.

## Conscience: The Chariot's Backrest

The next part of the chariot described by the Buddha was its backrest, which was conscience. In those days chariots had backrests for support. Without one, a driver or passenger might fall off the chariot as it suddenly stopped or jerked forward. A backrest could also be a luxury item. One could lean back as comfortably as in a favorite armchair and proceed to one's destination. In our case, the destination is the noble goal of nibbāna.

## Wholesome Shame and Wholesome Fear

In order to understand the function of the "backrest" of the vipassanā chariot, we must delve into what is meant by conscience. The Buddha used a Pāli word, *hiri*; the quality of *ottappa* is its close companion. Since ottappa is implied, we shall discuss it at the same time even though the sutta does not specifically mention it. These two words are often translated as "shame" and "fear" respectively. Unfortunately, these words are negative, and thus become inaccurate. There are no good words in English to convey these meanings. The best expedient is to say "moral conscience" and then, if there is time, to try to explain the meaning of the Pāli words.

Remember that hiri and ottappa are not at all associated with anger or aversion, as are conventional shame and fear. They make one ashamed and afraid in only a very specific way, ashamed and afraid of unwholesome activities. Together they create a clear moral conscience, self-integrity. A man or woman of integrity actually has nothing to be ashamed of, and is fearless in virtue.

Hiri or "shame" is a feeling of disgust toward the kilesas. As you try to be mindful, you find there are gaps during which the kilesas pounce on you and make you their victim. Returning to your senses, so to speak, you feel a kind of abhorrence, or shame, at having been caught off guard. This attitude toward the kilesas is hiri.

Ottappa or "fear" is fear of the consequences of unwholesome activities. If you spend long intervals in unwholesome thoughts during your formal meditation practice, your progress will be slow. If you perform unwholesome actions at any time under the kilesas' influence, you will suffer the consequences. Fearing that this will happen, you will be more attentive, alert against the kilesas which are always waiting to pounce. In sitting, you will be strongly committed to the primary object.

Hiri has a direct connection to one's own virtues and integrity, while ottappa is also linked to the virtues and good name of one's parents, teachers, relatives and friends.

Hiri works in various ways. Say a person, a man or woman, comes from a good upbringing. No matter what economic level they may have come from, their parents educated them in human values. Such a gentleman or lady would think twice before committing the unwholesome act of killing. They would think, "My parents taught me to be kind and loving. Will I jeopardize my self-respect by succumbing to such destructive thoughts and feelings? Should I kill another being in a weak moment when I am devoid of compassion and consideration? Am I willing to sacrifice my virtue?" If one can reflect in this way and decide to refrain from killing, hiri has done a good job.

The virtue of wisdom or learning can also cause one to refrain from unwholesome actions. If a person is learned and cultured in any meaningful sense, he or she has high moral standards. When tempted to commit an immoral act, a truly cultured person will consider it beneath him or her, and shrink from the temptation. Hiri can also arise on account of one's age. At an advanced age one gains a sense of dignity. One says to oneself, "I'm a senior citizen and I know the difference between right and wrong. I will not do anything unbefitting because I have deep respect for my own dignity."

Hiri also occurs because of courageous conviction. One can reflect that immoral actions are the province of timid, cowardly, unprincipled people. A person of courage and conviction will choose to stick to principles no matter what. This is heroic virtue, refusing to allow one's integrity to be undermined.

Ottappa, the fear aspect of conscience, arises when one considers how one's parents, friends and family members would be disgraced by immoral acts. It is also a wish not to betray the best that is in humanity.

Once committed, an immoral act can never be concealed. You yourself know you have done it. There are also beings who can read the minds of others, who can see and hear what happens to others. If you are aware of the presence of such a being, you may be hesitant to commit unwholesome behavior lest you be found out.

Hiri and ottappa play a great part in family life. It is because of these that father and mother, sisters and brothers, can live a life that is quite pure. If they have no sense of moral conscience, human family members relate without barriers of kinship, as dogs and cats do.

The world today is plagued by a lack of these qualities in people. In fact, these two aspects of conscience are called "The Guardians of the World." Imagine a world where everyone possessed them in abundance!

Hiri and ottappa are also called *sukka dhamma*, pure dhamma, because they are so essential in maintaining purity of conduct among the beings on this planet. Sukka dhamma can also mean the color white as a symbol of purity. The opposites, shamelessness and fearlessness, are called *kaṇha dhamma* or black dhamma. Black absorbs heat, and white reflects it. The black dhamma of shamelessness and audacity are excellent absorbers for the kilesas. When they are present you can be sure that the kilesas will be well-soaked into the mind; whereas if white dhamma are present, the kilesas will be reflected away.

The texts give the example of two iron balls. One is smeared with excrement and the other is red hot. A person offered these two iron balls refuses the first because it is disgusting and rejects the second out of fear of being burned. Not taking the ball smeared with excrement is like the quality of hiri or shame in one's mind. One finds immorality disgusting when one compares it with integrity. Not taking the hot ball is like ottappa, the fear of committing an unwholesome act out of the fear of the kammic consequences. One knows that one might end up in hell or in states of misery. Thus one avoids the ten types of unwholesome behavior as if they were these two iron balls.

### Useless Kinds of Shame and Fear

Some kinds of shame and fear are useless. I call them "imitation" shame and fear. One might be ashamed or embarrassed to observe the five precepts, listen to Dhamma talks or to pay respect to a person worthy of veneration. One might be ashamed to read aloud or give a talk in public. Fear of the bad opinion of others, if that bad opinion is not based on one's immoral acts, is imitation shame.

There are four things conducive to one's personal benefit which human beings should not be ashamed to do. These are not listed in a Buddhist text – they are worldly and practical.

The first is not to be ashamed to do one's business or to work for a living. One should not be ashamed to approach a teacher to learn a trade, a profession or subject. If one is ashamed to do this, how will one ever gain knowledge? One should not be ashamed of eating. If one cannot eat, one will starve to death. Lastly, one should not be ashamed to have intimate relations between husband and wife.

There is also imitation fear, such as the fear of meeting an important person when this is necessary in the course of life.

Villagers tend to experience imitation fear when traveling in a train, a bus, or ferry. I mean real villagers, people who have never taken public transport. These simple people might also be afraid to use the bathroom when they are traveling. This, too, is unhelpful. People may also be afraid of animals, dogs, snakes or insects, or of going to places they have never been before. Many fear members of the opposite sex, or are so much in awe of their parents and teachers that they can't talk or walk in front of them. Some yogis are afraid of interviews with the teacher. They wait outside the door as if it were a dentist's office.

None of these are real hiri and ottappa, which are only connected with performing unwholesome actions. One should be terrified of bad kamma and of the kilesas, knowing that when they attack, there's no telling to what extent they might manipulate one to commit unwholesome acts.

Reflecting on hiri and ottappa is a very good thing to do. The stronger these two qualities in a yogi, the more easily he or she will activate the effort to be mindful. A yogi who fears to break the continuity of practice will try hard to cultivate alertness.

Therefore the Buddha said to the deva, "This magnificent chariot of the Noble Eightfold Path has hiri as its backrest." If you have this backrest of hiri and ottappa, you will have something to rely on, something to depend on, something on which you can sit comfortably as you ride toward nibbānic bliss. Just as one who rides a vehicle is open to the risk of accidents, so too a yogi on the chariot of the Noble Eightfold Path runs a risk in practice. If these qualities are weak, he or she risks losing mindfulness, and all the dangers that then ensue.

May your abundant hiri and ottappa cause you to activate ardent energy so as continuously to practice mindfulness. May you thus make smooth and rapid progress along the Noble Eightfold Path, until you eventually realize nibbāna.

*Mindfulness is the Armor that Surrounds this Chariot...*

To ensure that the Dhamma journey is carried out safely, the chariot must have a body. In the Buddha's day, chariots were made of wood or some other hard material as a defense against spears and arrows. More recently, nations have devoted a lot of resources to develop armor plating for battlefield vehicles. Modern-day automobiles are also encased in metal for safety's sake. Today you can ride about as if in a comfortable room, free from wind, heat, cold and sun. If a car's body keeps you well protected from the elements of nature, you travel in comfort whether it is raining and snowing outside or not. All these examples illustrate the function of mindfulness in keeping yogis free from the kilesas' harsh attack. Sati, or mindfulness, is a kind of armor that keeps the mind safe, comfortable and cool: as long as mindfulness provides its protection, the kilesas cannot enter.

No one can travel safely in this vehicle of the Noble Eightfold Path without the protective covering of mindfulness. When the chariot goes into battle, armor is the decisive factor in protecting the occupants. Our vipassanā practice is a battle against the kilesas, which have dominated our existence since before we can remember. We need strong armor surrounding our chariot so we can be protected against their ruthless depredations.

It is good to understand how the kilesas arise in order to defeat them. Kilesas arise in connection with the six sense objects. Whenever there is no mindfulness at any of the six sense doors, you easily become a victim of desire, anger, delusion and the other kilesas.

When the seeing process, for example, occurs, visual objects come into contact with seeing consciousness. If the object is pleasant and you are not mindful, thoughts based on craving or desire will arise. If the object is disagreeable, aversion attacks you. If the object is insipid and neutral, you will be carried off on a tide of delusion. When mindfulness is present, however, kilesas cannot enter your stream of consciousness. Noting the seeing process, sati gives the mind a chance to understand the true nature of what is happening.

The immediate benefits of mindfulness are purity of mind, clarity and happiness. They are experienced at the very moment that mindfulness is present. Absence of kilesas is purity. Because of purity come clarity and joy. A mind that is pure and clear can be put to good use.

In the unchecked course of things, unwholesome mental states are unfortunately more frequent than wholesome ones. As soon as greed, aversion and delusion enter the consciousness, we start to create unwholesome kamma, which will give results in this life as well as in the future. Rebirth is one result. With that, death becomes inevitable. Between birth and death, a being will create more kamma, both wholesome and unwholesome, to keep the cycle turning. Therefore, heedlessness is the path that leads to death. It is the cause of death in this world as well as in future life.

So mindfulness is also like fresh air, essential to life. All breathing beings need clean air. If only polluted air is available, they will shortly be afflicted by disease and may even die. Mindfulness is just this important. A mind deprived of the fresh air of mindfulness grows stale, breathes shallowly, and chokes upon defilements.

A person breathing dirty air may become sick very suddenly, and suffer extreme pain before death actually comes. When we are not mindful, we breathe in the poisoned air of the kilesas and we suffer. In the presence of a pleasant object, we are pierced by pangs of craving. If the object is unpleasant, we burn with aversion. If we find the object humiliating, we will be eaten up by conceit. The kilesas come in many forms, but when they attack us it is always the same: we suffer. Pure comfort of mind, peace and happiness only exist if we can keep the kilesas out of our minds.

Some pollutants cause breathing creatures to become dizzy and disoriented. Others kill. The same is true for the kilesas. Some attacks are minor, others fatal. One can be dizzied by sensual pleasures or die in an apoplectic fit of rage. A strong excess of lust can kill a person. Greed, indulged over many years, can lay the foundations for terminal disease. Extreme anger or fear is also deadly, especially if the victim suffers from heart disease. Kilesas are also responsible for neurosis and psychosis.

Kilesas are actually much more dangerous than the bad chemicals in air. If a person dies from breathing contaminated air, the poison will be left behind in his or her corpse. But the taints of the kilesas carry forward to the next life, not to mention their negative effect on other beings. Breathed in by the mind, the kilesas result in kamma that will ripen in the future.

When mindfulness is present from moment to moment, the mind is gradually cleansed, just as the lungs of a person who stops smoking gradually shed their coating of tar and nicotine. A pure mind easily becomes concentrated. Then wisdom has the opportunity to arise. This process of healing begins with mindfulness. Basing your practice on mindfulness and deepening concentration, you will pass though the various levels of insight, your wisdom growing by degrees. Eventually you may realize nibbāna, at which point kilesas are uprooted. There are no pollutants in nibbāna.

The value of mindfulness can only be appreciated by people who have experienced its benefits in their personal practice. When people take the trouble to breathe fresh air, good health proves to them the value of their effort. So too, a meditator who has experienced deep practice, even nibbāna, will truly know what mindfulness is worth.

### Right View is the Charioteer

No matter how marvelous the vehicle, without a driver it can go nowhere. Similarly, the Buddha explained, right view must provide the impetus as well as the direction for our spiritual journey. The scriptures list six types of right view or *sammā diṭṭhi*. In this discourse, the Buddha was specifically referring to the right view that arises at the moment of the noble path consciousness. Noble path consciousness is one of the culminating insights of this practice. We will discuss it below.

## Right View of Kamma as One's Own Property

The first kind of right view is *kammassakatā sammā-diṭṭhi*, right view of kamma as one's property – kamma being, of course, all wholesome and unwholesome activities. Our concepts of ownership and control over material objects are basically illusory, for all matter is impermanent, subject to decay. Kamma is our only reliable possession in this world. We must understand that whatever good or evil we do will follow us through samsāra, giving rise to corresponding good or evil consequences. Kamma has an immediate effect upon the mind, causing joy or misery depending on whether it is wholesome or unwholesome. It also has long-term consequences. Unwholesome kamma results in birth in states of woe or misery. Wholesome kamma leads to rebirth in happy states. The highest wholesome kamma leads to relief from samsāra.

Seeing life in this way gives us the power to choose the conditions under which we want to live. Thus, kammassakatā sammā-diṭṭhi is called "The Light of the World," for by it we can see and evaluate the nature of our choices. Right understanding of kamma is like a railroad junction where the train can choose its direction, or an international airport, linked to many destinations. Since we, like all beings, want happiness, this understanding of kamma will generate in us a strong wish to develop more and more wholesome habits. We will also want to avoid acting in ways that will bring us future misery.

Practicing charity, *dāna*, and morality, *sīla*, one chooses a direction toward rebirth in good circumstances. This meritorious kamma helps beings walk the path to nibbāna.

## Right View with Regard to the Jhānas

To go beyond kammassakatā sammā-diṭṭhi, one practices concentration. Concentration has immediate benefits, enabling the yogi to live in tranquility, absorbed in the object. This second type of right view is *jhāna sammā diṭṭhi*, right view with regard to the jhānas and absorptions. It is the knowledge that arises in conjunction with each of the eight types of jhāna. The benefits of jhāna right view are three-fold. Upon death, if one is able to maintain strength in ability to gain absorption, one is reborn in the brahmā worlds and can live there for a very long time, many eons and world systems. Second, the jhānas are the basis for developing strong vipassanā. The jhānas can also become the basis for the development of *abhiññās* or psychic powers.

### Clearing the Way for Ultimate Insight: Developing Vipassanā Right View

We devote the most time and effort developing the third type of right view within ourselves. It is *vipassanā sammā diṭṭhi*, right view that occurs as a result of vipassanā insights. When effort, mindfulness and moral conscience are present, these insights naturally develop. It is important to remember that right view is something more than an opinion. It is a deep intuitive knowledge that comes from our seeing directly into the true nature of existence.

These days when heads of state leave their palaces, there is a great deal of preparation. Before the motorcade sets forth, teams of security agents make sure its route is clear and safe. Agents check for bombs, place barriers on the sidewalks for crowd control, assign police officers to their posts and remove any vehicles that might block the road. Only then will the president leave the official residence and climb into the chauffeured car.

In the same way, on this Noble Eightfold Path, vipassanā right view is like the secret service. Insight into impermanence, suffering and absence of self is what clears from the path all sorts of clinging – clinging to wrong views and pet theories, misconceptions and so forth. The clearing process takes place at sequential levels. Once the preliminary preparations are complete, then the noble path right view will make its appearance and uproot the kilesas.

## A Process of Elimination

On the way to noble path consciousness, each stage of insight eliminates a particular kind of wrong view or misconception about the nature of reality. The first vipassanā insight into the nature of mental and physical phenomena shows us that mind and matter are distinct from each other, and that life is nothing more than a ceaseless stream of these two kinds of phenomena. At this time, we do away with the extras, cleanse ourselves of the view which puts into reality something that is not really there, such as the notion of a permanent and substantial self.

The second insight, understanding cause and effect, eliminates any doubt as to whether things happen by chance – we know that they do not. Furthermore, we see clearly and directly that events are not caused by any external force.

Deepening meditation, we see the impermanence of objects, and understand intuitively that everything experienced in the past, and to be experienced in the future, is similarly impermanent. Building on this knowledge of ephemerality and transience, we realize next that we have no refuge and can rely on nothing. Thus, we are rid of the false idea that peace and stability can be found in the objects of this world. To be oppressed by phenomena is indeed great suffering; and at this stage of insight, we feel this from the bottom of our hearts.

Related to, and following upon, this deep sense of fearsomeness and oppression is a realization that no one can prevent or control the way things come and go. It will dawn on our intuition that there is no self in things. These latter three insights are the beginnings of vipassanā right view, which relates specifically to impermanence, suffering and absence of self.

## The Arising of Vipassanā Right View

With the arising of vipassanā right view, the chariot is ready to go. It is shaking a bit and moving as it faces the right road that leads to nibbāna. Now you can really turn the wheels and get that vehicle rolling. The armor is in place, the backrest firm, and the driver well seated. You just need to give a bit of a push to those two wheels, and the chariot will really take off.

Once you have gained insight into impermanence, suffering and absence of self, you see things arising and passing away much quicker, much more clearly. Moment to moment arising and passing: it comes in microseconds, nanoseconds – the deeper you go the quicker you see it – and eventually you are not able to see the arising at all. Wherever you look, there is just a flash of quick dissolution. You will have a feeling as if someone is pulling the carpet out from under you. This disappearance is not an abstraction. It comprises your entire life at that time.

Deeper and deeper you go, driving closer and closer to your destination. After all these stages of vipassanā insight have been completed, the right view of the path consciousness will take over and drive you home, to the safe haven of nibbāna.

Although in the presence of vipassanā insights the kilesas have no chance of arising, they are not yet uprooted. They may be kept at bay, but they are waiting for their chance to get back into power.

## The Final Stamp: Weakening and Eliminating the Kilesas

Only at the moment when the noble path right view occurs are the kilesas uprooted.

You may wonder what is meant by the notion of uprooting a kilesa. Kilesas which have already arisen can no longer be removed – they are past. Similarly, kilesas not yet arisen cannot be removed, since they are not here yet. And even in the present, kilesas arise and pass away, so how can they be uprooted? Latent or potential kilesas are what is removed. There are two types of kilesas, one connected with objects and the other with the continuity of existence. The first type occurs when the conditions are conducive, that is, in connection with a mental or physical object and in the absence of mindfulness. If an object becomes predominant, and there is no mindfulness to keep the contact between mind and object clear and pure, the kilesa which has been latent will come to life. It will become manifest. If one is mindful, however, the conditions are no longer appropriate and the kilesas are kept away.

The second type of kilesas are dormant and will remain buried in the stream of our consciousness all the way through samsāra. This kind can only be uprooted by path consciousness.

In the old days when patients suffered from malaria, they were treated with two kinds of medicine. Malaria patients undergo a repetitive cycle of temperature changes. Every two days or so, a very high fever comes, followed by sudden chills. The first course of treatment levels the extremes of temperature. It strengthens the patient and weakens the malaria germs. Finally when the cycles of fever and chills abate somewhat, a dose of knockout medicine is prescribed. Now that the patient is stronger, and the bacteria are much weaker, the malaria can be totally eradicated.

The preliminary course of treatment is analogous to vipassanā insight, which weakens the kilesas. The knockout medicine is path consciousness, uprooting kilesas once and for all.

Another example is the process of getting a document legally certified through the process of bureaucratic red tape. It could take all day. First you go to the ground floor and talk to the receptionist. He or she sends you up to the second floor to get a document and have it signed. The Department of This sends you to the Department of That. You produce the document and are given a set of forms to fill out. Then you wait for the person in charge to sign it. All day you go through various channels, from one level to another, filling out forms and getting signatures. It takes a very long time to get all the parts complete. Finally you arrive at the top and it takes the official half a second to make the final signature. Your document is now certified, but you have had to go through all that other red tape first.

It is the same in vipassanā. There is a lot of red tape. Path consciousness comes even faster than the time it takes for the top official to sign, but you have to work for it.

When all is in order, the path of right view appears and certifies that all the kilesas have been uprooted.

The first part of vipassanā insight might be called "The Worker Path." You have to work to complete it properly, without shirking. Noble path consciousness is like the boss, ordering work to be done. He or she cannot sign a blank piece of paper on which the preliminary processes have not been completed.

### Noble Path and Fruition Right View: Putting Out the Fire of Defilement, Pouring Water on the Ashes

When vipassanā insights are completed, noble path consciousness will arise automatically, followed by fruition consciousness. In Pāli, these consciousnesses are called *magga* and *phala*. Noble path right view and noble fruition right view, elements of these two respective consciousnesses, are the fourth and fifth kinds of right view on the list of six.

When noble path consciousness arises, noble path right view uproots the group of kilesas that causes rebirth in lower realms, states of woe and misery. This refers to hell realms, animal realms, peta and hungry ghost realms. Immediately after comes noble fruition consciousness, part of which is noble fruition right view. One might ask the function of this, since the dormant kilesas already have been uprooted. Fruition right view just cools the defilements. A fire may burn out but still leave embers and warm ashes. Noble fruition right view splashes water over the embers.

### Reviewing Knowledge Right View

The sixth and last kind of right view is reviewing knowledge right view. Reviewing knowledge comes on the heels of fruition consciousness and the experience of nibbāna. It reviews five things: the occurrence of path consciousness and of fruition consciousness; nibbāna itself as an object of consciousness; the kilesas which have been uprooted and those which have yet to be uprooted. It serves no other important function.

The first kind of right view, kamma sakatā sammā diṭṭhi, is said to be perpetual. That is, it will never disappear from existence. This world system may shatter and be devastated, but there will always be beings, perhaps in other world systems, who have the right view of kamma as one's own property.

People who do not even try to appreciate the difference between wholesome and unwholesome kamma are far from any light at all. They can be likened to a baby which is blind from birth: blind in the womb and blind when it comes out. If this baby grows up, still it will not be able to see well enough to guide itself. A person who is blind and guideless will get into a lot of accidents.

Jhāna right view will always be present as long as people practice and attain the jhānas. The Buddha's teaching may not be flourishing, but there will always be people practicing concentration and absorption.

However, the remaining types of right view can only be present while the Buddha's teaching remains alive. From the time of Gotama Buddha until this present age, his teachings have flourished. They are known throughout the world at this moment. Even in countries that are not Buddhist, there are groups or institutions based on his teaching. A person satisfied with right view related to kamma or the jhānas has no access to the light of the Dhamma. He or she can be brightened by the light of the world, but not by that of the Buddha. The remaining four types of right view, from vipassanā right view through reviewing right view, contain the light of the Buddha's teaching.

When yogis can distinguish mind and matter, they are free of the delusion of self, and the first veil of darkness is removed. We say that the light of Dhamma has dawned on the consciousness. But there are more layers to be removed. The second layer of ignorance is the opinion that things happen chaotically and at random. This veil is removed by the insight into cause and effect. When a yogi sees cause and effect, the light in his or her mind shines a bit brighter. He or she ought not to be satisfied at this point, for the mind still is darkened by ignorance of the characteristics of impermanence, suffering and absence of self. To remove this darkness the yogi must work harder, persistently watching things as they arise, sharpening mindfulness, deepening concentration. Then wisdom will arise naturally.

Now the yogi sees that there is no refuge to be sought in these impermanent phenomena. This brings on deep disappointment, but the light within is brighter still. He or she clearly realizes the suffering and nonselfness of phenomena. At this time only one last veil remains, covering the realization of nibbāna, and it can only be removed by the noble path consciousness. Now the light of the Buddha's teachings really begins to shine!

If you develop all six types of right view, you will be radiant. You will never be separated from the light of wisdom, no matter where you go in future wanderings. On the contrary, wisdom will shine ever more brightly in you throughout the remainder of your wanderings in samsāra. At the last there will be a big firework when *arahanta magga phala*, the path and fruition consciousnesses of the final stage of enlightenment, come to you.

## Taking Possession of the Chariot

> Anyone, woman or man, possessing such a chariot and driving it well, shall have no doubt of reaching nibbāna.

It is said that when the bhikkhu deva heard this discourse of the chariot, he perceived the point the Buddha was making and immediately became a sotāpanna, or stream entrant. He took ownership of this magnificent chariot called the Noble Eightfold Path. Although the Buddha's discourse was directed toward the ultimate goal of arahantship, this deva did not yet have the potential to gain final enlightenment. His predisposition carried him only as far as stream entry.

*Benefits of Stream Entry: Drying Up the Ocean of Samsāric Existence*

At this first stage of enlightenment, one is freed from the danger of falling into states of misery. The suttas say that three kilesas are uprooted: wrong view, doubt, and attachment to wrong practices. In the commentary, the kilesas of jealousy and miserliness are added to the list.

Safely assume that this deva had gained insight into the nature of mind and matter in his previous life as a bhikkhu. At the moment of gaining this insight, he was free from a false view that there is an internal abiding entity, or self. However, his abandoning of this wrong view was only temporary. Not until he glimpsed nibbāna for the first time was there a permanent change in his view. One who has experienced stream entry no longer believes in the illusion of an abiding entity.

The second type of defilement uprooted is closely connected to wrong view. When one has not correctly understood the nature of things, it is difficult to come to a firm conclusion about what is right and what is not. Like a person standing at a fork in the road, or someone who suddenly discovers that he or she has lost the way, there is doubt about which way to go. This dilemma can be quite debilitating and undermining.

When yogis see the mechanism of cause and effect, they temporarily abandon doubt. They see that the Dhamma is true, that mind and matter are conditioned, and that there is nothing in this world which is not conditioned. This lack of doubt only lasts as long as mindfulness and insight are sustained, however. Final, unshakable faith in the Dhamma's efficacy and authenticity only comes when a person has walked as far as the Eightfold Path's destination, nibbāna. A yogi who walks in the Buddha's footsteps to the end of the path will also have faith in the Buddha and the other noble ones who have attained the same goal by the same route.

The third defilement uprooted by the sotāpanna, stream enterer, is belief in wrong practice. This understanding is fairly obvious in a general way, and can be understood more completely if examined from the point of view of the Four Noble Truths. When potential stream entrants first develop the Noble Eightfold Path within themselves, they learn to understand the first noble truth, that all things are unsatisfactory. Mind and matter are suffering. A yogi's preliminary development consists of watching these suffering things. When the first noble truth is completely seen, then the remaining three are automatically achieved or realized. This means abandoning craving, the second noble truth; cessation of suffering, the third noble truth; and developing the Noble Eightfold Path, the fourth noble truth.

The preliminary or mundane part of the Noble Eightfold Path is being developed in every moment of mindfulness. At some point it ripens into supramundane knowledge. So, upon attaining nibbāna, this deva now knew that his practice was the only way to achieve this nibbāna. He knew that he had experienced a real cessation of suffering, the unconditioned, and that there is no nibbāna other than that. All yogis feel the same way at this moment.

The Noble Eightfold Path is the only one that leads to nibbāna. This understanding is very deep and can only be attained through practice. With this understanding, the stream entrant is free from attachment or belief in the efficacy of other methods of practice which are devoid of the elements of the Noble Eightfold Path.

In the commentaries two additional kilesas are said to be uprooted. These are *issā* or jealousy, the wish not to see others happy and successful, and *macchariya* or miserliness, which is the dislike of seeing others as happy as one is oneself. Personally I do not agree with these commentaries. These two mental states belong to the category of dosa, anger or aversion. According to the canon of suttas spoken by the Buddha, the stream entrant uproots only defilements which have no connection with dosa. However, since the potential for rebirth in lower states has been uprooted, the stream entrant's attacks of issā and macchariya will not be sufficiently strong to cause this lower rebirth.

An interesting comment is found in the *Visuddhi Magga*, which is a noncanonical work but still held in high esteem.

Based on canonical references, the *Visuddhi Magga* admits that a stream entrant can still be attacked by greed, hatred and delusion, and still is subject to conceit and pride. However, since the noble path consciousness has uprooted kilesas that lead to states of misery, one can safely conclude that the stream entrant is free from kilesas strong enough to lead to such rebirths.

The *Visuddhi Magga* also points out that a stream entrant has succeeded in drying up the vast ocean of samsāric existence. As long as a person has not attained the first stage of enlightenment, he or she must continually perpetuate existence in the beginningless rounds of samsāra. The scope of samsāra is vast – you just keep going on and on. But a stream entrant has only a maximum of seven more existences to live before he or she gains complete enlightenment as an arahant. What are seven existences compared to an eternity of innumerable lives? For all practical purposes we can say the ocean has dried up.

Unwholesome kamma can only occur under the influence of ignorance and craving. When a certain level of ignorance and craving disappears, so does the potential for certain unwholesome results, namely rebirth in states of misery. There is no limit to the evil people may do when still mercilessly assaulted by the kilesas of wrong view of the self and of doubt about the path and kamma. The atrocities they commit will lead to lower realms without a doubt. Lacking these kilesas, a stream entrant will no longer commit terrible deeds that may lead to such rebirth. Furthermore, his or her past kamma which might have led to such unfortunate rebirths is cut off at the moment of attaining the noble path consciousness. A stream entrant no longer need fear this intense suffering.

### The Inalienable Property of Noble Ones

Another benefit of stream entry is realization of the sevenfold property of noble ones. Noble ones are persons who are purified, noble of character, who have attained one of the four levels of enlightenment. Their properties are faith, morality, hiri, ottappa, learning, charity and wisdom.

Faith is a durable and unshakable confidence in the Buddha, the Dhamma and the sangha. It is unshakable because of direct experience and realization. A noble one can never be bribed or corrupted in any way to abandon the Buddha, Dhamma and sangha. No matter what suave and cunning means, or frightening threats, a person might employ to this end, a noble one can never be convinced to abandon his or her knowledge.

Morality is purity of conduct with respect to the five precepts. It is said that a stream entrant is incapable of deliberately breaking them, incapable of any wrong thoughts or actions leading to rebirth in states of woe. He or she will be free from the threefold immoral behavior manifested through the body, will be largely free from wrong speech, will be free from wrong livelihood, and finally will be free from wrong effort in practicing a wrong spiritual path.

The third and fourth properties, hiri and ottappa, we explained earlier. A stream entrant has these two aspects of conscience very strongly developed, and so will be incapable of performing bad deeds.

The fifth property, learning, refers to the theory of meditation as well as a practical understanding of how to meditate. A stream entrant is indeed learned in the mechanics of walking this Noble Eightfold Path toward nibbāna.

*Cāga*, usually translated as charity, actually means relinquishment. A stream entrant generously relinquishes all kilesas that produce results in lower realms. Moreover, he or she will be liberal in dāna; his or her generosity will be continuous and very real.

The last property is wisdom. This refers to vipassanā insight and wisdom. A stream entrant's practice will be free from wrong mindfulness and wrong concentration. He or she will also be free from very explosive kilesas which erupt within and manifest physically, vocally or mentally, and from fear of evil rebirth.

Personal peace is of utmost importance. It can be achieved in freedom from fear. If many people are capable of realizing such peace – if many people actually have that peace within – you can imagine how conducive it would be to world peace. World peace can only start from within.

## A True Child of the Buddha

Another benefit of stream entry is that one becomes a true child of the Buddha. Many are devoted. They may have great faith and make daily offerings to the triple gem of Buddha, Dhamma and sangha, but due to changes in circumstances it is always possible for a person to give up faith. He or she may be reborn without it. You may be very holy and goodhearted in this life, but next time you could turn out a rascal. There is no insurance for you until you attain the first stage of enlightenment and become a true daughter or son of the Lord Buddha.

The Pāli term used in the *Visuddhi Magga* is *orasa putta* which means a real, full-fledged, redblooded child. *Putta* is often translated as son, but actually it is a general term for progeny, including daughters.

There are hundreds more benefits that can be obtained, the *Visuddhi Magga* says. In fact, the benefits of stream entry are beyond number. A stream entrant is totally committed to the Dhamma, intensely interested in listening to the true Dhamma; and can understand Dhamma that is profound and not easily grasped by others. When a stream entrant hears a discourse that is well-delivered, he or she will be filled with joy and rapture.

And because a sotāpanna has stepped into the stream, his or her heart will always be with the Dhamma. In executing his or her duties in the world, the stream entrant will be like Mother Cow, who eats grass and still watches over her tender calf. The heart of the sotāpanna is inclined to Dhamma, but he or she will not shirk worldly responsibilities. Stream entrants gain concentration very easily if they put appropriate effort in meditation, wishing to walk further on the path.

## A Vehicle for Everyone, a Vehicle that Never Breaks Down

The Buddha concluded by saying explicitly that meditative achievement is not differentiated on a basis of sex. Either a woman or a man, he said, could trust this chariot to carry him or her to nibbāna. The chariot was, and is, available to all.

In the modern age we have a myriad vehicles available. Ever newer inventions appear in the field of transportation. Human beings can travel over land and sea or in the sky. An ordinary person can go around the world without much trouble. Men have walked on the moon. Spacecrafts have gone to other planets and even beyond.

No matter how far vehicles go through space, however, it is unlikely they will be of any help bringing you to nibbāna. If indeed there is a vehicle that stops in nibbāna, I would like to have it. However, I have not yet heard advertisements or assurances of any such extraordinary vehicle that could carry a person to the safe haven of nibbāna.

No matter how advanced scientific technology may be, there is no guarantee that even the most sophisticated vehicle is accident free. Fatal accidents occur on land, on sea, in the air and in space. Many people have died in this way. I do not suggest that this renders the vehicles useless. It is just that there is no guaranteed safety in them. The only vehicle with one hundred per cent insurance coverage is the Noble Eightfold Path.

Modern cars have a high standard of performance and safety. If you are rich you can afford an extremely comfortable, fast, luxurious automobile and can have it conveniently at your disposal. If you are not rich you can get a loan, or rent a limousine or a sports car for a short time, or you can ride on public transportation. Even if you are poor you can always stand by the road and hitch a ride.

However, there is no guarantee that performance will be faultless even if the car is your own. You have to fill up your car with gas, maintain it in various ways, repair it when it breaks down – there are many chores involved. All the vehicles will be towed to the junkyard someday, and the more you use them, the closer they get to that final resting place.

It would be preferable to produce a nibbāna vehicle with the same sophistication and high standards, for this is a vehicle that never wears out. How good it would be if such a vehicle were easily accessible to common people! If anyone could own a vehicle to nibbāna, imagine what a peaceful world it would be. This vehicle leads to something priceless. Nibbāna cannot be bought, no matter how wealthy you may be, nor can it be rented. You have to work for it so that it belongs to you. It will only be useful if it becomes your own property.

In this world most vehicles are ready-made. They come from the factory. But this vehicle leading to nibbāna has to be self-made. It is a do-it-yourself kit. You must have faith at the start that nibbāna is in your reach, and faith in the path that will lead you to your destination. You must also have motivation, a sincere and committed desire to strive for that goal. But motivation alone will not get you far unless you act upon it. You must work, put in the effort to be mindful, persevering and enduring moment after moment so that concentration builds and wisdom begins to blossom and mature.

Would it not be wonderful if the Noble Eightfold Path were ready-made on an assembly line? Unfortunately, it is not, and that is why you poor souls have to do your own manufacturing. You arm yourself with faith and the strong desire to realize your goal. You intend to practice through thick and thin, undergoing difficulties, fatigue and tiredness and the strain of struggling to assemble your vehicle. You come to put forth energy to keep its wheels rolling. You try to keep the body work of mindfulness intact. You fix firmly your backrest of hiri and ottappa so that you can rely upon it. You train your driver to go straight. Finally, after passing through various stages of insight, you gain possession of the *sotāpatti magga* vehicle, stream entrant path consciousness. When this vehicle becomes your own possession, you will have very easy and convenient access to nibbāna.

Once this stream entrant vehicle is completed, it will never depreciate in value or run down. It is quite unlike vehicles presently available on this planet. You never need to oil or lubricate it, repair it or replace it. The more you use it, the stronger and more sophisticated it gets. It is totally accident free. When you travel on this vehicle, you have one-hundred-per-cent guaranteed safety.

As long as we live on this earth, we will be subjected to ups and downs and vicissitudes of life. At times things go smoothly and well; at other times, disappointment and discouragement, suffering and sorrow are the rule. However, one who has gained possession of this stream entrant path vehicle glides smoothly through rough times, and does not fall over too sharply in good times. The gates to misery are closed and he or she always has free access to the safe haven of nibbāna.

It is impossible to sing all the praises of this great vehicle, but be assured that if you really complete it and own it, you will have access to the fulfillment of life.

Please do not entertain any thoughts of surrender, but rather put forth all the energy and effort you have. Strive to assemble this vehicle and have it safely in your possession.

*The Gates of Misery are Closed*

The essential form of this chariot, this Dhamma vehicle, was first revealed to the world by the Buddha about 2,525 years ago or more, in the discourse called *The Sutta on the Turning of the Wheel of the Law*, the first discourse after his enlightenment.

Before the Buddha appeared, the world lived in total darkness, in ignorance of the Noble Eightfold Path. Recluses and renunciates, sages and philosophers, all held their own views and opinions, speculations and pet theories about the truth.

Then as now, some people believed nibbāna was the happiness of sensate pleasure, and so they immersed themselves in pleasure. Others looked with disdain at this behavior and reacted against it, mortifying themselves. They deprived their bodies of sense comfort and delight, seeing this as a noble endeavor. In general, beings lived in delusion. They had no access to the truth, and so their beliefs and actions were arbitrary. Each person had a view or opinion and, based thereon, did a thousand and one different things.

The Buddha accepted neither sense indulgence nor asceticism. His way is between the two, inclining to neither extreme. When he revealed the Noble Eightfold Path to beings, true faith grounded in the truth of existence could arise. Faith could be placed on that which was true, instead of on just an idea.

Faith has a great influence on one's consciousness. That is why it is a controlling faculty. With faith there can be effort. Faith arouses motivation in practice and becomes the basis for all other dhammas, like concentration and wisdom. When the Buddha first revealed the Noble Eightfold Path, he set the controlling faculties into motion. This view of dhammas was set rolling in the hearts of beings, and thereby true freedom and happiness came within reach.

May your faith in the practice be sincere and profound. May this be the basis for your attainment of ultimate liberation.

# Appendices

*Seven Factors of Enlightenment*
*Hindrances and Antidotes*
*The Progress of Insight*

Numerical Lists
Glossary
Index

# The Seven Factors of Enlightenment

In the chart below, each of the seven factors which lead to enlightenment, and which become properties of an enlightened person, is analyzed according to three aspects – its most salient characteristic, its function as it affects the general mental state, and its manifestation, or visible result within the mental field. This complete description comes from the Buddhist texts known as the *Abhidhamma*. Following the characteristic, function and manifestation, practical ways for meditators to arouse each enlightenment factor during meditation are listed by source, either according to the Buddha or according to subsequent amplifications by commentators.

## 1. MINDFULNESS — *SATI*

*Characteristic:* non-superficiality
*Function:* non-disappearance, or to keep the object in view
*Manifestation:* confrontation
*Ways of arousing:*
  According to the Buddha: mindfulness
  According to the Commentaries:
  1) Mindfulness and clear comprehension, or broad-based mindfulness
  2) Dissociation from unmindful persons
  3) Association with mindful persons
  4) Inclination of the mind toward the development of mindfulness

## 2) INVESTIGATION — *DHAMMA VICAYA*

*Characteristic:* intuitive knowledge of the nature of dhammas, also of nibbāna
*Function:* to dispel darkness
*Manifestation:* nonconfusion
*Ways of arousing:*
    According to the Buddha: direct perception
    According to the Commentaries:
    1) To ask questions about Dhamma and meditation practice
    2) Cleanliness of internal and external bases (the body and the immediate environment)
    3) Balancing the controlling faculties
    4) Avoiding unwise persons
    5) Associating with wise persons
    6) Reflection on profound Dhamma
    7) Commitment to cultivating investigation

## 3) COURAGEOUS EFFORT — *VIRIYA*

*Characteristic:* enduring patience in the face of suffering and difficulty
*Function:* supporting the mental state
*Manifestation:* a bold and courageous mind
*Ways of arousing:*
    According to the Buddha: wise attention
    According to the Commentaries:
    1) Reflection on the fearsomeness of āpaya or the states of misery one can fall into in the absence of effort
    2) Reflection on the benefits of effort
    3) Reflecting on and trying to match the nobility of previous practitioners
    4) Respect and appreciation for alms food or other supports one has received
    5) Reflection on the sevenfold heritage of a noble person (see Numerical Lists, page 277)
    6) Reflecting on the greatness of the Buddha

7) Reflecting on the greatness of the Dhamma which links the lineage of Buddhas, monks and nuns to oneself
8) Reflecting on the greatness of those who practice brahmacariya, or the sangha
9) Avoiding the company of lazy persons
10) Associating with energetic persons
11) Incline the mind toward developing energy

## 4) RAPTURE — *PĪTI*

*Characteristic:* happiness, delight and satisfaction
*Function:* lightness and energy of body and mind
*Manifestation:* physical sensations of lightness
*Ways of arousing:*
   According to the Buddha: wise attention to being effortful in bringing about wholesome feelings of rapture connected with the Buddha, Dhamma and sangha
   According to the Commentaries:
   1) *Buddha anussati,* recollection of the virtues of the Buddha
   2) Recollection of the virtues of the Dhamma
   3) Recollection of the virtues of the sangha
   4) Recollection of one's own moral purity
   5) Recollection of one's own generosity
   6) Recollection of the virtues of devas and brahmas
   7) Reflection on the peace of cessation of the kilesas, either in nibbāna, in the jhānas, or in deep meditations one has experienced
   8) Avoid the company of rough, angry and coarse persons
   9) Cultivate friends who are warm, loving and refined
   10) Reflect on the suttas
   11) Incline the mind toward developing rapture

## 5) TRANQUILITY — *PASSADDHI*

*Characteristic:* calmness of body and mind; end of agitation
*Function:* to extract or suppress mental heat due to restlessness, dissipation or remorse

*Manifestation:* nonagitation of body and mind
*Ways of arousing:*

According to the Buddha: wise attention directed toward developing wholesome mental states, especially meditative states, which allow tranquility

According to the Commentaries:

1) Sensible and nutritious food
2) Suitable weather
3) Comfortable, but not luxurious, posture
4) Maintaining a balanced effort in practice
5) Avoiding bad-tempered, rough or cruel people
6) Associating with calm and gentle people
7) Inclining the mind toward the development of tranquility

## 6) CONCENTRATION — *SAMĀDHI*

*Characteristic:* nondispersal
*Function:* to collect the mind
*Manifestation:* peace and stillness
*Ways of arousing:*

According to the Buddha: continuous wise attention aimed at the development of concentration

According to the Commentaries:

1) Purity of internal and external bases (cleanliness of body and immediate environment)
2) Balance of the controlling faculties
3) Skill in the concentration object (applicable to jhāna practice)
4) Uplifting the mind when it is depressed
5) Calming the mind when it is excited
6) Bringing happiness to the mind when it is withered by pain
7) Continuous, balanced awareness
8) Avoiding unconcentrated people
9) Associating with concentrated people
10) Reflecting on the peace of the jhānic absorptions
11) Inclining the mind toward the development of concentration

## 7) EQUANIMITY — *UPEKKHĀ*

*Characteristic:* the balancing of opposed mental states
*Function:* to fill in where there is a lack and to reduce excess
*Manifestation:* a state of ease and balance
*Ways of arousing:*

According to the Buddha: wise attention; that is, continuous mindfulness based on the intention to develop equanimity

According to the Commentaries:

1) An equanimous attitude toward all living beings, not to be too attached to anyone
2) A balanced attitude toward nonliving objects, such as property
3) Avoiding people who are deeply possessive or otherwise lack equanimity
4) Association with those who are not too strongly attached to beings or possessions, and who otherwise demonstrate equanimity
5) Inclining the mind toward developing equanimity

# Hindrances and Antidotes

Aspects of the concentrated mind have the capacity to remedy problematic mental states. Here are the factors of the first *jhāna*, or state of concentration, paired with the hindrance each overcomes:

| Jhāna factor | Overcomes |
|---|---|
| *vitakka*, aiming | *thīna middha*, sloth and torpor |
| *vicāra*, rubbing | *vicikicchā*, skeptical doubt |
| *pīti*, delight | *vyāpāda*, aversion |
| *sukha*, happiness | *uddhaccakukkucca*, restlessness and worry |
| *ekaggatā*, one-pointedness | *kāmacchanda*, sense desire |

# The Progress of Insight

As yogis practice vipassanā meditation under the instruction of a qualified teacher, they become able to perceive different truths about reality not accessible to ordinary consciousness. These meditative insights tend to occur in a specific order regardless of personality type or level of intelligence, successively deepening along with the concentration and purity of mind that result from proper meditation practice. This list is provided with a strong cautionary note: if you are practicing meditation, don't think about progress! It is quite impossible for even the most experienced meditator to evaluate his or her own practice; and only after extensive personal experience and training can a teacher begin to recognize the specific, subtle signs of this progression in the verbal reports of another meditator.

*Insight into Mind and Matter*

Awareness of a distinction between the observing mind or consciousness and matter, the objects of consciousness.

Seeing that one hundred per cent of one's experience is composed of mind and matter, this insight temporarily removes the wrong view that a self exists independent of matter and mind. As long as mindfulness is sustained, doubt in the Dhamma remains in abeyance.

*Insight into Cause and Effect*

Direct apprehension of the causal relationship between mind and matter. For example, subsequent to a mental intention, a series of physical sensations arise and one has a sudden intuition of the causal relationship. Or, a painful sensation gives rise to a wish to move the body.

Seeing that there is only mind and matter, and that these are the elements that cause each other to come into existence, this insight removes the wrong view that an external force is responsible for our experiences. Seeing that there is only a continuous chain of causes and effects, this insight removes the false idea that events occur in a haphazard, uncaused manner.

*Insights into Impermanence, Unsatisfactoriness and Absence of Self*

*Aniccā-nupassanā-ñāna:* Seeing of impermanence in the perpetual and inescapable vanishing of objects of consciousness. Removes the wrong view of permanence, and lessens pride and conceit.

*Dukkhā-nupassanā-ñāna:* Observing the breakup of objects, especially painful sensations, one understands the unsatisfactoriness, the oppressiveness of impermanence. Realization that there is no refuge within objects and that impermanence is frightful and undesirable. Removes the false view that enduring satisfaction can be attained within the realm of impermanence.

*Anattā-nupassanā-ñāna:* Then, seeing the uncontrollability within the impermanence and painfulness of objects. Removes the illusion that oneself, or any other agency, can prevent or direct the passing away of objects; and clears away the false notion that an inherent essence is present in oneself, mind, or matter.

These three intuitions correspond to the first *vipassanā jhāna,* and are accompanied by reflective thinking about the universality of impermanence, unsatisfactoriness, and absence of self. One reflects that there was no time, nor will there ever be a time, when objects have not been characterized by these three marks of conditionality.

*Sammasanañāna,* verified knowledge by comprehension: The three marks of impermanence, suffering and absence of self, seen clearly together. One feels a conviction that the Dhamma is true as one has heard it.

This insight, together with the previous group, is the full development of the first vipassanā jhāna, and the dawning of vipassanā right view, which sees every object and experience under the triple aspects of impermanence, unsatisfactoriness and absence of self.

## Insight into Arising and Passing Away

The mind clearly sees the momentary arising and passing away of objects; that is, the very rapid beginning and ending of each mental and physical phenomenon.

This insight corresponds to the second vipassanā jhāna, characterized by the weakening of conceptual thought and the arising of extremely strong rapture and comfort. Because some aspects of mindfulness are as yet undeveloped in this stage, there also is grasping onto these pleasant experiences (the "defilements of insight.") Yogis feel strong faith and a desire to preach the Dhamma, and may believe themselves to be enlightened.

## Insight into Path and Not-Path

As yogis are encouraged to note the faith and rapture they experience, grasping onto these experiences begins to diminish. Yogis gain the conviction that simple noting is the true path of practice rather than the generation of blissful states. From this point they proceed onward with confidence.

In this insight, the third vipassanā jhāna begins to predominate. Its predominant factor is happiness or comfort, and the equanimity that underlies all the vipassanā jhānas begins to be strongly apparent. Yogis may be able to sit for long periods without suffering from painful sensations.

## Insight into Dissolution

The mind loses contact with the beginnings and middles of each object, and focuses instead on endings. Thus, awareness perceives nothing but dissolution everywhere it comes to rest. Conceptual images of the body become indistinct.

As Insight into Dissolutions matures, a neutral feeling begins to predominate in body and mind, neither comfortable nor uncomfortable. The yogi's mind can rest, coolly observing the dissolution of all phenomena. This insight is the onset of the fourth vipassanā jhāna. The factor of happiness and comfort disappears and equanimity begins to predominate. Conceptual thought no longer sprouts up within each moment of insight or direct awareness.

### Insight into Fear

Seeing the fearsomeness of all phenomena.

### Insight into Disgust

Seeing the disgusting nature of all phenomena as they decay and fall apart.

### Insight into the Wish For Liberation

The arising of a profound impulse to continue the practice, driving onward to reach the cessation of all unsatisfying experiences.

### Insight into Equanimity Regarding All Objects

Balance is reestablished as mindfulness becomes extremely agile, picking up objects quickly before the mind can be perturbed by pleasantness or unpleasantness. There is a sense of coolness and steadiness in the absence of reactions.

During this insight, practitioners experience a peaceful mental state similar to the mind of an arahant, or perfectly purified enlightened being. It is from this state of extreme balance that the mind may be able to penetrate into the peace of nibbāna.

### Insight into Nibbāna, the Happiness of Peace

Mental and physical phenomena come to a stop. Path and Fruition Consciousness; Nibbāna; Reviewing Consciousness.

This is the experience commonly known as enlightenment, and it is irreversibly transforming. According to the Buddha there are four levels of enlightenment. Each of them is reached after culmination of the series of insights described above.

On the first level, called *sotāpanna* or stream entry, path consciousness uproots the defilements of wrong view of self, doubt, and adherence to wrong practices. Moreover, the kilesas strong enough to cause rebirth in hell or as an animal are uprooted, and the remaining kilesas are weakened. It is said that a sotāpanna has only seven more existences remaining in samsāra, meaning that only seven more times can he or she be reborn in a different realm from the one in which he or she expired; and, since the gates to the lower realms have been closed by the first path consciousness, all of these rebirths will take place in the human realm or higher.

Fruition consciousness is compared to water being poured on the ashes of a campfire. It cools the place from which the defilements have been uprooted.

Reviewing consciousness reviews path and fruition consciousnesses, nibbāna as an object of consciousness, and also surveys the path ahead. One realizes that one's work of purification has, in a sense, just begun, for there are still kilesas remaining to torment one.

## FURTHER LEVELS OF ENLIGHTENMENT

*Sakadāgāmitā, anāgāmitā, arahatta.* Progressions of Insight leading to the respective three Path and Fruition Consciousnesses:

A sotāpanna is only partially enlightened. Three levels of purification remain to be striven for – three successively deeper immersions in the peace of nibbāna, resulting in three successively deeper levels of happiness and contentment. The happiness of a pure mind is the true birthright of every human being. Every yogi should aspire to arahantship, perfect peace, the eradication of all inner torment.

# Numerical Lists

TWO KINDS OF IGNORANCE – Not seeing what is true, that is, universal impermanence, unsatisfactoriness and absence of inherent essence or self; and seeing what is not true, namely that objects and experiences possess permanence, happiness and inherent self-essence.

TWO KINDS OF *KILESAS* – Those connected with objects, which arise in conjunction with desirable, unpleasant or neutral objects and in the absence of mindfulness; and those connected with the continuity of existence, which remain dormant and are uprooted by the respective path consciousnesses.

TWO KINDS OF RARE AND PRECIOUS PEOPLE IN THIS WORLD – Benefactors; grateful persons who remember the good that has been done for them and repay it when possible.

TWO KINDS OF ULTIMATE REALITIES    (*paramattha dhammas*) – conditioned ultimate realities, *sankhata paramattha dhammas*; unconditioned ultimate reality, *asankhata paramattha dhamma*, nibbāna.

TWO MAIN WEAKNESSES OF BEINGS – Lack of security, lack of true possessions.

THREE BATTALIONS OF MĀRA'S NINTH ARMY – Material gain in the form of donations from followers, the reverence of devotees, and fame or renown.

THREE CHARACTERISTICS OF ALL PHENOMENA – *anicca*, impermanence; *dukkha*, suffering; *anatta*, absence of enduring self essence.

THREE GREAT ACCOMPLISHMENTS OF BUDDHAS – By virtue of cause, by virtue of result, by virtue of service.

THREE *KILESAS* UPROOTED BY THE FIRST PATH CONSCIOUSNESS – Wrong view of self, doubt, and adherence to wrong practices.

THREE KINDS OF *KILESAS* – Transgressive, obsessive, and latent or dormant.

THREE KINDS OF ULTIMATE REALITIES – Mind, matter, and nibbāna.

THREE KINDS OF PSYCHIC POWERS – Superhuman physical feats, mind reading, and the power of instruction.

THREE KINDS OF SECLUSION – *kāya viveka*, seclusion of the body through renunciation; *citta viveka*, seclusion of the mind through concentration; *upadhi viveka*, seclusion due to the weakening of the kilesas.

THREE LEVELS OF EFFORT – Launching, persistent, liberating. Sometimes a fourth, fulfilling.

THREE PERPETUATING *DHAMMAS* – Conceit, wrong view and craving.

THREE-PHASE DESCRIPTION USED IN MEDITATION INTERVIEW – Occurrence of the object, your noting of the object, what happened to the object.

THREE TYPES OF PROPERTY – Movable, immovable, knowledge.

THREEFOLD TEACHING (OR TRAINING) – *sīla, samādhi, paññā:* morality, concentration, wisdom.

TRIPLE GEM — Buddha, Dhamma, Sangha.

FOUR FOUNDATIONS OF MINDFULNESS – Mindfulness of body, feeling, mind, objects of mind.

FOUR KINDS OF HAPPINESS PERTAINING TO THE FIRST FOUR *VIPASSANĀ JHĀNAS* – First *jhāna*, the happiness of seclusion; second *jhāna*, the happiness of concentration, which leads to rapture and comfort; third *jhāna*, the happiness of equanimity; fourth *jhāna*, the purity of mindfulness due to equanimity.

FOUR POSTURES – Lying, sitting, standing, walking.

FOUR POWERS MOTIVATING A SUCCESSFUL MEDITATION PRACTICE – Willingness, vigor, strength of mind, wisdom or knowledge.

FOUR STAGES OF NIBBĀNIC ATTAINMENT – *sotapatti*, stream-entry; *sakadāgāmī*, once-returner; *anāgāmī*, non-returner; *arahatta*, perfection.

FIVE BENEFITS OF WALKING MEDITATION – Stamina for long journeys, stamina for meditation practice, good health, assistance in digestion, durable concentration.

FIVE CONTROLLING FACULTIES – Faith, energy or effort, mindfulness, concentration, wisdom.

FIVE FACTORS OF THE EIGHTFOLD PATH PREDOMINANTLY DEVELOPED DURING A MOMENT OF MINDFULNESS – Right effort; mindfulness; concentration; right aim; right view.

FIVE HINDRANCES – *kāmacchanda*, sense desire; *vyāpāda*, aversion; *thīna middha*, sloth and torpor; *uddhaccakukkucca*, restlessness and worry; *vicikicchā*, skeptical doubt.

FIVE JHĀNIC FACTORS – *vitakka*, aiming; *vicāra*, rubbing; *piti*, rapture or delight; sukha, happiness; *samādhi*, concentration.

FIVE KINDS OF DOUBT LEADING TO THE THORNY MIND – Doubt of the Buddha, of the Dhamma, of the Sangha, of oneself, and of others.

FIVE MENTAL FETTERS – To be chained to sense objects; overattachment to one's own body; overattachment to the bodies of others; overattachment to food; wishing for rebirth in a realm of subtle material pleasure.

FIVE PRECEPTS – Not to kill, not to take what is not given, to abstain from sexual misconduct, not to lie, not to take intoxicants.

FIVE PROTECTIONS FOR MEDITATION *(anuggahitas)* – *sīlā·nuggahita,* morality; *sutā·nuggahita,* understanding gained from discourses and texts; *sākacchā·nuggahita,* a teacher's guidance; *samathā·nuggahita,* concentration; *vipassanā· nuggahita,* forceful and continuous insight practice.

FIVE TYPES OF RAPTURE – Lesser, momentary, overwhelming, uplifting or exhilarating, pervasive.

SIX KINDS OF RIGHT VIEW – *kammassakatā sammā·diṭṭhi,* right view of kamma as one's only true property; *jhāna sammā diṭṭhi,* knowledge arising in conjunction with each of the eight stages of absorption; *vipassanā sammā diṭṭhi,* right view of the universality of impermanence, suffering and absence of self; noble path right view which uproots certain kilesas forever; noble fruition right view which cools the embers left behind by the extinguished defilements; reviewing consciousness right view, which reviews path and fruition consciousness, nibbāna as an object of consciousness, the defilements uprooted and the remaining defilements.

SIX SENSE DOORS – Eye, ear, nose, tongue, body, mind.

SEVEN FACTORS OF ENLIGHTENMENT – Mindfulness, investigation, investigation, energy, rapture or joy, tranquility, concentration, equanimity.

SEVEN RESULTS OF MINDFULNESS MEDITATION PRACTICE – Purification of the mind, overcoming of sorrow, lamentation, physical pain and mental displeasure, and finally reaching the right path and the realisation of nibbāna.

SEVENFOLD PROPERTY OF NOBLE ONES – Faith; morality; *hiri* or moral shame; *ottappa* or moral dread; learning or expertise in the theory and practice of meditation; *cāga* or liberality with respect to relinquishing *kilesas* as well as generosity in giving; and wisdom.

SEVEN TYPES OF SUITABILITY WHICH SUPPORT MEDITATION PRACTICE
– Suitability of place, of resort, of speech, of person
(teacher and community), food, of weather, of posture.

SEVEN ANTIDOTES TO DROWSINESS – Change one's attitude and
make meditation more dynamic; reflect on inspiring
passages of Dhamma; recite passages alound; physical
stimulation such as rubbing the ears; washing one's face
and/or eyes; looking at a light; brisk walking meditation.

EIGHT PRECEPTS – Includes the Five Precepts, with the third
converted to refraining from breaking celibacy, plus:
refraining from taking food after noon, refraining from
entertainments and adorning or perfuming one's body,
and refraining from sleeping on a high or luxurious bed.

NOBLE EIGHTFOLD PATH – Right view or understanding, right
thought or aim, right speech, right action, right livelihood, right effort, right mindfulness and right concentration.

NINE CAUSES FOR GROWTH OF THE CONTROLLING FACULTIES –
Attention directed toward impermanence; care and respect for meditation; continuity of awareness; supportive environment;   remembering and recreating
beneficial circumstances; cultivation of enlightenment
factors; intense effort; patience and perseverance; determination to reach liberation.

TEN ARMIES OF MĀRA – Sensual pleasures; discontent; hunger
and thirst; craving; sloth and torpor; fear; doubt; conceit
and ingratitude; gain, renown, honor and whatever
fame is falsely received; self-exaltation and disparaging
others.

TEN KINDS OF CROOKED BEHAVIOR –

THREE KINDS OF CROOKED BODILY BEHAVIOR: 1) Based on
lack of loving-kindness and compassion, namely killing, harming and oppressing others. 2) Based on greed,
namely stealing or deceitful acquisition of others' property. 3) Based on lust, namely sexual misconduct.

FOUR KINDS OF CROOKED VERBAL BEHAVIOR: 1) Lying. 2) Speech that causes disharmony. 3) Speech that is hurtful, coarse, crude or obscene. 4) Frivolous chatter.

THREE KINDS OF MENTAL CROOKEDNESS: 1) Thoughts of harming or cruelty toward self or others. 2) Covetous thoughts. 3) The wrong view of kamma, namely that one's actions have no consequences.

TEN PRECEPTS – Includes the Eight Precepts, above, with the eighth on entertainments and adornments split, becoming eight and nine, plus: refraining from handling money.

TWO HUNDRED AND TWENTY-SEVEN RULES FOR MONKS – The ten precepts, plus supplementary rules.

# Glossary

*Abhidhamma:* Buddhist analysis of consciousness. The "Third Basket" or group of texts in Buddhism.

*abhiññā:* Special knowledge; word for psychic powers.

*abhirati:* One who delights in something, for example, the Dhamma and prefers meditation to seeking sensual pleasures.

Ālāra the Kalama: Famous meditation teacher of the Buddha's time; one of the Bodhisatta's two main meditation instructors.

*Anāgāmī:* Nonreturner; one who has attained the third stage of enlightenment by experiencing nibbana at its third level of depth. This person will experience no more rebirths in sensual realms, but will attain final enlightenment from the Brahma realm. An anāgāmī has uprooted the defilements of greed for sense desires and anger, but may still experience subtle defilements such as restlessness.

*anagārika:* In Buddhist countries, a lay person who takes eight or ten precepts. An anagārika usually wears a white coat and shaves his or her head, and lives in a monastery assisting the monks and nuns.

*anattā:* The absence of inherent or independent self; the lack of self-essence; the unresponsiveness of objects to one's wishes. The third of three aspects common to all conditioned things, anattā is dependent upon *anicca* and *dukkha*.

*Anatta lakkhaṇa:* The sign or characteristic of absence of self. The uncontrollability of phenomena.

*anattā·nupassanā·ñāṇa:* The intuitive comprehension that realizes the fact of absence of self. A sudden sense that no one is in control.

*anicca:* Impermanence. The first of the three aspects common to all conditioned things.

*anicca lakkhaṇa:* The sign of impermanence; that by which impermanence can be recognized. The fact of the arising and passing away of all objects.

*aniccā·nupassanā·ñāṇa:* The intuitive comprehension that realizes the fact of impermanence. A sudden, direct sense of the rapidity of the vanishing of objects.

animal speech: Speech about worldly subjects, especially during a retreat.

*anuggahita:* Protection, specifically for meditation practice.

*apāya:* Rebirths in hell or as an animal. Miserable mental states devoid of wholesome kamma that can bring about happiness.

*arahant:* Fully enlightened being; one who has uprooted all the defilements and experiences no more mental suffering. Having attained the fourth and final stage of enlightenment, he or she will not be reborn again in any form, passing entirely into the unconditioned state upon death.

*araha:* Completely purified, and therefore worthy of respect from all humans, devas and brahmās. The first of the virtues of the Buddha on traditional lists.

*ātāpa:* Fiery heat; the energy of meditation that burns defilements.

*avijjā:* Ignorance. Not seeing what is true, namely universal impermanence, unsatisfactoriness and absence of self; and seeing what is not true, namely that objects and experiences possess permanence, happiness, and self-nature.

*bhāvanā:* Mental development, or meditation.

*bhikkhu:* A male monk under the Buddha and up to the present day who keeps Vinaya, the 227 rules; shaves his head, wears ocher-colored robes (or of related colors from orange, to dark brown, to maroon), and lives dependent on alms food. Also a word for any person who strives to develop wholesomeness and abandon unwholesomeness in order to gain liberation and true happiness.

*bhikkhunī*: A female nun under the Buddha. The Southeast Asian lineages of bhikkhunis have died out, and women renunciates now ordain as sīlashin nuns.

*Bodhisatta:* Enlightenment-being. One who has vowed to become a Buddha, or attain perfect enlightenment for the sake of all beings. A word describing the Buddha before his enlightenment.

*bojjhanga:* Enlightenment factor. A quality of mind that leads to enlightenment. Also, the aspect of knowledge that perceives the Four Noble Truths.

Brahmā: Name of the highest god; also a type of divine realm where there is mind, but no matter.

*brahmacariya:* The holy life; a life devoted to spiritual practice. Also, celibacy.

brahman (*brāhmaṇo*): A member of the priestly caste of Hindus. Often spelled Brahmin.

Buddha: One who is awakened. Historically, the prince Siddhattha Gotama, who lived in Nepal and Northern India 2,500 years ago.

*Buddhānussati:* Recollection of the virtues of the Buddha.

*cāga:* Liberality. Willingness to relinquish the kilesas, as well as openhanded generosity on the material level.

*chanda:* Willingness to act.

characteristic (*lakkhaṇa*): 1) "Individual characteristics" are the specific traits of mind and matter which can be experienced directly, such as movement, lightness. "Common characteristics" are traits shared by all objects, namely impermanence, unsatisfactoriness and absence of self. 2) In classical *Abhidhamma* analysis, the characteristic is the trait by which a mental factor can be recognized.

*Citta:* Mind.

Cittā: The name of a bhikkhunī in the Buddha's time who overcame serious physical pain and weakness and became an arahant.

*citta viveka*: Seclusion of the mind from the various hindrances which obstruct the development of insight. Equivalent to continuous mindfulness, which cannot be infiltrated by unwholesome thoughts.

*dāna:* Generosity, the practice of generosity, or objects given generously. Said by the Buddha to be the first practice for those who want to diminish the force of craving as part of the holy life.

*deva:* A kind of god inhabiting one of several subtle sensual realms which are higher than the human realm, and are characterized by great pleasure and distraction.

Devadatta: A monk who promoted schism in the order of bhikkhus, and later tried to murder the Buddha.

*Dhamma:* The teaching of the Buddha; the practice of meditation; fundamental truth.

*dhamma:* Philosophical word for any conditioned object or the unconditioned; a phenomenon of nature.

*dhamma vicaya:* Investigation of phenomena; the mental factor that discerns the true nature of dhammas, or of nibbāna. Second factor of enlightenment.

*dosa:* Anger or aversion; the mind's turning away from a painful experience. With lobha and moha, one of the three forces which keep the minds of beings in darkness.

*dukkha:* Unsatisfactoriness; suffering; pain. The second characteristic of all conditioned things. Results from impermanence and craving.

*dukkha lakkhaṇa:* The sign or characteristic of suffering; that by which *dukkha* can be recognized. Oppression by impermanence.

*dukkhā-nupassanā-ñāṇa:* The intuitive realization of suffering. A sense that no object is dependable, that all objects are fearsome, and that within objects there is no refuge from vanishing and dissolution.

Four Elements *(mahābhūta):* These are the classes of physical phenomena, the types of sensations which can be experienced directly: earth, or hardness and softness; water, or fluidity and cohesion; fire, or heat and cold; air, or movement and such sensations as tautness, stiffness and piercing.

Four Noble Truths *(ariya saccāni):* All conditioned things are suffering, or unsatisfactory; the cause of dissatisfaction is craving; there is an end to suffering; the means to this end is the Noble Eightfold Path.

function (*kicca*):     In classical *Abhidhamma* analysis, the operation of a mental factor.

Gotama:     The Buddha's maternal family name.

hindrance (*nīvaraṇa*):     A mental state that obstructs meditation, in the presence of which mindfulness is weakened or absent. There are five specific states – desire, aversion, sloth and torpor, restlessness, and doubt – which arise in the absence of the respective five factors of the first jhāna.

*hiri:*     Moral shame. A feeling of revulsion when one thinks of committing an immoral act, based on comparing such an act with the alternative of moral behavior.

*issā:*     Jealousy. The wish not to see others happy or successful.

*Jetavana,* Jeta Grove:     Name of a grove near the city of Sāvatthī in Northern India where the Buddha often preached.

*jhāna:*     The quality of mind able to stick to an object and observe it. Also, the absorption of the mind into an object of awareness; one of the eight levels of absorption, each of which is defined by the presence of particular mental factors. See *Samatha jhāna, vipassanā jhāna.*

*jhāna sammā diṭṭhi:*     Right view that arises in conjunction with each of the eight levels of jhānic absorption. Related to concentration practices, not to vipassana.

Kaccāyana:     Name of one of the Buddha's early disciples, an arahant, known for his ability to explicate the Buddha's shortest sermons, some of which were only a few words long.

*kāmacchanda:*     Sensual desire. The first hindrance.

*kamma:*     Action that bears results; the results of action.

*kammassakatā sammā-diṭṭhi:*     Right view that *kamma* is one's only true property.

*karuṇā:*     Compassion. The quivering of the heart in response to others' suffering; the wish to remove painful circumstances from the lives of other beings.

*kāya viveka:*    Seclusion of the body; a prerequisite for good meditation. An attitude of detachment toward the "body" of sense objects: sights, sounds, smells, tastes, physical sensations and thoughts. Also the physical removal of oneself from intense stimuli, in retreat or when choosing a quiet spot for daily meditation practice.

*kilesa:*    A torment of mind; a defilement.

King Ajātasattu:    King who killed his own father, repented and became a devotee of the Buddha.

*khema:*    Security or safety. One of the characteristics of nibbāna, in contrast to the insecurity of conditioned existence.

*kodha:*    Anger. The "thorny mind." Aversion and the mental states associated with it, such as doubt, frustration, rigidity and hardness of mind.

*kusīta:*    A lazy person.

*lobha:*    Greed. The mind's grasping onto a pleasant experience. With dosa and moha, one of the three forces which keep the minds of beings in darkness.

*macchariya:*    Miserliness. The wish not to see others as happy as one is oneself.

*magga:*    Path. Word for the moment of enlightenment when defilements are uprooted, and for the initial specific consciousness of nibbāna.

Mahākassapa:    One of the Buddha's early disciples.

Mahāmoggallāna:    One of the Buddha's primary disciples, known for his psychic powers.

Mahāpajāpati Gotamī:    The Buddha's stepmother; founder of the order of bhikkhunīs, and a famous enlightened practitioner.

*māna:*    Conceit.

manifestation:    In classical *Abhidhamma* analysis, the result of the functioning of a mental factor in consciousness. What is noticeable in the mental state when a mental factor, such as a factor of enlightenment, is present.

Māra:    In Pāli, derived from a word meaning "death." Personification of the force of ignorance, delusion and craving that kills virtue as well as life. The lord of all conditioned realms.

Mātikamātā: Name of an enlightened laywoman in the Buddha's time who supported meditating monks so that they, too, could become enlightened.

mental factor (*dhamma*): A discernible element, or quality, present in consciousness.

*mettā*: Loving kindness. The wish that other beings should enjoy internal and external safety, mental and physical happiness, and ease of well-being.

*middha* (See *thīna*): Constricted, unworkable state of consciousness when torpor is present.

mindfulness (*sati*): The observing power of the mind, which clearly and simply experiences an object without reacting to it.

*moha*: Delusion. The mind's inability to recognize an experience, especially a neutral one. With lobha and dosa, one of the three forces which keep the minds of beings in darkness.

Namuci: Another name for Māra.

*nekkhamma sukha*: The happiness of renunciation. The happiness and comfort of being free from sensual objects, as well as from the unwholesome kilesas that react to those objects.

*nibbāna*: The Unconditioned. Perfectly undefiled state that is neither mind nor matter.

*nikanti taṇhā*: Craving particularly for the pleasures of meditation.

*nirodha samāpatti*: The attainment of cessation. Arahants and anāgāmis have this capacity to enter the nibbānic state at will.

Noble Fruition Consciousness (*ariya phala*): Subsequent to Noble Path Consciousness, the experience of the mind's dwelling in cessation for an extended period of time.

Noble Path Consciousness (*ariya magga*): The culmination and goal of *vipassanā* practice. Insight into nibbāna; the experience of cessation of matter, mind and subtle mind-borne matter – that is, the temporary cessation of all conditioned experience. There are four levels of Noble Path Consciousness, each one uprooting particular defilements.

*ottappa:* Moral dread. The wish to refrain from immoral actions because one considers the consequences, including what wise and refined people would think of one.

*pabbajita:* One who has gone forth from the home life in order to extinguish the kilesas.

*paccakkha·ñāṇa:* Direct experiential perception, or direct in sight. A synonym for vipassanā.

Pāli: The language of the Theravadin scriptures; the closest written language to Magadhī, thought to be the language spoken by the Buddha and his disciples.

*Pāmojja, pāmujja:* The weaker forms of pīti.

*paññā:* Intuitive knowledge of ultimate truth; wisdom.

*paramattha dhamma*: An ultimate reality: an object which can be perceived directly without the mediation of concepts. These are of three kinds: physical phenomena, mental phenomena and nibbāna.

*pāramīs:* Perfections. Forces of purity within the mind which are gradually developed over many lifetimes.

*parinibbāna:* The passing out of conditioned existence of a fully enlightened being at physical death.

*parisuddhi sukha:* Happiness unmixed with defilements. Nibbāna.

*passaddhi*: Cool calmness; tranquility. Fifth factor of enlightenment.

*peta*: Unhappy ghost.

*phala*: Fruit. The moment of consciousness just after magga, which continues to perceive nibbāna, and during which the defilements are cooled.

*phassa*: Contact, a mental factor which arises when the mind touches an object

*pīti:* Rapture; joy. Physical and mental lightness and agility resulting from purity of mind; a delighted interest in what is happening. Fourth factor of enlightenment, third factor of the first jhāna.

Siddhattha, Prince:   The Buddha's personal name and rank (Skt: Siddhartha)

*rāga:*   Lust.

*saddhā:*   Trust, confidence, faith.

*sakadāgāmī:*   "Once returner," one who has attained the second stage of enlightenment. Because of weakened craving and anger, this being will be reborn in only one more plane of existence.

*samādhi:*   One-pointedness of mind; concentration. Sixth factor of enlightenment.

*sāmaṇera:*   A novice bhikkhu.

*sāmaṇerī:*   A novice bhikkhunī.

*samatha:*   Calmness of mind due to concentration. Meditation practices in which one concentrates on a conceptual object. Because the object is conceptual, these practices lead to stillness of mind, but not to insight wisdom.

*samatha jhāna:*   Pure concentration, fixed awareness of a single object. States of extraordinary calmness and peace, where the mind becomes absorbed into the object.

*sambojjhanga:*   Factor of enlightenment, same as bojjhanga.

*sammā-ditthi:*   Right or complete view.

*sammā-kammanta:*   Right action. Restraint from killing, stealing and sexual misconduct.

*sammā-sambuddha:*   A perfectly self-enlightened being.

*sammasana-ñāṇa:*   Verified knowledge by comprehension. A stage of insight consisting of seeing the disappearance of all objects – and with this seeing, arriving at a direct personal experience that all objects are impermanent, unsatisfactory and lacking in an inherent self-essence. It is called "verified" because one personally verifies the doctrine on this major point.

*sammā vācā:*   Right speech. Speech that is truthful, leading to harmony, kind, sweet to the ear and beneficial.

*sampajañña:*   Clear comprehension.

*samsāra:*   The cycle of craving and suffering caused by ignorance of ultimate truth.

*sangha:*    Community of bhikkhus. Or, community of all those who are striving for liberation.

*sankhāra paramattha dhamma:*    Conditioned ultimate reality. An impermanent mental or physical phenomenon which can be perceived by direct awareness, without the mediation of concepts.

*sankhārupekkhāñāṇa:*    Insight into equanimity toward all formations. One of the highest stages of insight in the classical progression. A subtly balanced mental state that is not disturbed by the alternation of pleasant and painful experience.

*santi sukha:*    The happiness of peace. A word for the nibbānic experience.

Sāriputta:    The Buddha's chief disciple, known for wisdom.

*sati:*    Mindfulness; observing power. The first factor of enlightenment.

*satipaṭṭhāna:*    Four foundations of mindfulness: mindfulness of the body, feelings, mind and mind objects.

*Satipaṭṭhāna Sutta:*    Discourse in which the Buddha described mindfulness meditation.

*Sayadaw:*    Burmese word meaning great teacher; a monk who teaches meditation, or an abbot of a monastery.

*sīla:*    Morality.

*Sīlashin Nun:*    A member of the Burmese lineage of woman renunciates who take eight or ten precepts, shave their heads and wear pink or brown robes.

Sonā Therī:    Name of an elderly woman who became a bhikkhunī and attained enlightenment after being cast out by her children.

*sotāpanna:*    Stream enterer. One who has attained the first stage of enlightenment by experiencing nibbāna for the first time. Such a person uproots the illusion of self as well as doubt in the efficacy of meditation practice; will not be reborn as an animal or in hell due to the weakening of his or her defilements; and ceases to believe that any rite or ritual can bring about liberation.

Subhadda:   A non-Buddhist renunciate to whom the Buddha preached on his deathbed, and who thereby became the last disciple to be converted by the Buddha.

*sukha*:   Happiness, contentment, pleasant feeling. The fourth factor of the first jhāna.

Sumedha:   Name of a hermit who undertook the Bodhisatta vow to attain perfect enlightenment, and eventually became the historical Buddha.

*Sutta Nipāta*:   Early text containing discourses of the Buddha.

*sutta*:   Discourse of the Buddha. Collected, the suttas form the "Second Basket" of basic texts in Buddhism.

*taṇhā*:   Thirst; craving.

*tatra majjhattatā*:   Mental balance. An aspect of equanimity.

*Tāvatimsa*:   The Heaven of the Thirty-Three Gods. Deva realm where the Buddha delivered a discourse on *Abhidhamma* to his mother, who had died and been reborn there; and where the bhikkhu of "Chariot to Nibbāna" was reborn upon his death during meditation practice.

*Thera*:   Elder. Respectful suffix added to the name of an elder monk.

Theravāda:   Literally, "the speech of the elders." Buddhist tradition based on Pāli canonical scriptures, found in Southeast Asia, Sri Lanka and now in the West.

*Therī*:   Female elder. Respectful suffix added to the name of an elder nun.

*thīna*:   Mental factor of torpor.

*thīna middha*:   Sloth and torpor. Specifically, the mental factor of *thina* or torpor, considered together with middha, its effects on surrounding mental factors and therefore on the mental state as a whole. Stiff and unworkable mental state; the Fifth Army of Māra and the fourth hindrance.

Tissa:   Young man in the Buddha's day who renounced the world to become a bhikkhu, and eventually became an arahant by meditating on the pain of his broken legs.

*uddhacca kukkucca*:   Restlessness and worry. The fourth hindrance.

Udaka the Rāmaputta: A famous meditation teacher of the Buddha's day, and one of the Bodhisatta's two main instructors.

*upādāna:* Clinging. The mind's grasping onto an object and refusing to let go.

*upekkhā:* Equanimity, balance of energy; the quality of mind that remains centered without inclining toward extremes. Seventh factor of enlightenment.

*vicāra:* The aspect of concentration consisting of the mind's "rubbing" against the object. Second factor of the first jhāna.

*vicikicchā:* Doubt; skeptical criticism; the exhaustion of mind that comes about through conjecture. The Seventh Army of Māra and the fifth hindrance.

*vikkhambhana viveka:* State where the defilements are weak and distant, no longer as troubling to the mental state. Results from kāya viveka and citta viveka, defined above.

*Vinaya:* Rules of discipline for monks; the monks' way of life; the "First Basket" or group of texts in Buddhism.

*vipāka:* The result of *kamma.* Conditions which arise due to past actions.

*vipassanā:* Literally, "seeing through various modes." The energetic observation of mental and physical objects in their aspect of impermanence, unsatisfactoriness, and lack of an inherent, independent essence or self.

*vipassanā jhāna:* 1) The continuous focusing of the mind on paramattha dhammas, that is, objects which can be known directly without the mediation of concepts. 2) The mind which, while ranging freely from object to object, remains fixed on the characteristics of impermanence, suffering and absence of self.

*vipassanā kilesas:* Defilements of insight. Chiefly appear during the stage of insight into the rapid arising and passing away of phenomena. Great bliss and rapture occur at this time. The defilements of insight consist of grasping at these pleasant experiences resulting from insight, without being fully aware that one is grasping at them.

*vīrānaṁ bhāvo:*   State of the heroic ones; word for the quality of effort required in meditation practice.

*viriya:*   The energy or effort expended to direct the mind continuously toward the object. Derived from the word for hero. Third factor of enlightenment.

*Visuddhi Magga:*   "The Path of Purification." A major and exhaustive instructive text written in the 5th century CE by Buddhaghosa of Sri Lanka.

*vitakka:*   The aspect of concentration consisting of the mind's aiming toward, sticking into, and establishing itself upon an object. First factor of the first jhāna.

*viveka:*   Seclusion; descriptive term for the calm state that occurs when the mind is secluded and protected from the disturbances of the kilesas.

*vivekaja pīti sukha:*   The rapture and happiness born of seclusion. Term for the third and fourth factors of the first jhāna, considered together.

*vyāpāda:*   Aversion. The second hindrance.

Yogi:   One who practices meditation.

# Index